WHEN PRESIDENTS ARE GREAT

Marcia Lynn Whicker
Virginia Commonwealth University

Raymond A. Moore
University of South Carolina

Prentice Hall, Englewood Cliffs, New Jersey 07632

Library of Congress Cataloging-in-Publication Data

WHICKER, MARCIA LYNN.
  When presidents are great.

  Includes bibliographies and index.
    1. Presidents—United States—Rating of.
2. Political leadership—United States. 3. United
States—Politics and Government—20th century.
I. Moore, Raymond A. II. Title.
E176.1.W57 1988   353.031   87-32852
ISBN 0-13-956228-1

Editorial/production supervision and
  interior design: Rob DeGeorge
Cover Design: George Cornell
Manufacturing Buyer: Margaret Rizzi

 © 1988 by Prentice-Hall, Inc.
A Division of Simon & Schuster
Englewood Cliffs, New Jersey 07632

All rights reserved. No part of this book may be
reproduced, in any form or by any means,
without permission in writing from the publisher.

Printed in the United States of America

10 9 8 7 6 5 4 3 2 1

ISBN 0-13-956228-1

PRENTICE-HALL INTERNATIONAL (UK) LIMITED, *London*
PRENTICE-HALL OF AUSTRALIA PTY. LIMITED, *Sydney*
PRENTICE-HALL CANADA INC., *Toronto*
PRENTICE-HALL HISPANOAMERICANA, S.A., *Mexico*
PRENTICE-HALL OF INDIA PRIVATE LIMITED, *New Delhi*
PRENTICE-HALL OF JAPAN, INC., *Tokyo*
SIMON & SCHUSTER ASIA PTE. LTD., *Singapore*
EDITORA PRENTICE-HALL DO BRASIL, LTDA., *Rio de Janeiro*

Contents

Chapter 2

PRESIDENTIAL LEADERSHIP

Chapter 3

PRESIDENTS AS SALESPEOPLE

Chapter 4

THE NONPERSUASIVE PRESIDENCY

Chapter 5

PRESIDENTS AS MANAGERS

Chairpersons of the Board

Chapter 6

NEUROSES IN THE WHITE HOUSE

Presidential Mismanagement Styles

Chapter 7

IN SEARCH OF HEROES

When Presidents Are Great

Chapter 8

THE PRESIDENCY TOMORROW

The Challenges and Promises of the Twenty-first Century 184

Preface

As the United States moves inexorably toward the twenty-first century, it becomes increasingly clear that the country faces an uncertain future. This is nothing new if scanned against the panoply of a national history which has featured the fragility of a post-revolutionary struggle for survival, the divisiveness of civil war, two world wars, the Great Depression, a civil rights revolution, and the agony of two long and costly undeclared wars. It is nevertheless certain that the United States is entering a new and troubling period of its national existence. The challenge of this period is whether or not the United States can remain a free and open society and still continue to be a great world power with growing and expanding economic wealth and a high standard of living and an industrial and technological base which is the envy of the world.

There are many who doubt our capacity to meet this challenge. They say our national will to compete and to lead has been depleted by Vietnam and Watergate, by deficits and debts, by owing our living to foreign investments in the United States, by inability to modernize our manufacturing base, by our failure to sell our products, and by national leadership that compares unfavorably with the new generation of leaders emerging in the Soviet Union.

There are others who say that if we are to be successful in facing the challenges and problems of the future, we must change our ways, tighten our economic belts, reduce our standard of living, lower our deficits, increase our savings for investments, retool our manufacturing sector, enlarge research and development, and learn to market our technological inventions. Failure to do this could mean gradual decline to the level, not just of an ordinary power, but of a power in decline economically and in increasing danger politically.

In the middle of this evolving crisis stands the president of the United States who provides leadership for the country and sometimes the world. How can we as a country increase our chances of "surviving, perchance to flourish," as Dean Acheson once put the question? One clear way is to have great leadership from our chief executive officer. But of what does great presidential leadership consist? This is the question we address in this book.

We are concerned not only with presidential character, technical competence and historical comparisons, but with the question of *when are presidents great*? If we can operationalize the concept of greatness more successfully than previously attempted, we may see more clearly what skills it takes for a contemporary president to be a great leader.

Our aim is to examine those skills that are needed by a modern president to successfully perform his duties and to provide great leadership. We develop a number of new typologies for such categories as salesmanship, management, non-persuasion and mismanagement, and apply these to presidents from Hoover to Reagan, with illustrative examples drawn from history and recent scholarship. Our goal is to help us understand better the proficiencies and abilities needed for great leadership, and hopefully provide some guidelines enabling us as a people to choose the kind of leaders who embody these qualities — leaders who will help us compete in the world arena of the twenty-first century.

The thesis we argue is that today's president must have, in addition to the traditional values of integrity, moral purpose, experience, and a sense of history, two skills that will enable him to meet the challenges of the present and future. These are salesmanship and managerial skills. When levels of these two dimensions are combined, the result is four categories of presidential leadership. "Inactive leadership" is low on both management and salesmanship skills. "Political leadership" is high on salesmanship and low on management skills. "Operational leadership" is high on managerial skills but low on salesmanship. "Great leadership" combines high skills in both areas.

In relating basic leadership types to the future, candidates who display inactive leadership are not likely to be elected president. They probably will not ascend to the White House unless they succeed a disabled, assassinated, or terminally ill president. Even this possibility grows more remote as both presidential and vice presidential candidates must exhibit superior salesmanship skills, at least to the media.

Operational candidates who are poor communicators but good managers are also unlikely to be elected. Only under extraordinary electoral circumstances, where the public reacts to excessive and abusive use of salesmanship skills bordering on demagoguery or where obvious crises elevate public concerns over competence in policy measurement, will an operational president be elected.

The leadership most likely to win will be political. With a shift to media campaigns, candidates who are not good salespersons are less likely to be elected, while candidates who appear attractive and who communicate persuasively are more likely to become presidents. Rarely, however, are managerial skills of presidential candidates tested before entering the White House on a scale comparable to what is needed once in office. Unfortunately, there are no advanced management schools for future presidents who must finely hone their skills on the job under fire.

Plainly, however, the need for great presidents who combine high salesmanship and managerial skills will grow as problems become more complex and more interdependent. There always has been, is now, and will continue to be a preference for great presidential leadership. In the future, preference may become a necessity. More than ever, good intentions in the White House will not be enough. For future presidents, high competence in selling themselves, their programs, and their policies, coupled with high competence in managing the White House, the bureaucracy, and the defense establishment, equate with presidential greatness.

The future will present dangers, as well as opportunities, to determine the worth of the American system. It will test the ability of its people to demand presidential greatness and the capacity of future presidents to deliver it.

ACKNOWLEDGMENTS

We would like to thank Ola L. Whicker for indexing this manuscript and Ruth Moore for assistance in proofreading. We would also like to thank both the secretarial staff in the Department of Government and International Studies at the University of South Carolina for their assistance in manuscript preparation and colleagues kind enough to provide thoughtful comments.

WHEN PRESIDENTS ARE GREAT

CHAPTER ONE
THE LANDSCAPE
OF TODAY'S PRESIDENCY:
Configurations
and Problems

INTRODUCTION

The purpose of this book is to explore the nature of presidential leadership by contrasting presidents who are great with those who fail. Successful presidential leaders today must display two primary aptitudes: selling skills and managerial skills. Presidents are great when they possess both of these important leadership skills to a high degree. Presidents fail when they possess neither skill in abundant quantities. Presidents who possess only a moderate degree of both skills, or who are low on one skill while high on the other, merely muddle through.

Circumstances determine the nation's view of presidents. American presidents who do not possess high levels of selling and managerial skills may still be viewed as adequate as long as circumstances shield them from major crises that expose their flaws. Truly great presidents surmount and mold crises rather than merely cope because they have the ability to sell solutions to the press, the public, and the Congress and also possess the managerial skills to implement, evaluate, monitor, and modify solutions once they are sold.

Traditional leadership qualities, especially integrity, moral purpose, experience, and a sense of history, are important for greatness. However, the presence of these traditional qualities alone will not produce great leadership in the competitive and complicated national and international environment in which presidents must operate. High degrees of both selling and management skills are necessary for greatness in the modern presidency.

This book will not replicate the usual material found in textbooks dealing with the presidency. Nor will it treat in depth such subjects as the growth of the modern presidency, the powers and structures of the chief executive, and constitutional bases for presidential authority. It will instead begin the presentation of the main thesis concerning presidential greatness by focusing on the present-day configuration of American society and the problems that create the agenda of the modern president, following a public-policy approach to the study of the presidency.

The public-policy approach to the study of politics in general has experienced a revival. In 1985, the journal *Chronicle of Higher Education* conducted a survey of major trends in research across twenty-two different scholarly fields. Demetrios Caraley of Columbia University (1985) reported on trends in political science and argued that some of the most significant research in that field had been conducted in public policy. Caraley espoused the theory that political scientists are returning to an interest in substantive problems, substantive issues, and questions that affect many people. Increasingly, the public-policy approach to the study of politics is pertinent to a study of when and why presidents are great.

We will employ cross-cutting analysis to the dimensions of the American presidency today rather than a historical, institutional, or legal approach. This chapter will highlight the problems that create what is and ought to be the president's agenda as he confronts the challenges of governance in the closing years of the twentieth century. In the concluding chapter, we will project from the landscape of the present to the landscape of the future by analyzing recommendations for changing and reforming the presidency.

POLITICAL PROBLEMS AFFECTING THE PRESIDENTIAL AGENDA

Economic, social, and international problems all affect the viability and workability of American political institutions. Does the American political system work today? Are the states, the Supreme Court, the Congress and the bureaucracy fulfilling their functions? Increasingly, all political institutions in American society confront intractable problems. While social problems have become comprehensive and cut across many boundaries, American political institutions remain decentralized and provincial. As other political institutions have become paralyzed, more and more is expected of the presidency. The job description of the modern presidency has expanded to the point where many scholars believe we have created an "impossible presidency" (Barger, 1984) and have called for lowered expectations of what the president can accomplish within a decentralized system. Yet public expectations of the presidency have not decreased, nor have the intractable problems diminished.

No doubt many a presidential candidate has favored a limited presidency. Some of those same candidates who, after having occupied the White House, and frustrated by the checks and balances built into the American system of government, have altered their views, seeing the limitations on the office as a deterrent to the solution of problems rather than as a means of avoiding the danger of excessive power. During the twentieth century the powers of the presidency have grown at the expense of the policy-making powers of the other two branches of government, particularly the Congress.

Growing Pains of the Presidency

The growth in the power of the presidency took many forms. For example, after World War II, the use of *impoundments* increased steadily, growing from a rarely exercised presidential management tool that blocked the use of appropriated funds for increased efficiency to a policy tool in the Nixon era used for the wholesale gutting of congressionally funded programs. The custom of executive privilege became firmly rooted, protecting not only the president's closest advisors but also many lesser White House aides from scrutiny and interrogation by the legislative branch. Accompanying a growth in the White House staff was a shift of policy-making functions from federal departments to the Executive Office of the President. Following enactment of the 1921 Budget and Accounting Act and the 1946 Full Employment Act, presidential power in budget formulation and national priority-setting increased.

Several developments in the larger society also facilitated the growth of presidential power. As the United States rose from being isolationist in international affairs to being a superpower with worldwide interests, the heightened importance of national security contributed to the centralization of power in the presidency. After the Great Depression of the 1930s, much of the responsibility for governmental management of the economy was centered in the presidency. In addition, the growing importance of the mass media led to a focus upon the president as the articulator of the nation's values, problems, and options.

Despite both the increased tools and societal pressures that catapulted the twentieth-century presidency into a greater leadership role, many limits upon the office remain. One leading presidential scholar, Richard Neustadt, has argued that the foremost power in the presidential arsenal is the power to persuade. Yet failures of the modern presidency due to poor persuasion are also visible and numerous: Carter's inability to persuade the public to turn down thermostats to save energy; Kennedy's inability to persuade a recalcitrant Congress to pass his civil rights legislation and many of his social programs; Johnson's futile efforts to persuade Congress and the public to continue their support of the Vietnam War; and Nixon's failure to convince the Congress and the public that the Watergate debacle was a minor campaign mistake are but a few examples.

In the 1970s, additional formal restrictions were placed on both the presidency and executive power with the passage of the War Powers Act, the Freedom of Information Act, and the Congressional Budget and Impoundment Control Act. Congress increased its vigilance of the presidency as a result of Vietnam and Watergate. Public opinion began to show increased distrust of the government, creating the "confidence gap" illustrated by results from public opinion polls across time. In 1958, University of Michigan surveys showed that 73 percent of respondents trusted the government all or most of the time. Even in 1964, 76 percent of the populace felt the same way, but in 1966 and thereafter, the "trust" factor began declining, falling to 30 percent in 1978. By 1986, the figures had improved slightly, but they still showed that only 34 percent of the American people trusted the government most of the time and 58 percent only some of the time. These figures have remained fairly constant since 1984 (*Washington Post Weekly*, September 22, 1986). Public distrust of both government as an institution and as a means to resolve increasingly complex and interdependent national problems remains a barrier that modern presidents not only must consider in planning their strategies and programs but must also overcome.

Lack of Confidence in the Presidency

In 1989, the Constitution of the United States will have been in operation 200 years. For a national constitution, two centuries represent a ripe old age. During those 200 years, the United States has survived and flourished, a testimony to the vigor of the American people and the stability of American institutions. But as we enter the third century of our existence under the Constitution, the machinery of government, once shiny and new, is now tarnished and sometimes rusty.

In the post-Watergate era, the once "heroic" and "imperial" presidency is beset by increasingly intractable problems and frustrations. Presidential scholars have noted this more recent decline in the power and luster of the presidency. Cronin (1980) described the modern presidency as overloaded and "imperiled." The weakened institution is unable to meet the exaggerated expectations of the "storybook" presidency. Barger (1984), as noted earlier, called the modern presidency "impossible." Contributing to this impossibility are several factors, among them fragmentation leading to a weakening of the two-party system, the decline of America as the world's only superpower to a world of shared power, energy shortages, periodic rampant inflation, declining productivity, and continuing unemployment.

Similarly, a "no-win" presidency is described by Light (1983). The complexity of modern problems leaves presidents with little room to maneuver and bargain. Congress is more openly hostile. Light identifies five trends that make the presidency a no-win office. These include (1) congressional competition for scarce domestic agenda space, (2) the rise of subcommittee government in Congress, thus increasing legislative complexity, and (3) the decline of party influence, especially in Congress. Two additional trends are (4) increased surveillance of the presidency by both Congress and the public, and (5) new domestic issues that have few active constituents such as energy and welfare reform and hospital cost containment.

Others have called the modern presidency "impotent" (Hodgson, 1980). According to this formulation, presidents are increasingly isolated from other components of the political system such as the bureaucracy, the Congress, and their own political parties. Presidents have little chance of making real progress toward problem resolution. Hodgson (1980, p. 3) contends, "Never has so powerful a leader been so impotent to do what he wants to do, what he is pledged to do, what he is expected to do, and what he knows he must do." We might also note that the accumulated burdens of office sometimes grow so great that "the killing of the presidency" has occurred when health problems have affected a president's performance.

The Confidence Gap

Describing the modern presidency as "imperiled," "impossible," "no-win," and "impotent" is symptomatic of the intractable nature of problems the institution faces. At the core of these problems is a declining public faith in government institutions. A "confidence gap" has developed between what Americans expect of their institutions and what they believe those institutions are capable of delivering. Survey research reveals that the public is more concerned with the lack of performance and leadership in our key institutions than with the core values of those institutions. Seymour Martin Lipset and William Schneider (1983) conducted an exhaustive study of the confidence gap, examining surveys over the past thirty years. These authors found that the confidence gap extended beyond government institutions to all major institutions within society. Sources of the confidence gap ranged from events such as the Vietnam War, Watergate, continuing high inflation, and unemployment, which raised questions about systemic performance. Lipset and Schneider found, however, that personal satisfaction and optimism about the future persisted simultaneously with the confidence gap in government and other societal institutions.

Increasingly, presidents need public support to carry out their programs. According to Abraham Lincoln, "Public sentiment is everything. With public sentiment nothing can fail. Without it, nothing can succeed." Edwards (1983) argues that the higher the president's public approval, the greater the probability of the president receiving congressional approval. Edwards as well as Hughes (1972) contends that the greatest source of influence for the president is public support.

Yet the confidence gap in political institutions has undermined presidential popularity and the president's ability to act. The gap corrodes public faith in government and the belief that politics matters. President Carter, in his well-known "malaise" speech, diagnosed the lack of confidence in American institutions as a fundamental problem. Carter attributed his administration's inability to make progress on many fronts to this cultural malaise, called the "cult of narcissism" by Lasch (1979). While Carter's critics accused him of blaming the American people instead of himself for government nonperformance, his general diagnosis was well supported by survey data. During the Reagan years, the nation responded more positively to a new patriotism and a revival of faith in American institutions. The prime precipitator of this seems to be Reagan's personal popularity, an economic recovery fueled by huge budget deficits, and the public's hesitant embrace of the new conservatism, which featured a return to traditional values. While Reagan's leadership appears to have arrested the confidence gap, it has not closed it. Until the confidence gap is closed— no doubt an open question for some years—the president will face an uphill fight to win and maintain the support of a profoundly skeptical citizenry. Strong, even great, presidential leadership is needed to win this uphill battle.

Problems with the Separation of Powers

Designed to protect against tyranny rather than to promote efficiency, the American governmental system is built around the principle of separation of powers. This principle protected the country from the excesses of the Nixon presidency during the Watergate scandal and even the excesses of presidential war-making in Southeast Asia, but it has handicapped the efforts of the federal government to come to grips with fundamental problems of American society. The increasing failure of the government to address these problems efficiently and expeditiously threatens the country, not with tyranny, but with chaos. In the modern era, separation of powers has produced stalemate as often or more often than it has produced innovation and progress.

While most parliamentary systems have evolved beyond separate legislative and executive branches, the United States continues to be locked into constitutionally separate branches of government with little prospect of change during this century. Prime ministers are executives who simultaneously lead the dominant party in Parliament. Presidents are executives who must cajole and persuade Congress to accept their programs. With the expansion of both the demands upon government and the scope of governmental powers, this separation of powers formulates a larger impediment for presidents who wish to lead boldly.

As a result of separation of powers, coordination between the president and the Congress is often difficult. In the American system, the president and the Congress are not required to hold the same party affiliation. Thus, in the past, several presidents have had to cope with a Congress dominated by the opposite party. Harry Truman, a Democrat, ran against the Eightieth Congress, which was controlled by the Republicans in 1948. In the 1980s, Ronald Reagan was forced to deal with a Democratic House of Representatives and a Republican Senate during his first six years in office, and with Democratic majorities in both House and Senate during his last two years. Different party affiliations make the achievement of comity between the legislative and executive branches very difficult if not impossible at times. Even when the president and the majority in Congress are from the same political party, the two may hold significantly different attitudes toward policies. The president has a national constituency and must appeal to national interests whereas senators must be attentive to their states' interests, and members of the House of Representatives to the interests of their local districts.

The enactment of the Twenty-Second Amendment, which limits the president to two terms, has weakened the president's bargaining power in the last two years of his term of office. Reagan in both 1985 and 1986 began to feel the effects of his lame-duck status when both Democrats and Republicans grew increasingly restive under his leadership. The decline of his immense popularity after the public learned of the secret sale of arms to Iran and use of some of the profits to buy weapons for the Contras in Nicaragua further contributed to his declining effectiveness that resulted from his lame-duck status.

As Congress is confronted with a growing agenda of complex issues, it has allocated greater discretionary authority to the bureaucracy. The massive growth of administrative law is a result. The bureaucracy, an unelected and in many ways an unrepresentative institution—now called the "fourth branch of government" by some scholars—has assumed a life of its own and is increasingly difficult for the president to control and direct. Theodore Lowi, among others, has diagnosed the problem of the delegation of power to administrative agencies in his classic book, *The End of Liberalism* (1979).

The Growth of Special Interests

Members of Congress are increasingly pressured by a multitude of interests that reduce presidential influence. In recent decades, effective political party support for members of Congress has declined, thus weakening party ties to the president. The costs of campaigning have skyrocketed, thus increasing the dependence of candidates on political action committees (PACs). For example, the average cost of a winning Senate campaign went from $609,000 in 1978 to $2.9 million in 1985, an increase of 376 percent!

As the costs of campaigning have escalated, the role of special interests in politics has grown. Special interests have used political action committees to influence both electoral outcomes and legislation. In 1974, about six hundred PACs contributed a total of $12.5 million to congressional campaigns. In 1984, about four thousand PACs contributed $113 million, with incumbents being the beneficiaries of most PAC financial support. Since public funding of presidential campaigns began in 1976, every major party nominee has accepted this aid, with the result that PACs shifted their support to congressional candidates.

This growth in the role of PACs has complicated the presidency in two ways. First, PACs have lessened dependence of congressional candidates on political party organization and on the president's political leadership. Second, the heightened importance of the mass media in campaigns, especially television, has further accelerated this trend, making the individual style of members of Congress more important to winning reelection than linkages to the president. The effects of both PACs and television become interactive: Rising television costs make candidates further dependent upon PACs for campaign contributions.

As members of Congress rely more heavily upon PAC contributions, PACs can exert greater influence on legislation, either blocking measures they find inimical to their interests or pressing for laws that maximize their advantages. Conflicts develop between the presidential programs and policies supported by powerful PACs. All too often the result is stalemated government, or partial ad hoc solutions instead of comprehensive ones.

Economic Problems

Modern presidents must deal with the checkered and poor performance of the U.S. economy, an issue that profoundly affects their chances for reelection and their flexibility to implement policies in other areas. The U.S. economy has featured recent and recurrent recessions, high unemployment, double-digit inflation, merger mania, mounting and massive trade deficits, and an increasing lack of competitiveness in international markets. The strength of the American dollar on international currency markets contributed to the nation's trade deficit and made exporting more difficult. Even after successful efforts to reduce the value of the dollar in 1985–1986, U.S. exports failed to expand. Presidents confront an economic environment where labor and management are often at loggerheads and where transnational corporations are not amenable to national policy controls. Protectionist pressures and trade barriers, as well as the strength of the dollar, all require increased attention and surveillance from the White House. Nonpayment of massive debts by third-world countries to American and foreign banks threaten both the U.S. economy and the world economy. Worldwide shortages of goods, energy supplies, and basic resources are exacerbating the Malthusian dilemma of population outstripping food. Third-world countries, confronted by a quadrupling of oil costs in the 1970s, found both economic development and political stability difficult.

As America becomes more enmeshed in the global economy, Keynesian fiscal policy and monetary tools become less effective in stabilizing the U.S. economy. Modern presidents have been urged to assume increased responsibility for monetary policy by moving the Federal Reserve Board organizationally to the Treasury Department. However, others fear that such a move would politicize the board and reduce its effectiveness. No agreement exists on the extent to which government should control the economy and what the nature of those controls should be, although the government in general and the president in particular are blamed when the economy performs poorly.

Nor is there agreement over the desired nature of the uneasy relationship of government with the private sector, and debates over whether to adopt a national industrial policy remain unresolved. Private sector management, labor, and government maintain quasi-adversarial relationships at times, yet the changing economic environment demands greater cooperation for survival in a global economy. Reich (1983) attributes much of the slow unraveling of the American economy since the 1960s to both this lack of consensus and common goals among management, labor, and government, and to the various perceptions this disharmony has generated. Reich argues that from the 1920s to the 1970s, American management, both in the public and private sectors, has employed the principles of specialization by simplification, predetermined rules, and management-information systems to generate high-volume standardized production geared toward homogeneous national markets. Yet the future lies with flexible production systems to generate precise technology-driven products. This shift requires enlightened leadership in all three major segments of the economy.

The farm crisis in America in the mid-1980s resulted in the demise of thousands of family farms and created economic hardship and general malaise among America's 2.3 million farmers. The crisis of foreclosures and sales under duress occurred despite an increase in federal farm aid from less than $5 billion in 1980 to over $20 billion in 1983. Many farmers bought land at high prices and, encouraged by the farm credit system, incurred heavy debt, but increasingly the viability of the family farm itself was questioned. Long one of America's most productive economic sectors which provided the American family with inexpensive food and contributed to exports, agriculture was increasingly dominated by large corporate enterprises. Thus, the challenge to future presidents is how to maintain this agricultural productivity while trimming or restructuring a federal aid program whose basic roots are in the Great Depression and whose wisdom has been criticized and questioned ever since. Among the contradictions and criticisms leveled against this aid program are policies that encourage production for exports, which totaled about $35 billion in the mid- 1980s, and that also drive farmers and investors to destroy fragile forests and rangelands and to irrigate, thus diminishing limited water supplies. In the past, farm policies, most recently the payment-in-kind (PIK) program, that pay farmers to reduce surpluses by not planting crops are undermined by tax policies that encourage surplus production on marginal lands at taxpayers' expense. Great political pressures exist, however, to continue agricultural subsidies, and their contradictions await future presidents.

Federal Deficits and the National Debt

The growing federal deficit and accelerating national debt are related problems with significant economic implications on the landscape of today's presidency. The national debt is now in excess of a trillion dollars. The cost of servicing this debt approached 15 percent of the annual federal budget, or approximately $150 billion annually in recent years. In addition to the high costs of debt service, federal deficits consume a large share of available capital for investment, thus preempting private borrowers.

Advocating balanced budgets while insisting on large defense increases and no tax increases, President Reagan presided over the largest deficits in U.S. history. He argued that a constitutional amendment to balance the budget and a presidential item veto would be the solutions to the flow of red ink. Disagreeing, Congress in 1985 passed the Gramm-Rudman-Hollings deficit reduction act, which established declining deficit targets across a five-year period, leading to a balanced budget by 1991. The act required mandatory across-the-board percentage cuts in congressional appropriations in nonexempt categories, distributed equally across defense and social spending if congressionally approved appropriations produced deficits exceeding the target. However, that portion of the act delegating to the Comptroller General responsibility for triggering the automatic cuts was declared unconstitutional, and early deficit targets were met by accounting chicanery and one-time sale of government assets that ranged from land and oil and mineral leases to loan portfolios. Deficit reduction plainly remains a major issue for future presidents.

The Federal Reserve can partially influence the impact of the deficit by employing either tight or easy money policies and by setting interest rates. Yet regardless of the prevailing monetary policy, many observers argue that large federal deficits contribute to high interest rates, systemic inflation, and destruction of capital markets and the economy. Some scholars, including John Kenneth Galbraith and Lester Thurow, argue that democracies cannot cope with the redistributive decisions that take from some and give to others. Mounting federal deficits and inflation are the indirect methods of making zero-sum redistributive decisions. Presidents must increasingly cope with these economic and budgetary decisions that, until the modern era, have been secondary to foreign-policy concerns.

Crime, Violence, and Drug Abuse

Most Americans at some point in their lives are affected by crime. According to Federal Bureau of Investigation statistics, between 1960 and 1975, every major category of crime, including the murder rate, more than doubled. However, the arrest rate for this FBI index rose only about 19 percent. Fewer than one criminal in five is ever caught. Still fewer are convicted and imprisoned for any length of time. Not even presidents are immune from the surge of crime and violence. The assassination of President Kennedy and the attempted assassinations of Presidents Roosevelt, Ford, and Reagan attest to this unpleasant fact. Presidents attempting to address the problem of crime must deal with the public's distrust of government solutions and the difficulty of coordinating the efforts of a multitude of law enforcement agencies. Criminals today are more mobile and are oblivious to political subdivisions, thus heightening the need for a national coordination of a war against crime. As already stated, the probability of a criminal being arrested is slight; being convicted for the original crime committed is even slighter. Plea-bargaining not only reduces court backlogs but it undercuts the cause of justice by encouraging the guilty to plead to a lesser charge. Sentencing guidelines are resisted by judges who are protective of their power. With a per capita incarceration rate in the United States exceeded only by South Africa and the Soviet Union, state prisons remain backlogged, the overflow spilling over into county jails that are under federal court order to reduce overcrowding. At times, near-riot conditions have prevailed in the worst of prisons.

Americans are affected by the fear of crime as well as crime itself. Fear of gratuitous acts of violence is particularly widespread. This fear of crime, coupled with governmental impotence in dealing with the problem, has led many citizens to arm themselves, thereby exacerbating the problem. The United States has less restrictive gun laws than any other advanced country and it also has the highest murder rate. Guns are used in 62 percent of all murders and 56 percent of all suicides. An estimated 150 million firearms are in the hands of the nation's citizenry. Half of all American families own guns. One-third say the purpose of gun ownership is self-defense.

Fueling high crime rates and contributing to a deterioration in the American social fabric is drug abuse. The names of the drugs keep changing—marijuana, heroin, LSD, amphetamines, cocaine, crack, and, more recently, designer drugs—but the problem of drug abuse remains, affecting ever-younger segments of the population. No longer predominantly an inner-city phenomenon, the proliferation of drugs, throughout all social strata of American society has caused considerable alarm, leading the Reagan administration to launch a "war on drugs." Yet presidents prior to Reagan also launched major efforts to stem the flow of illegal drugs into the country with limited success at best. Thus, national efforts to reduce drug abuse will certainly occupy presidential agenda for some presidencies to come. While the number of heroin addicts has stabilized at half a million, an estimated 22 million Americans in 1986 had used cocaine within the last thirty days (*Time*, September 15, 1986, pp. 60–73). To combat the spread of drugs into the professional classes, the Reagan administration has proposed drug testing for federal employees in sensitive positions, thus raising questions of whether drug testing violates civil rights in the workplace. Future presidents may alter the five strategies now employed for combatting drug abuse: (1) interdiction at the border to stem the flow of drugs into the country, (2) increasing law enforcement and police crackdowns, (3) drug testing of employees, (4) drug treatment of abusers, and (5) education of all citizens and especially youth to the dangers of drug abuse.

As tragic as illegal drugs are, legal drugs continue to create problems of life-and-death dimensions. Whereas 570 people died from cocaine use in 1985, 98, 186 fatalites in 1980 were caused by alcoholism, and 300,000 deaths annually are attributed to tobacco. The medical bill for treating abuse of illegal drugs was a whopping $59.7 billion in 1983 according to a National Center for Health Statistics estimate, and the bill for alcohol abuse ($116.7 billion) was almost double that (*Time*, September 15, 1986, p. 64), making alcoholism the number-one problem. Nearly half of all highway fatalities are linked to alcohol. In a society where alcohol is frequently the oil lubricating social and political intercourse, creative solutions to alcohol abuse on federal highways and in air traffic will challenge future presidents.

Social Problems

Social problems, many resulting from demographic shifts affecting family structure and minority groups, challenge the modern presidency. The faltering family presents many problems that impinge on the modern president and help to shape presidential agenda. In the past two decades the divorce rate has more than doubled to where one marriage out of every two now ends in divorce. Young women who are single heads of households, along with their children, constitute a third of the poor in America despite government programs to try to raise them from poverty. More children are likely to be raised in single parent households. As more women move into the labor force, either by choice or by necessity, the provision of adequate child-care facilities has not kept up with demand. Child abuse and teenage pregnancies are on the rise. Traditional family values have been assaulted by the sexual revolution and feminist movements, fomenting debate about abortion, school prayer, and the role of government in reinforcing traditional values. Proposed constitutional amendments to ban abortion and reinstate school prayer have entangled recent presidents and presidential candidates in myriad disputes, debates, and quarrels—both within and outside of government.

Despite thirty years of government effort to achieve equality for minorities in American society, the major minority groups continue to lag behind mainstream America. Recent economic disturbances, combined with a slowdown in the momentum of civil rights legislation, have deepened the anxieties of blacks and Hispanics, who fear that they will never achieve a position of equality. While government attempts to require legal equality have been successful, attempts to bring about economic and social equality have not. Minorities continue to have the highest incidences of unemployment, crime, poverty, educational inadequacies, and health-related problems. High concentrations of many minorities in cities have created urban stress and demand for social services in those areas.

Welfare reform, never popular, remains an issue that will not go away. Developed in an ad hoc fashion to meet crises, coordination between welfare programs is often limited, and despite an expansion of programs since the 1960s, welfare coverage has gaps, in large part due to its categorical rather than needs-based nature. The needs of the working poor in particular are not addressed. Critics contend that such programs as Aid to Families with Dependent Children encourage illegitimate births and the breakup of families in states that have not adopted an "unemployed fathers" program. The polyglot of state/federal programs has allowed great disparity in recipient benefits to continue, often creating stress on more generous states and localities. Effective tax rates in welfare programs—the rate at which benefits are lost when income is earned—discourage work among low-skilled recipients for whom minimum-wage jobs are all that is available. Nor is quality day care available to encourage employment. Cutbacks in most social programs under Reagan boosted the percentage of the population below the poverty line to above 15 percent.

During the mid-1980s, both housing costs and the numbers of homeless rose sharply, registering more homeless than at any previous time since the Great Depression. Deteriorating housing continued to cause problems of urban decay, especially in older declining cities. In 1970, about half of the nation's housing stock had been built before 1929 (Brewster 1984, p. 156). Despite housing shortages, federally subsidized urban renewal demolished over a million housing units between 1949 and 1967 while providing only a little more than half a million units of public housing. Changing family patterns, with increases in the number of divorced and single-parent households and increases in the age for first marriages, contribute further to the pressure on the housing market. The development of a federal policy to address housing needs is a challenge for future presidents who will be confronted with a multiplicity of state and local regulations and strong and powerful homebuilders' preferences for labor-intensive traditional stick-built housing over manufactured housing.

Mounting health costs and health cost containment will no doubt be on the agenda of future presidential domestic programs, along with the development of plans to expand health care to groups with minimal access and expansion of the type of care for the average citizen. The United States alone, among the major industrial nations, still has no comprehensive national health care system for its citizens. Contributing to rising health care costs which, by the 1980s consumed 11 percent of the gross national product (GNP), are increased reliance upon medical technology; a shift in focus from curable infectious diseases to noncurable long-term systemic diseases such as heart disease and cancer; third-party payments; and fee-for-service reimbursement systems (Kronenfeld and Whicker, 1984). A reimbursement system employing diagnostic-related groups to provide incentives for hospitals to hold down costs was implemented in major federal programs in the 1980s, but was criticized for achieving cost containment at the expense of quality of care by encouraging hospitals in some instances to discharge patients before they were ready. The development of catastrophic insurance to cover expenses when major medical insurance was depleted took on new urgency as public fear of AIDS spread. Despite criticisms that federal efforts in health care have often been misguided (for example, funding to increase the number of physicians in the 1980s through capitation and institutional grants when a surplus supply existed), pressure for greater federal involvement in both health care expansion and cost containment will confront future presidents.

Inferior U.S. Education

Another factor contributing to U.S. economic woes and trade imbalances, and caused at least in part by an altered family structure, is American education, which is on the decline. Yet the sources of decline in the once enviable American education system are many and span a variety of causes from outdated and too-short school calendars to low teacher pay and a deemphasis on science, math, and engineering. While educators, parents, teachers, and administrators struggle to pinpoint and sometimes pass the blame, the signs of trouble continue to mount. The signals are particularly distressing when the United States is compared with other countries, including postindustrial, newly industrial, and, in some instances, developing nations (*U.S. News and World Report*, January 19, 1987, pp. 58–65). Japanese youth finishing high school have the equivalent of three to four more years of school than American high school graduates. Only 6 percent of American teenagers study calculus and most do not take even a year of physics or chemistry, whereas Soviet students regularly study physics and algebra for five years, chemistry and biology for four years, and calculus for two. Although the U.S. population is twice as large as Japan's, Japan produces 9 percent more engineers. Most people receiving doctoral degrees in engineering in the United States are foreigners. Nine out of ten Japanese earn high school diplomas, but one-fourth of American teenagers drop out before completing high school. Many American teenagers who stay in high school do so to take driver's education and get a driver's license. In 1982, an algebra test given internationally to thousands of twelfth graders in fifteen countries confirmed America's declining performance. The United States ranked fourteenth out of fifteen—barely ahead of Thailand—whereas Hong Kong and Japan ranked first and second, respectively. Nor are American students developing a solid background in foreign languages, geography, and sometimes even English. This has caused American industry to spend $25 billion a year training poorly educated workers. Those who cannot find jobs never get this opportunity.

Presidential leadership will be particularly tested in the educational arena, for the stakes are high. A battle of brains is being waged for the technological future, and clearly the United States is losing. Yet federal involvement in education on a massive scale is relatively recent and has not always been welcome. Suggestions for solutions abound: lengthening the school year; abolishing summer recesses, which are based on the agricultural production cycles of the nineteenth century; reemphasizing basic skills; strengthening math and science requirements and curricula; imposing competency tests on teachers and uniform graduation exams on students; increasing the pay and status of teachers; and insisting on greater classroom order and more homework for students. Each of these proposals is controversial or costs money or both. Yet in a nation where 55 percent of all jobs involve information processing, an undereducated and poorly educated labor force is a prescription for economic decline, leading concerned and informed observers to contend that nothing less than a major national initiative with full presidential backing—equivalent to or greater than that undertaken after Sputnik—will stop U.S. education from declining even further and thus restore health to the system.

Environmental and Energy Problems

A variety of environmentally related problems are gaining greater priority on the presidential agenda, demanding attention, money, and solutions. Among these are the licensing and safe operation of nuclear power plants, the disposal of nuclear and toxic wastes, the protection of air and water, recurring energy shortages, and the need to find alternative energy supplies to supplement limited supplies of gas and oil. While many of these problems were downplayed or ignored by the Reagan administration, future presidents may not be able to treat environmental problems so cavalierly. Contributing to environmental problems in many areas is a decaying urban and transportation infrastructure, leaking water pipes and sewers, and unsafe bridges, dams, and reservoirs.

Particularly troublesome for future presidencies is the disposal of toxic wastes, a problem with regional as well as national dimensions since approximately 70 percent of the nation's hazardous wastes are generated in the Middle Atlantic, Great Lakes, and Gulf Coast regions. Reports by the Environment Protection Agency (EPA) at the end of the seventies revealed that New York, Pennsylvania, Michigan, Ohio, Indiana, and New Jersey were highest on the list of toxic landfills, closely followed by California, Texas, and Louisiana.

Yet dumpsites in all states have the potential to harm both the environment and citizens living adjacent to them through groundwater contamination, surface runoff into waterways, air pollution via evaporation of chemicals and wind erosion, direct contact poisoning, disruption of the food chain, and the creation of fires and explosions. However, pollution does not recognize political boundaries and thus requires national solutions. Acid rain, created by the release of sulfur dioxide into the atmosphere, has assumed international dimensions, creating ill feelings between the United States and Canada, whose officials view the United States as unresponsive to the primarily American-generated problem. Creative solutions to ocean and space pollution, including pollution from dumping of waste plastic products, also demand negotiations with other countries and active presidential involvement.

Long oriented toward mobility and individuality, Americans have maintained a love affair with the automobile, which has contributed to the development of an automobile-petroleum complex built originally on the notion of cheap and unlimited fuel supplies. Yet since the formation of OPEC, the United States has had to deal with wrenching energy shortages, to plan for energy conservation, and to search for alternatives to fossil fuels. Presidents Ford and Carter actively sought to reorient the nation's energy future to less dependence on imported oil. Despite a glut of petroleum in the mid-1980s, largely attributable to the collapse of OPEC and contributing greatly to the decline in inflation, the long-term questions of finding feasible energy replacements for diminishing fossil fuels remains for future presidents to solve.

International Problems

With increasing technological and economic interdependency among the nations of the world, the number of problems without significant international dimensions is rapidly diminishing. In addition to domestic problems, modern presidents must confront many problems looming on the international horizon. These include the continued lack of an international community with powers to enforce international law; the threat of nuclear holocaust and a concomitant imperative for international arms control and reduction; new, vigorous, modern leaders in the Soviet Union, who promise to mount renewed challenges to the United States; and a growth in international terrorism that threatens not only international travel and tourism but also the domestic tranquility of Middle Eastern, Western European, and even Western Hemisphere countries, including the United States. Also on the horizon is a growth in the world role of the People's Republic of China with its population in excess of a billion people. Trouble spots in the Middle East, Central America, and East Asia continue to threaten international stability.

Related to America's role in the international arena is its inability to protect the integrity of its own borders, an ability upon which the influx of illegal immigrants during the 1980s cast doubt. Compounding efforts to deal with the illegal immigration problem was the growing dependency of the U.S. economy, particularly in the Southwest, on the cheap labor illegal aliens provide. With the passage of amnesty legislation in 1987 for illegal aliens able to prove continuous residence in the United States since 1982 without dependency on welfare, Congress began to address the problem. The law also provided for penalties on employers who hire illegal aliens. Yet the wage differential between the United States and Mexico, a country mired in a major economic crisis in the mid-1980s as a result of the slump in international oil markets, promises to keep the issue of illegal immigration the focus of future presidential attention.

No president can escape the difficulties involved in establishing a viable defense policy. Consuming about 30 percent of a trillion-dollar budget by the close of the Reagan administration, defense expenditures, while necessary to protect American interests and integrity, have often been criticized for being wasteful and bloated. The perennial question remains: How much is enough and how shall we spend it? Each new proposed weapon system, from the antiballistic missile system, to the B-1 bomber, to the cruise missile, to the strategic defense initiative (SDI, or "Star Wars"), brings on a bitter debate. Some programs, such as the B-1 bomber, have been riddled with substandard performance and have been pronounced obsolete before becoming operational. Yet despite an explosion of defense spending under Reagan, America's ability to mobilize quickly and to strike in distant locations was frequently found lacking, weaknesses attributed to a bureaucratic military hierarchy, intense interservice rivalries, a confusing command structure that undercuts accountability, and sometimes spotty intelligence. Pressures to produce a quick show of force against smaller and less powerful nations have been strong, especially under Reagan, yet long-term solutions require more methodical, painstaking, and occasionally bold presidential management.

SETTING THE NATIONAL AGENDA

More than any other individual or leader, the president is responsible for translating major national problems into items on the national agenda. In recent years, political scientists and students of the presidency have increasingly turned their attention to the study of public policy and agenda setting, identifying four stages in the policy process: initiation, formulation, implementation, and evaluation. According to Paul Light in his book *The President's Agenda*, agenda control is the most important means of securing and extending presidential power.

Every agenda item does three things: it addresses an issue, involves a specific alternative, and has some priority in the policy queue (Light, 1983, p. 3). In addressing issues, the president asks which problems deserve national attention. Those issues selected by a president as important reflect not only the national needs at the time but also the president's value hierarchy. By involving specific alternatives, the president centers on programs to solve the identified problems. Various solutions may be explored before a final determination of the appropriate one. Lastly, presidents must give priorities to various issues and solutions. Obviously, any item on a presidential agenda holds some importance, but clearly presidents give certain programs higher priority than others. Here the president determines which proposals are most deserving of immediate attention and which ones can wait for future action.

Several factors influence the success of presidents in setting national agenda as well as the shape those agenda take. Paul Light contends that the key to presidential success in persuading Congress to enact the White House agenda is speed in the first year. During their first year in office, presidents often experience a honeymoon period with the media and the Congress when their proposals and programs are more favorably received than at a later time. The greater the delay in pushing presidential agenda items, the greater the probability that frictions have built up between the White House and other key Washington actors. Perhaps the best time of all for presidents to advance their agenda is in the first year of their second term when presidential expertise and the postelection honeymoon coincide. If presidents fail to act decisively during either one of these two periods, their programs run the risk of being overwhelmed by the structural problems of decentralized, fragmented American democracy.

Light also suggests that the size of a president's agenda is dictated less by party ideology than by political resources. Political resources can come from the president's personal powers of persuasion, as Neustadt (1980) suggests, or from constitutional prerogatives that emphasize managerial skills to a greater degree. Larry Berman (1987, p. 193) suggests presidents need balanced tactics of persuasion and command if they are to provide leadership in a fragmented political system. They also need viable solutions to pressing problems, some of which do not lend themselves to easy answers and may be insoluble.

Light provides several recommendations in the form of snappy, pithy phrases for overcoming structural and political obstacles of a "no-win" presidency (Light, 1983, pp. 218–232). Presidents should move the agenda or lose it. Light believes learning must wait, and presidents should take the first alternative, eschew innovations, concentrate on reelection, and avoid cabinet government, too many details, and too much internal delegation. His recommendations to convert a no-win presidency to a winnable presidency are to plan ahead, hire people with expertise, set priorities, and avoid placing amateurs in the administration.

Light's analysis and prescription reveal a deep and accurate understanding of the problems that make it difficult for a president under the conditions of today's political system to be efficient, constructive, and purposeful. His recommendations of methods for new presidents to overcome the no-win presidency are realistic and to the point, if somewhat cynical, and his nostrums for the construction of a winnable presidency are pragmatic and sensible. However, he mostly addresses administration competencies rather than the personal competencies of presidents. A winnable presidency ultimately needs both.

If Neustadt's idea of presidential power as the power to persuade is taken as a starting point instead of Light's prescriptions, then high competence in presidential abilities to sell positions, policies, and programs become most important. In addition to other characteristics, great presidents must be great salespersons. If Richard Pious's (1979) and Edward S. Corwin's (1957) notion of presidential command provide another starting point, then presidential managerial skills also become paramount. The competence of presidents in running their office, their administrations, the bureaucracy, and federal programs is a crucial determinant of presidential greatness. These twin concepts of persuasion and command can be enlarged into the twin skills of salesmanship and management. These are the two main motifs of this book, which will be expanded upon in subsequent chapters.

REFERENCES

"America's Crusade: What Is Behind the Latest War on Drugs?" *Time*, September 15, 1986, pp. 60–73.

BARGER, HAROLD M., *The Impossible Presidency*. Glenview, Ill.: Scott, Foresman, 1984.

BERMAN, LARRY, *The New American Presidency*. Boston: Little, Brown, 1987.

"The Brain Battle," *U. S. News and World Report*, January 9, 1987, pp. 58–65.

BREWSTER, LAWRENCE G., *The Public Agenda: Issues in American Politics*. New York: St. Martin's Press, 1984.

CARALEY, DEMETRIOS, quoted in *Chronicle of Higher Education*, September 4, 1985. Vol. XXXI, p. 1.

CORWIN, EDWARD S., *The President: Office and Powers, 1787–1957*, 4th revised edition. New York: New York University Press, 1957.

CRONIN, THOMAS E., *The State of the Presidency*, 2nd edition. Boston: Little, Brown, 1980.

EDWARDS, GEORGE C., *The Public Presidency: The Pursuit of Popular Support*. New York: St. Martin's Press, 1983.

HODGSON, GODFREY, *All Things to All Men: The False Promise of the Modern Presidency*. New York: Simon and Schuster, 1980.

HUGHES, EMMET JOHN, *The Living Presidency*. Baltimore: Penguin, 1972.

KRONENFELD, JENNIE JACOBS, and MARCIA LYNN WHICKER, *U. S. National Health Policy: An Analysis of the Federal Role*. New York: Praeger, 1984.

LASCH, CHRISTOPHER, *The Culture of Narcissism*. New York: Warner Books, 1979.

LIGHT, PAUL C., *The President's Agenda*. Baltimore: Johns Hopkins University Press, 1983.

LIPSET, SEYMOUR, and WILLIAM SCHNEIDER, *The Confidence Gap*, New York: The Free Press, 1983.

LOWI, THEODORE, *The End of Liberalism*. New York: W. W. Norton & Co., 1979, 2nd edition.

LOWI, THEODORE, *The Personal President: Power Invested, Promise Unfulfilled*. Ithaca, N. Y.: Cornell University Press, 1985.

NEUSTADT, RICHARD E., *Presidential Power: The Politics of Leadership from FDR to Carter*. New York: John Wiley, 1980.

PIOUS, RICHARD M., *The American Presidency*. New York: Basic Books, 1979.

REICH, ROBERT B., *The Next American Frontier*. New York: New York Times Book Co., 1983.

Washington Post Weekly, September 22, 1986, p. 12.

CHAPTER TWO
PRESIDENTIAL LEADERSHIP:
That Energizing, Elusive Enigma

This chapter explores the nature of presidential leadership, that energizing, elusive enigma that makes the United States governmental system work when it is present and falter and stumble when it is not. Presidential leadership is exciting, bold, innovative, and sometimes charismatic. Most of us recognize it when we see it and feel it when it is missing. But what exactly is presidential leadership? Perhaps it is easier to recognize than to define and describe. Yet many scholars have grappled with this important problem and the prior question of what is leadership. Before proposing our own answers to these questions we will review the efforts of others to illuminate this puzzling enigma.

Leadership is a comprehensive topic impinging on most studies of human behavior in social settings. Many attempts to conceptualize leadership have relied upon typologies—nominal categorizations. Both societal-level and contextually specific leadership typologies emphasize, either directly or indirectly, the "relations" nature of leadership.

SOCIETAL-LEVEL TYPOLOGIES OF LEADERSHIP

In one of the most encompassing and pervasive of the various attempts to categorize leadership styles, Max Weber discussed leadership and authority in terms of societal change. Weber (1964) posed three different pure types of leadership, each with a different base of authority: (1) *rational leadership* rests on belief in the legality of patterns of normative rules and in the right-to-rule of those elevated to authority under normative laws and regulations; (2) *traditional leadership* rests on a long-standing belief in the sanctity of tradition and custom; (3) *charismatic leadership* is based upon devotion to a particular individual person, attributable to that person's sanctity, heroism, or exemplary character. Weber's typology defines the foundations of the relationship bonds between the leader and the led. The basis for bonding changes as society develops.

David McClelland (1961) is similarly societal in his scope. Addressing leadership as a force initiating and shaping societal change, McClelland differentiates individuals on the basis of their primary motivation or drive into those with (1) high need for achievement, (2) high need for affiliation, and (3) high need for power. He develops operational measures of need for achievement based upon the number of achievement images in children's stories, and he demonstrates empirically a positive correlation between increases in achievement images and economic development at the societal level. McClelland attributes the otherwise hard to explain spurts in economic growth to an increase in the numbers of entrepreneurial leaders in society for whom goal attainment is a primary motive. His typology primarily emphasizes the nature of the leader's motivation. Yet it is also relational, for categories are defined on the basis of what the leader wants from followers. High-need-affiliation individuals want love; high-power-affiliation individuals seek compliance; high-need-achievement people desire esteem and respect.

David Riesman (1950) categorized individual character into three distinct types: (1) *tradition-directed*, (2) *inner-directed*, and (3) *other-directed*. For the *tradition-directed* person who feels the impact of one's culture through daily contact with a small number of individuals, fear of acting in an unapproved way and of being ashamed tends to dominate. The *inner-directed* person has internalized paternal values and often acts from feelings of guilt. The *other-directed* person, often motivated by feelings of diffuse anxiety, is compelled by the opinions and values of others. Autonomous individuals are able to establish independent standards for themselves by which they judge their own behavior. According to Riesman, an increase in the number of other-directed individuals in society has consequences for leadership emergence, insofar as "captains of industry" are more likely to be replaced by "captains of nonindustry, consumption, and leisure." Yet Riesman's categories could apply to both leaders and to followers. They distinguish between individuals on the importance of perceptions of significant others.

Perhaps the boldest effort to conceptualize leadership at the societal level has been the work of James MacGregor Burns (1978). Burns employs

Maslow's hierarchy of individual needs in his conceptualization. Maslow conceived of individuals progressing upward through a hierarchy of ranked needs from basic physical, safety, social, and esteem needs to self-actualization. According to Burns, the role of the leader is to assist and motivate followers to progress upward through this hierarchy. Burns develops two categories for leadership: (1) *transforming leadership*, which emphasizes reform, revolutionary, heroic, ideological, and intellectual goals; and (2) *transactional leadership*, which facilitates the functioning of legislative, executive, party, and opinion groups. Whereas Burns places greater emphasis on the moral character of leadership than does Weber, his category of transforming leadership bears resemblance to Weber's charismatic authority, while Burns' transactional leadership is not dissimilar to Weber's rational-legal authority. As with Weber, Burns' categories define the bases for the leader-follower relationship.

In a discussion of types of leaders in the American political system, Thomas E. Cronin develops a threefold categorization that could apply cross-culturally (Cronin 1980; Burns, Peltason, and Cronin 1984). As with earlier typologies, the primary basis of his categories is the nature of the leader-follower relationship. A discussion of these three types follows: (1) *agitators* are leaders who start movements, stimulate public hopes and expectations, and who put external pressure on government to respond to citizen demands; agitators mobilize followers to activity that may not necessarily be electorally oriented; (2) *coalition builders* strive to win elec-

Table 2–1 Societal-Level Leadership Typologies

Author	Environmental Focus	Leadership Categories	Perceptual Basis for Typologies
Weber	Society	Rational Traditional Charismatic	Societal role
McClelland	Society	Need-Achievement Need-Affiliation Need-Power	Individual motivation
Riesman	Society	Tradition-Directed	Individual
Burns	Society	Transforming Transactional	Societal role
Cronin	Society	Agitators Coalition builders Officeholders	Societal role

tions and tend to be brokers; (3) *officeholders* hold formal governmental positions and have limited ability to exercise leadership. On the one hand, officeholders have the authority that accompanies their official position, but they are constrained on the other by the need not to alienate voters in order to be reelected. (See Table 2–1.)

INSTITUTIONAL-LEVEL TYPOLOGIES OF LEADERSHIP

In addition to attempts to conceptualize leadership at a societal level, classic typologies of leadership for each of the major institutions of government have been developed. Walhke, Eulau, Buchanan, and Ferguson (1962) have divided legislators into three types: (1) *delegates,* (2) *trustees,* and (3) *politicos.* The distinction is made on the basis of the legislator's perception of his or her role (or relationship) with followers. Whereas *trustees* have a Burkean notion of representation that legislators should act primarily on the basis of their own conscience when in office, and *delegates* believe that constituent preferences should directly affect all critical legislative decisions, *politicos* represent a middle ground between these two extremes.

David Vogler (1983, p. 17) has tried to clarify what he calls "the inherent conflict between maximizing representation through interest articulation and maximizing representation through enactment of electoral mandates" by using the terms "representation" for the former and "law making" for the latter. The legislative leader must know how to balance effectively these two claims on one's own time and energy. Schubert (1974) and other judicial scholars have similarly used typologies to characterize judges and their leadership styles, along two dimensions. The first dimension contains liberal-conservative policy preferences. This dimension is sometimes further subcategorized into liberals versus conservatives on economic, political, and social issues. A second dimension (*active* versus *passive*) regards the judge's perception of the appropriate leadership role of the court in addressing policy issues. *Actives* tend to support expansion of the courts into new areas that were previously addressed solely by alternative government institutions. Constitutional conservatives or passives considerably limit the role of the courts in societal decisions.

Anthony Downs (1967) has developed a five-category typology for leadership behavior in government agencies and bureaus. The basis for Downs' typology is the breadth of the leader's perception of interest. Self-interested officials include (1) *climbers* who value power, income, and prestige; and (2) *conservers* who value convenience and security. These types of officials would be subsumed by Burns' transactional leadership. In the Downsian schema, mixed-motive officials have goals that combine self-interest and altruistic loyalty to larger values, and they would be subsumed by Burns' transforming leadership. The remaining leadership types are (3) *zealots*, who are loyal to narrow functions and organization; (4) *advocates*, who are loyal to broader functions and organization; and (5) *statesmen*, the Downsian category most like transforming leaders, who are loyal to society as a whole.

Maccoby (1976) presents a major attempt to categorize leadership in large nongovernmental organizations. He creates five categories for corporate executives based on the relationship the executive has with both followers and with tasks. Types often found in middle management include (1) "the craftsman," who is an independent perfectionist concerned with the quality of work and product produced; and (2) "the company man," who is loyal to the organization but values security more than success. In previous times, rugged power-oriented, individualistic, entrepreneurial executives, called (3) "jungle fighters," dominated top leadership. With a rise in the complexity of both corporations and their environments, and a consequent need for team playing and cooperation, jungle fighters are being replaced in the top leadership ranks by a new type of leader—(4) "the gamesman." "The gamesman" loves contests, seeks the novel, is aggressive, and enjoys putting together winning teams. In particular, "the gamesman" and "the jungle fighter" in the Maccoby schema—the two categories that could most easily be depicted as leadership categories—are characterized by the relationship leaders have with followers.

MacGregor (1957) is also concerned with leadership in hierarchical bureaucratic organizations. Drawing on Maslow's work, MacGregor contrasts two different leadership styles based on the leader's perception of the basic human nature of followers. Theory X managers assume that management is motivated by strictly economic ends and that employees must be directed and modified by management through rewards and punishment. Embedded in Theory X leadership is a worldview that the average person is indolent, works as little as possible, lacks ambition, dislikes responsibility, is inherently self-centered, and is resistant to change. *Theory Y leadership*, by contrast, assumes that management's role is to help employees fulfill their own potential in a way that is beneficial to the organization. Management is to create opportunities for individuals to develop. These categories have been further expanded by the addition of *Theory Z* (Ouchi, 1981), which emphasizes the leadership role of management in generating cohesive teams and team playing, much like Maccoby's gamesman. (See Table 2–2.)

PRESIDENTIAL LEADERSHIP: TYPES AND QUALITIES

Clinton Rossiter (1956) was one of the first scholars on the modern presidency to classify presidents as to their leadership abilities and to outline the qualities he believed were needed for success. In his book *The*

Table 2–2. Nonpresidential Institutional Leadership Typologies

Author	Environmental Focus	Leadership Categories	Basis for Typology
Walhke Eulau	Legislatures	Trustee Delegate Politico	Representational role
Schubert	Courts	Active Liberal Passive Liberal Active Conservative Passive Conservative	Judicial role and political orientation
Downs	Government bureaucracies	Climbers Conservers Zealots Advocates Statesmen	Individual motivation and job orientation
Maccoby	Corporate bureaucracies	Craftsman Company Man Jungle Fighter Gamesman	Individual motivation and job orientation
MacGregor Ouchi	Corporate bureaucracies	Theory X Theory Y Theory Z	Assumptions about human motivation

American Presidency, Rossiter not only presents his now well-known role analysis but he also divides presidents into "earth movers" and "earth smoothers." The "movers" are strong presidents who made things happen. The "smoothers" are weak presidents who were content to keep things tranquil and undisturbed. These categories are very similar to those of Sidney Hyman (1958) and Erwin C. Hargrove (1966).

Hyman classifies leadership styles on a continuum between active and passive and identifies Buchanan, Lincoln, and Cleveland as models of three types of president. Buchanan, along with McKinley and Coolidge, was an apolitical administrative official. Lincoln, Jefferson, Wilson, and F.D. Roosevelt were the opposite and stressed political leadership and innovation over narrow legality. Cleveland and Eisenhower fell between these two extremes and, while mostly administrators, they were not apolitical. They talked change but did little about it. They were defensive in strategy and relied on their veto power.

In his book *Presidential Leadership*, Hargrove advances the notion of "presidents of action" and "presidents of restraint." He classifies the two

Roosevelts, Wilson, Truman, Kennedy, and Johnson as the former, and Taft, Hoover, and Eisenhower as the latter. He also tries to capture the personality of both the presidents and the presidencies by labeling Theodore Roosevelt as The Dramatizing Leader, Wilson as The Moralizing Leader, Franklin Roosevelt as The Manipulative Leader, Taft as The Judge, Hoover as The Engineer, and Eisenhower as The General.

Rossiter also thinks that a successful modern president must have or cultivate certain qualities. Among them are bounce, affability, political skill, cunning, a sense of history, the newspaper habit, and a sense of humor.

In his classic work *Presidential Power*, Richard Neustadt (1960, p. 4) writes that a president's strength or weakness "turns on his personal capacity to influence the conduct of the men who make up the government." His influence becomes the mark of leadership. To rate a president according to these rules, one looks into the person's own capabilities as seeker and wielder of affective influence upon the other people involved in governing the country. This leads to Neustadt's well-known formulation that presidential power is "the power to persuade." He concludes that the presidency is no place for amateurs, but that a president-as-expert is no cure-all (Neustadt, 1960, p. 14). Franklin D. Roosevelt is his role-model for a great president who mastered the art of presidential persuasion.

By 1966, James MacGregor Burns advanced the idea that there are three models of presidential leadership: the Hamiltonian, the Madisonian, and the Jeffersonian. In *Presidential Government: The Crucible of Leadership,* Burns describes the Hamiltonian model as "a vigorous executive with the federal government revolving around the presidency" (Burns, 1966, p. 28). The Madisonian model makes a virtue of countervailing powers within and between Congress and the executive branch. A prudent, orderly, and stable government of ordered liberties and responsibilities is the result. In his Jeffersonian model, Burns sees strong leadership through majority rule, two-party competition, and the popular democratic and egalitarian support for the president. Burns' preferred model is the Hamiltonian ideal. He includes Washington, Lincoln, and the two Roosevelts as the "heroic leaders of the American Republic." These presidents led the nation to great achievements, not only by the vision of their role, but also through strong party leadership, loyal followers, judicious use of power, and vigorous and at times ruthless campaigning.

Thomas A. Bailey (1966) wrote one of the best and most comprehensive treatments of the problem of presidential greatness. He carefully surveys the results of various evaluations from public-opinion polls to the polls of experts. He also discusses numerous criteria and tests for judging greatness and makes summary reassessments of presidents from Washington to Lyndon Johnson. While he addresses such topics as character, temperament, health, intelligence, and such roles as teacher, preacher, and administrator, Bailey does not classify presidents as leadership types per se. His forty-three yardsticks or measuring rods of presidential greatness cover the waterfront, yet make it difficult to bring any order or preciseness into the measurements.

In *The Living Presidency,* Emmet John Hughes (1972) asks what shapes and makes an effective presidential style. His answer is that it is not the instructions, prescriptions, or designs, but rather insights and specific senses of political life that set the tone and dictate the force of presidential leadership. These senses include:

1. a sense of confidence that enlivens and strengthens a president;
2. a sense of proportion that avoids excess and extravagance;
3. a sense of drama that includes the spark of combativeness;
4. a sense of timing for the pace and rhythm of politics;
5. a sense of constancy that can distinguish between changing course and changing conscience; and
6. a sense of humanity that avoids the chillness of spirit.

The sum of these six senses, according to Hughes, is a sense of history and a sense of humor, without which presidents lack true perspective on events and on themselves.

Thomas E. Cronin (1980, p. 378) addresses the problem of presidential leadership in his influential book, *The State of the Presidency.* In it he compares the stages of presidential leadership to a theatrical play. Presidents are *Act III* leaders who provide "the acceptance, approval, and spirit of renewal that can accommodate change." However, presidents confront several leadership paradoxes:

1. Presidents are expected to be decent and just, but also decisive and guileful.
2. While we want programmatic leadership committed to issues and details, we also want pragmatic, flexible, and adjustable leaders.
3. The public appreciates innovative and inventive leadership; at the same time, presidents must be cognizant of majority public opinion.
4. We want presidents who inspire, but we get angry when they overpromise.
5. The public wants courageous and independent presidential leadership but simultaneously expects presidents to be open and sharing.
6. Presidents are inherently political creatures who are expected to rise above politics.
7. Everyone loves a common president, but everyone expects the common president to perform uncommonly.
8. We exhibit a longing for a president who will unite us across differences, yet who will make priority setting choices which are divisive.
9. We love our presidents but longevity dulls our passion.
10. Skilled presidents must walk a tightrope exuding hope and reassurance while combating crises.

11. We are torn between letting things happen and having our presidents make them happen.
12. The campaign skills necessary to achieve the presidency are different from the managerial skills required to govern.
13. The modern presidency is both too powerful for our constitutional system and too weak to achieve the burdens and expectations placed upon it.

High- and low-democracy presidential types have been identified by Louis Koenig (1981). Drawing upon the earlier work of Harold Lasswell, Koenig argues that high-democracy types act in ways that enlarge the civil rights of citizens and groups. High-democracy types also develop and support economic and social programs that respond to the needs of many groups. They are accessible to a large variety of issues and groups, discuss campaign issues meaningfully and constructively, and encourage candor among subordinates. Presidents in this category believe in democracy and act with restraint toward other branches of government and other nations.

By contrast, low-democracy types are inactive or regressive concerning civil rights, are overresponsive to the needs of the powerful, are remote, and relatively inaccessible. Low-democracy types also run campaigns that appeal to fear and irrationality. They are manipulative and secretive toward subordinates, and they display low tolerance of criticism. They show little regard for the Bill of Rights, allow problems to drift, encroach on other branches of government, and resort readily to presidential war.

Four scholarly models of the presidency that emerged in recent history are reviewed by Hargrove and Nelson (1984). The models tap two dimensions—an empirical dimension that asks whether the presidency is strong or weak, and a normative dimension that asks: Is the condition of strength or weakness good or bad? The *Savior* model of the presidency depicts the office as strong and as an uplifting force in American society. In this model, the strength of the presidency is regarded as an asset.

In the *Satan* model, the presidency is strong, but its strength is viewed as an evil. The evil is particularly manifested in foreign affairs. Examples include Vietnam and Watergate.

The third model of the presidency is the *Sampson* model. This model describes a powerful but tethered presidency that is unable to meet the challenges of the office. The president is weak and this weakness is viewed as bad, because other institutions such as Congress, the bureaucracy, and political parties are too weak or decentralized themselves to fill the void.

In the last model, the *Seraph* model, weak presidents are regarded as desirable. Contending that smaller is better, this model sees the presidency as weak, as it should be.

Hargrove and Nelson conclude that, regardless of the model of the presidency employed by holders of that office, all presidents face the same problems of managing policy formation and policy implementation. Some chief executives are presidents of "preparation," who care more about the development of new policies. They are more interested in developing plans of policies than in seeing them passed or implemented. Conversely, presidents of "achievement" stress enactment of policy options. In their rush to secure legislative passage, presidents of achievement overlook implementation problems by making unworkable compromises. Presidents of "consolidation" are concerned primarily with the modification and consolidation of existing programs. They pay great attention to the administrative feasibility proposals. (See Table 2–3.)

BARBER'S TYPOLOGY OF PRESIDENTIAL CHARACTER

For measuring presidential leadership, James David Barber (1985) has produced a provocative typology of presidential character. Character is more important than style or worldview in determining behavioral approaches to problems encountered subsequently in life. Character is mainly but not totally developed in childhood, whereas worldview is mainly developed in adolescence and style in early adulthood. Barber identifies two dimensions that constitute character: an active-passive dimension defines how much energy a president devotes to the job, whereas a positive-negative dimension defines how much a president enjoys the job. When these two dimensions are each dichotomized and crossed with each other, a fourfold typology of presidential character emerges:

1. Active-positive presidents devote much energy to their jobs and enjoy the presidency. Barber classifies Thomas Jefferson, Franklin D. Roosevelt, Harry Truman, and John F. Kennedy as active-positive presidents.
2. While active-negative presidents put much energy into the job of being president, they do so out of an aggressive drive for power rather than enjoyment and fun. Into this category Barber places John Adams, Woodrow Wilson, Herbert Hoover, Lyndon Johnson, and Richard Nixon. Prophetically, Nixon was predicted to be susceptible to the abuse of power during periods of stress and crisis.
3. Passive-positive presidents are rare, comparatively, as are passive-negative presidents. Passive presidents put less energy into their job than do active presidents. Passive-positive presidents are optimistic and seek affection. Barber classifies James Madison, William Howard Taft, and Warren G. Harding as passive-positive presidents.
4. Passive-negative presidents, in addition to putting little energy into their jobs, are less optimistic and participate in politics out of a sense of duty and obligation. George Washington, Calvin Coolidge, and Dwight Eisenhower are typed as passive-negative.

Temporally, Barber views presidential character as intermediate between childhood experiences on the one hand and presidential performance

TABLE 2–3   Presidential Leadership Typologies

Author	Environmental Focus	Leadership Categories	Basis for Typology
Rossiter	Presidency	Earth Movers Earth Smoothers	Attitudes toward change and problem solving
Hargrove	Presidency	Presidents of Action Presidents of Restraint	
Neustadt	Presidency	Power to Persuade	Professional reputation
Burns	Presidency	Hamiltonian Madisonian Jeffersonian	Early presidential styles
Koenig	Presidency	High Democracy Low Democracy	Philosophy and psychological attitude
Hargrove and Nelson	Presidency	Savior Satan Sampson Seraph	Attitudes on power and morality
Barber	Presidency	Active Positive Active Negative Passive Positive Passive Negative	Psychology of adaption
Lowi	Presidency	Keeping the initiative Keeping the initiative in the White House Democratizing the presidency	Institutional structures

and behavior on the other.   Childhood experiences especially mold and determine a president's character. A president's character, in turn, molds and partially determines the chief executive's performance in the Oval Office.

Subsequent to his initial presentation of the presidential character typology, Barber classified Jimmy Carter, Gerald Ford, and Ronald Reagan within his scheme. Barber predicted that Carter would be an active-positive president, and he saw Carter's religion as a positive force (Barber, 1985). Ford, a step-by-step thinker, was the only Republican to be classified as active-positive since Theodore Roosevelt. Later, Ronald Reagan, noted for long vacations, short office hours, and ebullient optimism, was considered to be passive-positive (Barber, 1985).

In Barber's view, the best type of president is the active-positive and the most dangerous is the active-negative. His typology is meant to help us classify candidates and to pick better presidents. Thus far his predictions have been confined to four presidents. His prediction about Nixon has proven to be the most accurate. Whether Carter's and Ford's performances as president fit the active-positive mode is a matter of lively dispute. So too is Reagan's classification as a passive-positive. Reagan's first-term performance, where he controlled the political agenda of the country, seems to belie Barber's prediction of a passive presidency, but Reagan's second term more accurately conformed to the passive-positive role. Barber's prediction of trouble for Reagan through inattention and passivity was borne out surprisingly well in the Iran-Contra scandal that became public in 1986.

Other than the soundness of Barber's theoretical base, the adequacy of his classification system, and the difficulties of fitting presidents into the correct categories (see George, 1974; Talalovich and Daynes, 1984), there is a further criticism from "institutionalists" such as Theodore Lowi (1985), who argues that while character and individual psychology are very relevant in the analysis of presidential performance, these are marginal "in the context of the tremendous historical forces lodged in the laws, traditions and commitments of institutions." Moreover, while character is formed from experiences prior to the assumption of the presidency, no allowance is made for psychological change that may occur during the campaign and during the presidency. In other words, the impact on the candidate of the presidential campaign, the presidential office, and "the presidential experience," as Bruce Buchanan (1978) calls it, has been ignored in Barber's analysis. That Lincoln and Truman grew and matured in office and that Hoover and Carter were overburdened by the office is not accounted for by Barber.

Incidentally, Lowi himself devises an "institutionalized model" of presidential performance that includes three categories:

1. *Keeping the initiative*: Presidents try to keep the initiative by proposing programs. Such proposals fill the political agenda and dominate hearings, debates, and the media. By such tactics, presidents may get a substantial part of their programs enacted, and they can earn and retain their reputation for having power and using it effectively.

2. *Keeping the initiative in the White House:* It is important to keep the initiative, but even more important to make it understood that any initiative comes from the president's program, the president's budget, and the president's administration. This centers both power and responsibility in the White House

and makes the president the center of political gravity with the rest of Washington revolving around him.

3. *Democratizing the presidency:* Because the president is now expected to be The Wizard of Oz by the masses, he must keep the initiative in the White House for appearances sake, if nothing else. The mythology of "presidential efficacy" is reinforced when credit is given to the president for leadership. As Lowi (1985, p. 151) puts it, "The more the president holds to the initiative and keeps it personal, the more he reinforces the mythology that there actually exists in the White House 'a capacity to govern.'" This puts presidents at the center of democratic government. What presidents do must appear to be of, for, and by the people. If presidents can gain and keep the support of the masses, they can mobilize the elites in and out of Washington to support them, their administrations, and their programs.

Another criticism of Barber's typology is whether it reflects a separate theoretical construct such as salient background characteristics and experiences, which in turn can be used to predict presidential performance, or is it a surrogate measure for presidential performance itself. This distinction remains unclear in Barber's original presentation of his character typology. In the exercise of predicting the Carter presidency, Barber at times appears more interested in predicting Carter's presidential character than using presidential character to predict performance in the White House.

Several attempts to employ Barber's typology empirically have appeared. Qualls (1977) applied the typology to Connecticut legislators, using Barber's own data from an earlier study, *The Lawmakers*. Qualls believes the measure of attitude toward the job of being president is unreliable and that the measure for activity, namely, how much energy presidents expend on their jobs, is both unreliable and invalid. When a measure is unreliable, it is like a stretchy yardstick; different applications of the measure to the same thing yield different results. When a measure is invalid, it is not a good instrument to measure the concept in question.

Qualls argues that Barber's interpretation of his own questionnaire data introduces ambiguity into the scientific classification he subsequently employs and that generalizations to other populations are invalid. Qualls bases his criticism of Barber's typology on its inadequacy as a measuring device.

Carpenter and Jordan (1978) attempt to predict presidential character by employing inaugural speeches of newly elected presidents. They examine the number of repetitions to measure style in discourse, hypothesizing that passive presidents will be more repetitive. While these authors find evidence to support their research hypothesis, they argue that character must be predicted with caution. First, speechwriters rather than presidents or presidential candidates may write the addresses given by presidents or presidential hopefuls. Second, their operational test applies only to the active-passive dimension of the Barber typology. Finally, presidential candidates do not make inaugural addresses.

Another attempt to employ the character typology was made by Cohen (1980). Cohen uses personality scores developed by Donley and Winter who, in turn, use speeches or written statements by presidents as if they were protocols from projective tests, such as the Thematic Aptitude Test. The Donley-Winter scores rate presidents on achievement motivation and power motivation, as developed by the psychologist David McClelland. Cohen derives mixed results in testing Barber's theory when he examines the correlations between the personality indices developed by Donley and Winter with Barber's typological classifications. Cohen finds that other than the positive-negative dimension, what Barber offers may be more easily explained by a theory based on the ideological differences between parties. Cohen concludes that Barber's measure of leadership is confounded with party distinctions implicitly measured by party identification.

USING TYPOLOGIES TO EVALUATE LEADERSHIP

All of the preceding schemas represent attempts to evaluate the concept of leadership. But schemata differ in their quality. A good schema is distinguished from an inferior one by being both valid and reliable. Typological classifications are less preferred than valid and reliable quantitative measurements, as typologies generate low-level data. Typologies consist of categories that are mutually exclusive (have no overlap) and exhaustive (cover all possibilities in the relevant universe). Despite their less preferred status in the hierarchy of scientific measurement, most attempts to estimate, let alone measure, leadership have been categorical.

Typologies may be subcategorized into three types, which also vary in quality (Kegley 1973). *Definitional* typologies, the least developed and sophisticated of the three types, employ a researcher's mental model of the distinguishing features of the concept being analyzed. Their primary utility is as a conceptualizing or "heuristic" device. Although definitional typologies often represent the first attempt to theorize about complex phenomena, their limitations are substantial. They are not amenable to validation, include normative assumptions and emotional connotations, do not include empirically specific operationalization procedures, and employ ordinary verbal phrases that invite confusion. *Ad hoc* typologies are also formulated on the basis of the researcher's prior assumptions. By contrast with definitional typologies, however, they identify the type of data to be collected to use the typology. The third type, *empirical* typologies, differs from both definitional and ad hoc types by departing from the researcher's assumptions. Categories are formulated on the basis of empirically observed differences. The criteria for placing objects into categories are explicit and replicable.

Of the previously discussed leadership typologies, most are definitional in nature, incorporating assumptions and ambiguities into their operationalizations. Exceptions to this generalization are McClelland, who specifies children's literature as a data base; Schubert, who draws upon court rulings; and Maccoby, who develops a questionnaire to probe corporate leadership styles. Barber's typology of presidential character is a definitional typology and fits the generalization. Barber's own categorization of presidents occurred only after reading voluminous and detailed materials on each president to derive an intuitive feel for a president's appropriate label. No explicit operationalization procedure is specified to enable other researchers to classify presidents in the future.

Difficulties in conceptualizing and measuring leadership have contributed at least indirectly to an enhanced emphasis on two related concepts—presidential power and presidential popularity. Researchers working with a concept of presidential power in particular have also encountered substantial measurement difficulties. Yet leadership, despite its elusive nature, remains an important concept for political and social scientists interested in understanding and explaining social systems.

Perhaps attempts to conceptualize and develop operational measures of leadership, both presidential and otherwise, have not been more successful because they have often occurred in a theoretical vacuum. No fully developed theory of leadership currently exists, yet the measurement of theoretical constructs and the development of theories about these constructs occur simultaneously. The potential exists for including time in the development of dynamic leadership theories. Two of the societal-level typologies—those of Weber and Cronin—implicitly incorporate time and therefore have greater potential for resulting in a leadership theory. The other societal-level, as well as institutional, typologies remain predominantly crosssectional, describing leadership at only one point in time.

Weber implies that traditional leadership chronologically precedes rational-legal leadership. The transition between these two categories is charismatic leadership, which acts as a bridge between the older ascriptive basis for authority and the newer achievement basis. Yet the occurrence of a charismatic leader critical to this transition is almost viewed as an unpredictable random event.

Time is also implicit in Cronin's categories. While the three leadership categories of agitator, coalition builder, and officeholder may occur simultaneously at any point in time, the passage of time is implied. As a single issue flows through the policy process, different leaders act upon it at different points in time. Agitators are crucial to first establishing the issue as a legitimate item on the national agenda. Coalition builders then mobilize interest groups and create the coalitions necessary to bring the issue to resolution. Even later, officeholders act upon the issue, deciding the shape and type of policy change needed.

A NEW CONCEPTUALIZATION OF PRESIDENTIAL LEADERSHIP

Because of the growing size of the modern presidency that Cronin (1973) has described as "The Swelling of the Presidency," and what others have called the "Institutionalization of the Presidency," an urgent need exists to devise a simple and straightforward schema that can evaluate the performance of today's presidency. To ameliorate, yet alone solve, the problems on the president's agenda today, which we have described in Chapter 1, necessitates that a chief executive have a combination of skills not customarily associated with successful presidents in the past. In the contemporary media environment of the late twentieth century, where a premium is put on ability to communicate via television and to supervise trillion-dollar budgets, the traditional skills of the past are not enough to confront and cope with current problems, let alone those over the horizon in the twenty-first century. The traditional skills and qualities that we have surveyed in this chapter are of course still needed and desirable today. In fact, we may say that they are still indispensable if a president is to be successful.

We argue, however, that today's president must have, in addition to these traditional qualities, two other skills that will enable him (or her) to meet the challenges of the moment and of tomorrow. These two we have identified as selling skills and managerial skills. These are the distillation of many of the qualities that Bailey (1966) and others have cited as a necessity for a twentieth-century president. The president who is a good salesperson can more easily lead, manipulate, and motivate people. The president who is a good manager can assemble materials and people to achieve particular goals. These two dimensions result in the following four categories: (1) inactive leadership that has low management and selling skills; (2) political leadership that is high on sellings skills but lacks managerial skills; (3) operational leadership that is high on managerial skills but lacks selling skills; and (4) great leadership that, we postulate, is high on both selling skills and managerial skills (See Table 2–4.)

Unlike Barber's typology, this typology is not concerned with psychological motivation to perform or not to perform. Rather, it focuses on a job analysis of skills needed to perform well.

In our evaluation of presidents and candidates we will employ aggregate data, biographies, and past performance ratings of presidents by professional scholars. By relying on the conclusions of the best scholarship

TABLE 2–4.   A New Conceptualization of Presidential Leadership

		Selling Skills	
		Low	*High*
Management skills	High	Operational leadership	Great leadership
	Low	Inactive leadership	Political leadership

available and aggregate data studies, we can arrive at reliable conclusions about how presidents have performed.

This schema, which falls under the classification of an ad hoc category, will also include a breakdown of selling skills as they apply to the press, public, Congress, and world leaders. Grades of high, low, and medium will be assigned and numerical equivalents will be given to each grade. An overall selling-skill score will be assigned to presidents from Hoover to Reagan. Management skills will be tested in defense policy, foreign policy, social policy, and economic policy. The same grades and numerical scores will be used, and overall management scores will be allotted. A combination of these scores will be used to classify presidential leadership styles. We can then contrast when presidents are effective and ineffective and when they are great and when they fail. Particular attention will be devoted to those presidents who exhibit great effectiveness and great leadership.

Circumstances partially determine how we view presidents. Presidents who do not possess high levels of both selling and managerial skills may still be viewed as adequate as long as circumstances shield them from major crises that expose their flaws. Yet truly great presidents surmount and mold crises rather than merely cope. They have the selling skills to sell solutions to the press, the public, and the Congress. They also have the managerial skills to implement, evaluate, monitor, and modify the solution once it is sold.

Traditional leadership qualities, especially integrity, a moral purpose, experience, and a sense of history, are important for greatness. However, the presence of traditional qualities alone will not produce great leadership in the modern competitive national and international environment in which presidents must operate. High levels of selling and management skills are necessary for greatness in the modern presidency.

REFERENCES

BAILEY, THOMAS A., *Presidential Greatness*. New York: Appleton-Century-Crofts, 1966.

BARBER, JAMES DAVID, *The Presidential Character: Predicting Performance in the White House*. 3rd edition. Englewood Cliffs, N.J.: Prentice-Hall, 1985.

BUCHANAN, BRUCE, *The Presidential Experience*. Englewood Cliffs, N.J.: Prentice-Hall, 1978.

BURNS, JAMES MACGREGOR, *Leadership*. New York: Harper and Row, 1978.

_____, *Presidential Government: The Crucible of Leadership*. Boston: Houghton Mifflin, 1966.

BURNS, JAMES MACGREGOR, JACK PELTASON, and THOMAS E. CRONIN, *Government by the People*, 12th edition. Englewood Cliffs, N.J.: Prentice-Hall, Inc., 1984.

CARPENTER, RONALD H., and WILLIAM J. JORDAN, "Style in Discourse as a Predictor of Political Personality for Mr. Carter and Other Twentieth-Century Presidents: Testing the Barber Paradigm," *Presidential Studies Quarterly*, 10 (1978), 588–599.

COHEN, JEFFREY, "Presidential Personality and Political Behavior: Theoretical Issues and an Empirical Test," *Presidential Studies Quarterly*, 95 (1980), 209–237.

CRONIN, THOMAS E., *The State of the Presidency*, 2nd edition. Boston, MA.: Little, Brown, 1980.

DONLEY, RICHARD and DAVID G. WINTER, "The Swelling of the Presidency," *Saturday Review*, 1 (1973), 30–36.

_____, "Measuring the Motives of Public Officials at a Distance: An Exploratory Study of American Presidents," Behavior Scientist, 1970, 227–236.

DOWNS, ANTHONY, *Inside Bureaucracy*. Boston, MA.: Little, Brown, 1967).

GEORGE, ALEXANDER L., "Assessing Presidential Character," *World Politics*, 26 (1974), 234–282.

HARGROVE, ERWIN C., *Presidential Leadership*. New York: Macmillan, 1966.

HARGROVE, ERWIN C., and MICHAEL NELSON, *Presidents, Politics, and Policy*. New York: Knopf, 1984.

HUGHES, EMMET JOHN, *The Living Presidency*. Baltimore: Penguin, 1972.

HYMAN, SIDNEY, "What Is the President's True Role?," *New York Times*, September 7, 1958, p. 10.

KEGLEY, CHARLES W., Jr., *A General Empirical Typology of Foreign Policy Behavior*. Beverly Hills, Calif.: Sage Publications, Inc., 1973.

KOENIG, LOUIS W., *The Chief Executive*, 4th edition. New York: Harcourt Brace Jovanovich, 1981.

LOWI, THEODORE, *The Personal President: Power Invested, Promise Unfulfilled*. Ithaca, N.Y.: Cornell University Press, 1985.

MACCOBY, MICHAEL B., *The Gamesman: Winning and Losing the Career Game*. New York: Bantam, 1976.

MACGREGOR, DOUGLAS, "The Human Side of Enterprise," *Management Review*, 46 (1957), 22–28.

MCCLELLAND, DAVID C., *The Achieving Society*. Princeton, N.J.: D. Van Nostrand, 1961.

NEUSTADT, RICHARD, *Presidential Power: The Politics of Leadership from FDR to Carter*. New York: John Wiley, 1980.

OUCHI, WILLIAM G., *Theory Z: How American Business Can Meet the Japanese Challenge*. New York: Avon Books, 1981.

QUALLS, JAMES H., "Barber's Typological Analysis of Political Leaders," *American Political Science Review*, 71 (1977), 182–211.

RIESMAN, DAVID, *The Lonely Crowd: A Study of the Changing American Character*. New Haven, Conn.: Yale University Press, 1950.

ROSSITER, CLINTON, *The American Presidency*. New York: Harcourt Brace & World, 1956.

SCHUBERT, DAVID, *Judicial Policy Making*. Glenview, Ill.: Scott, Foresman, 1974.

TATALOVICH, RAYMOND and BYRON W. DAYNES, *Presidential Power in the United States*. Monterey, Calif.: Brooks/Cole, 1984, chapter 8.

VOGLER, DAVID J., *The Politics of Congress*, 4th edition. Boston: Allyn & Bacon, 1983.

WALHKE, JOHN C., HEINZ EULAU, WILLIAM BUCHANAN, and LEROY C. FERGUSON, *The Legislative System: Explorations in Legislative Behavior*. New York: John Wiley, 1962.

WEBER, MAX, *The Theory of Social and Economic Organization*. New York: The Free Press, 1964.

CHAPTER THREE
PRESIDENTS AS SALESPEOPLE:
Head of the Trillion Dollar Club

This chapter explores the role of selling ability in leadership. Scholars from Machiavelli to Richard Neustadt have long recognized the importance of convincing others to follow and to perform acts they otherwise would not have done. Machiavelli notes that people will readily change masters in the belief that they will better their condition. The shrewd prince convinces his subjects that they are better off under his dominion than under the dominion of a rival. Neustadt bluntly states that presidential power rests not upon formal authority but largely upon a president's potential and capacity to persuade.

Similarities and differences will be noted between the concept of presidents as preachers using a "bully pulpit" and presidents selling their product through the mass media. Presidents must increasingly sell ideas, programs, and budgets to four different audiences: the media, the public, the Congress, and world leaders. This chapter will discuss each of these areas of presidential selling ability in detail. The selling abilities of modern presidents will be rated in each of these four areas.

Modern presidents are like salespeople who strive to achieve visible recognition of their success by gaining membership in a "million dollar" sales club. All members must sell a million dollars annually to belong. The sales job of the president is even larger. A modern president must "sell" trillion dollar budgets to a sometimes recalcitrant Congress. Increasingly, presidents must cope with the problems of managing a trillion-dollar national debt as well. Consequently, not only is the president the head of this very special trillion dollar sales club but he is the only member.

WHAT IS A SALESPERSON?

Selling ability has not always been a highly regarded skill in the United States, yet it is critical to the functioning of a healthy capitalistic economy. Selling is often viewed as a simplistic activity that does not require an extensive formal education, compared to other professionals. Salespeople, especially manufacturers' representatives who cover large territories, are often among the highest paid occupations. The ultimate goal of a salesperson is to persuade clients and customers to buy a particular product or service. Persuasion is a complex psychological process involving many different skills.

The potential for high earnings for salespeople reflects the importance of various persuasive skills. First, sales reps must be intimately familiar with their products or services. Failure to know a product line thoroughly may result in failure to promote its strengths over competitive lines. Second, salespeople must have a high degree of interpersonal intelligence. They must be able to read the responses of clients, to sense their moods and problems, and even to set those moods. Third, salespeople must be articulate, comfortable with words, both to describe and explain their products and to relate to customers. And last, salespeople must be willing to take risks. Often working on a commission basis rather than a fixed salary, they are willing to repeatedly risk their economic well-being on their skills, on the state of the economy, and on their products. Many travel extensively and are willing to venture away from their home base.

Peters and Waterman (1982), in their best-selling book *In Search of Excellence,* identify basic principles that the best run American companies employ to stay on top. Most involve some element of selling. Like good salespeople, well run companies have a bias for action. They prefer doing something to doing nothing. These companies stay close to the customer and know and cater to client preferences. On the job, sales reps, often geographically remote from the home office, must think and act independently. Many have the authority to set customer prices and shipping conditions. Similarly, well run companies promote autonomy and entrepreneurship by retaining small groups within the organization that can think and act independently.

Sales reps who work on commission share directly in the company's success. If the company makes a superior product, the salesperson benefits personally and economically by higher sales. Well run companies use this principle of sharing in company rewards throughout the entire organization, not just with the sales force. These companies keep in touch with the essential business of the company, just as good salespeople are very knowledgeable with their products and services.

Sales reps in the field have very little immediate support help for they are geographically removed from the company's secretarial and administrative staff. They must develop an efficient, systematic method for handling paperwork and details. To neglect this aspect is to alienate customers and lose future sales. Similarly, well-run companies have few administrative layers and stay lean at the top. The most effective salespeople believe in their products and are dedicated to the values of the company. Finally, efficiently run companies also foster an atmosphere of values and beliefs supportive of company policies.

Selling skills are not confined to the sales force of companies and to manufacturers representatives. Modern presidents must also be salespeople capable of persuading various audiences of the merits of their policies.

How does presidential selling ability differ from presidential teaching and preaching? Thomas A. Bailey (1966), in his book *Presidential Greatness,* included a chapter on the teacher- and preacher-in-chief. He stressed the importance of teaching and preaching in judging the greatness of presidents. Woodrow Wilson, probably the most famous of presidential teachers, sought to educate the citizenry about significant issues and about the need for corrective action. Wilson's effort to inform Americans of the goals and importance of his Fourteen Points, which explained the leadership role of the United States in the post-World War I environment, is illustrative of how this role can be used to affect history. His failure, in spite of herculean efforts to convince both the public and the Senate of the importance of the United States joining the League of Nations, suggests that teaching skills must be supplemented by selling skills.

By contrast, Theodore Roosevelt is a prime example of a presidential preacher, who used the White House as a bully pulpit to pontificate his moral judgments throughout the country. Thomas B. Reed, sometimes called "Boss Reed," an infamous political kingpin of Roosevelt's day, sarcastically congratulated Roosevelt on his "original discovery of the Ten Commandments." Also observing Roosevelt's moralistic tone in the White House, the British writer, John Morely, found Roosevelt to be an interesting combination of St. Paul and St. Vitus. Nevertheless, Theodore Roosevelt was enormously successful as a lay preacher while president. He used the bully pulpit to rouse the country about conservation, about powerful economic trusts, and about America's destiny in world affairs.

While the ability to sell includes important skills also involved in teaching and preaching, it is more expansive than either of these. Teaching implies the transfer of intellectual knowledge in a nonpersuasive context. The goal of teaching is to impart to the pupil knowledge and skills held originally only by the teacher. Teachers do not try to persuade students to alter their behavior. Rather, a teacher is successful when the pupil has acquired the intended knowledge base and expertise. Like teachers, salespeople must also impart new knowledge and technical skills to their customers and clients. Successful salespeople, however, must sell their product. The transfer of knowledge alone is insufficient for success. Sales reps must generate a behavioral response on the part of customers, enticing them to alter their behavior to buy one product over another or not to buy anything.

Nor is selling identical to preaching. Preachers strive to impart a value code to parishioners. Rarely do preachers impart technical knowledge and skills. Like sales reps, preachers care about the behavioral response to their message. Sales reps must sell products, while preachers sell a set of behaviors and a way of life. Unlike salespeople, however, preachers care that their followers adopt the appropriate values and morals. Behavioral action alone is insufficient to the preacher, as the internal belief system is equally and often more important. By contrast, sales reps, like presidents trying to build political coalitions, are mostly concerned with the behavioral response. Presidents and salespeople are only secondarily concerned with why the desired behavioral response was achieved.

Selling ability also overlaps with popularity but is more encompassing. Popularity is approval but does not necessarily imply competence or performance. Elmer Plischke (1985) has commented:

> Over time, the attempt merely to please, unaccompanied by initiative and accomplishment, is likely to boomerang. In practice, a President may be popular without being respected, he may be well regarded without being acclaimed, and he may be esteemed without being prestigious. Or he may be admired without being liked, or honored by his contemporaries without becoming historically noteworthy.

Popularity facilitates selling ability but is not sufficient to make a good salesperson. As Arthur Miller's characterization of Willy Loman in *Death of a Salesman* indicates, striving to be popular and to be liked is not enough. Salespeople must combine popularity with technical knowledge, a good product, and persuasive skills to achieve success.

SELLING TO THE MEDIA

Above all else, a modern president must sell ideas and programs to the media. The media are the primary intermediaries between the president and the public. Failure to communicate effectively with the media will ultimately cloud and shroud in ambiguity, confusion, and misperception a president's message to the citizens who decide the president's reelection fate as well as the electoral fate of his party. Similarly, presidential communications with both Congress and world leaders are also filtered through the media. The media become a magnifying lens through which messages to all other audiences are viewed. Failure to use the media effectively is to court imminent disaster. Successful use of the media eases the way for success in all other arenas.

The professional media include the managers, reporters, and editors of the printed media, as well as employees of television and radio organizations who shape and transmit political news through mass channels (Rubin, 1981). Nor is the exercise of political power through the media unilateral. Presidential media relationships are relationships of mutual dependence. Presidents use the media to achieve their own agenda, but members of the media also use and are dependent upon presidents to practice their craft. The single greatest producer of information within the nation is the U.S. government. The largest source of information within the government is the executive branch, and within that, the president.

The media and the president are usually involved in a tug of war, each trying to maximize its own interests. The president is constantly trying to sell programs to the public via the media, and the media are constantly trying to unearth as much information as possible on policymakers, policy decision making, and policy outcomes. The president wishes to reveal only information which serves this purpose, presenting a facade that all is well. The media wish to penetrate this veil that all is well and challenge the image of the president as an infallible commander.

Not all presidents are equally skilled at selling their programs to and through the press. Jefferson, Lincoln, and Wilson were naturally gifted orators, and Lincoln is widely conceded to be a great writer. Woodrow Wilson was a superb scholar and was repeatedly voted the finest lecturer at Princeton University. Other presidents, such as William Howard Taft, were considerably less skilled. What follows is an analysis of the abilities of modern presidents to sell their programs to the media. Each president will be ranked high, medium, or low.

Hoover to Kennedy

Herbert Hoover was an ineffective salesman in his relationships with the media. Although Hoover was a serious, dignified, and conscientious person, as a radio performer, the dominant electronic media in his day, he was handicapped, according to Bailey (1966), by a voice that was "flat, tired, and monotonous." Hoover, following the examples of Harding and Coolidge, required written questions in advance at his press conferences, a style which depreciated the newsworthiness and limited the subject matter and spontaneity of the event. Rubin (1981) described the initially friendly and supportive relationship between the media and Hoover as one that eventually eroded.

The erosion was reflected in a decline in both the quality and quantity of press conferences. Newspeople came to dislike the ceremonial trappings, the presence of Secret Service agents, and presidential playing to favorites in press conferences as well as Hoover's complaints to publishers about reporters who criticized him. Hoover held fewer and fewer meetings with the press as his administration progressed. In his last two years, he barely held one a month. Increasingly, the press conferences consisted of White House press secretaries distributing official handouts. Schlesinger (1957, p. 244) quotes Paul Anderson of the *St. Louis Post- Dispatch* reporting in 1931 that Hoover's relations with the press had reached "a stage of unpleasantness without parallel during the present century. . . characterized by mutual dislike, unconcealed suspicion, and downright bitterness." Martin Fausold (1985, pp. 204–205), in his recent study of the Hoover presidency, notes that, "It is difficult to imagine that Hoover, who had so expertly practiced public relations over a decade prior to his presidency, could not adjust to the kind of public relations required by the presidential office." He also quotes Ted Clark, Coolidge's former press secretary, as being shocked by the "bitter personal hatred which [Hoover]. . . has inspired in so many newspapermen." Hoover's inability to communicate effectively to the media contributed to the ultimate rejection of his programs and philosophy.

Hoover's successor, Franklin Delano Roosevelt, excelled at selling his programs and philosophy to the press. He is widely conceded to be the most effective president at media relations in this century. Roosevelt changed the rules governing presidential press conferences, eliminating the practice of requiring written questions in advance and furnishing reporters with in-depth background information, both on the record and off. By the end of his first term in office, Roosevelt's mail was ten times that of Hoover's at the end of Hoover's administration.

Roosevelt enjoyed the give-and-take with journalists and was able to develop friendships with many White House reporters. He did, however, dislike columnists who added their own interpretation to "the facts" that Roosevelt dispensed. Roosevelt's wife, Eleanor, proved to be a valuable asset in his relations with the press. Her column, entitled "My Day," appeared in 135 newspapers. It usually discussed the themes of the Roosevelt administration. Roosevelt's magnificent speaking voice and his natural abilities as an actor made radio a natural medium for him. Here, he answered his critics, and his thirty Fireside Chats in over twelve years in office established a lasting rapport with his audience.

In contrast to Roosevelt, Harry Truman exhibited a moderate or medium ability to sell his programs and ideas to the media. One of his biggest shortfalls in communication with the press was his failure to clarify America's war aims in Korea, leading to bitter homefront resentment over the stalemated war and paving the way for Eisenhower's 1952 election. However, like Roosevelt, Truman enjoyed the give-and-take with reporters at his press conferences. He frequently was surrounded by a coterie of reporters on his early morning walks where he would pepper the reporters with his off-the-cuff remarks about life and politics. This shoot-from-the-hip style sometimes injected him into political controversy, but his salty, down-to-earth honesty established him as role model for later presidents for unpretentious communications with the media and others. Although Truman at first was ineffective in his delivery of speeches, he improved with experience and instruction. His "give-'em-hell, Harry" speeches during his 1948 whistlestop campaign were rough and tumble campaign speeches at their most effective.

Dwight Eisenhower also ranks medium or moderate in his media salesmanship skills. His press conferences received mixed views. On the one hand, his reputation as a military commander and his natural charisma lent dignity and glamour to the occasion. However, his jumbled syntax often made his remarks incomprehensible. Revisionist scholarship on Eisenhower has argued that this fogging of issues was done by intent rather than accident. Revisionists contend that in a cat-and-mouse game with the press, he did not wish to reveal his true intentions prematurely. Eisenhower was most effective in personal appearances where his smile and avuncular appearance were assets. On radio, his presentations were often characterized by hesitancy and stumbling.

John Kennedy was the only president ever to win a Pulitzer Prize, which was awarded in history for his book *Profiles in Courage*. He has been likened to a young F.D.R. for his skill and adeptness in dealing with the media. Kennedy had obvious literary gifts, but he also relied heavily upon speech writers, like all modern presidents. He was a master of the modern press conference. His sharp wit, bon mots, and command of facts all proved salutary in his relationships with members of the press. He enjoyed reading newspapers and liked many newspeople. His rapport with them was typically excellent. Like Roosevelt, he relished the swift give-and-take. His quick sense of humor made his press conferences entertaining and a verbal delight, compared to the normal humdrum of Washington verbiage.

During Kennedy's presidency, television came of age, and he was the first president to master the new medium. His besting of Richard Nixon in the presidential debates of 1960 contributed substantially to his narrow margin of victory in the election. Not just an excellent speaker, Kennedy was also a superb actor. He projected an image that was handsome, young, vigorous, and bright. He proved innovative in his relations with the media, developing the technique of live television press conferences and "rocking chair" chats with selected newspeople.

Johnson to Reagan

If Kennedy introduced the age of television to the presidency, Lyndon Johnson wholeheartedly embraced it. According to Hoxie (1986, p. 7), Johnson became the slave of television, with "television cameras in the White House always in the ready position, and with the reporters, at his own invitation, always at his heels." Yet Johnson ranks medium in his media skills. His image in the press was often that of a crude, larger-than-life, unlettered, and unpolished Texan, especially when contrasted with the sophistication of the preceding Kennedy administration. As the Vietnam War became increasingly unpopular, his relations with the media grew more testy. However, his strong convictions and his persuasive abilities, particularly on behalf of civil rights and the Great Society, often proved moving and eloquent. His press conferences ranked neither among the best nor the worst of modern presidents and, across time, as his unpopularity grew, declined in frequency. Johnson had both good and bad moments with the media. His good moments most typically occurred in domestic politics and his bad moments usually concerned foreign policy.

In most of Richard Nixon's adult political life, his relations with the media were troubled and characterized by abrasiveness and hostility. Nixon had a profound distrust of the professional reporters with whom he dealt. Even after he became president and learned how to package his appearances and master the press conference, the relationship continued to be uneasy, skeptical, and distrustful. During his fateful debates with Kennedy, he appeared ill at ease, haggard, and heavy bearded. These characteristics never quite disappeared from his presidential press conferences. He had no sense of humor or rapport with the press, and he appeared tense, moralistic, and duty-bound rather than playful or relaxed. His relationship with the media deteriorated to perhaps an all-time low in modern presidential history during Watergate when his lying and chicanery became obvious to members of the media.

Gerald Ford, Nixon's successor, experienced periods of good media relations, especially in the beginning of his administration before the Nixon pardon. During this transition period, from the Watergate crisis to a more stable and open government, Ford's innate decency and openhandedness contributed to his favorable press response. Perhaps a highlight of his press relations followed the retaking of the *Mayaguez*, an American merchant vessel, from the Cambodians who had seized it earlier. Here his popularity jumped 12 percent. Ford operated best with small groups of reporters and press officials (Kerbel 1986, p. 86). However, the Nixon pardon was so divisive and controversial that Ford's press secretary resigned. Ford had an image in the media as being bland, lacking presidential qualities, awkward, and stumbling. To the very end of his administration, he struggled to overcome this image.

Ford ranks moderate in his ability to sell his ideas and programs to the press. His WIN campaign (Whip Inflation Now) is symbolic of his checkered dealings with the media. Ford deeply believed in the power of individual voluntary action, and he invested considerable enthusiasm in his campaign, but to seasoned political observers the campaign was not backed by forceful governmental leadership.

Jimmy Carter presented a paradox of a detail-oriented, conscientious president who was unable to sell most of his programs to the press. In spite of having one of the most able press secretaries in recent history in Jodie Powell, the relationship between Carter and the Washington press corps grew increasingly uneasy as Carter incurred difficulties in getting his programs through Congress. The media progressively perceived Carter as a well-intentioned, hard-working, but incompetent chief executive who could not see the forest for the trees. The amateurism of many of his closest advisors was perceived in an unfavorable light by the Washington establishment, especially the Washington press corps. Hamilton Jordan, Carter's first chief of staff, was alleged to have engaged in social indiscretions that created image problems difficult to overcome. The resignation of Bert Lance from the Office of Management and Budget and Billy Carter's numerous shenanigans further contributed to Carter's image problems.

While the press respected Carter's hard work and good intentions, they faulted his execution and policy implementation. Carter tried to demystify and humanize the remnants of the imperial presidency, only to discover that neither the press nor the public liked the extent to which he made the presidency common. In the last year of his only term, Carter confronted a variety of national emergencies that contributed to his negative media image. The Soviets invaded Afghanistan and the United States appeared impotent. Inflation reached double digits, compounded by stagflation and recession. American hostages were seized in Iran by a revolutionary government that came to power there while Carter presided over the White House. His "Rose Garden strategy" of managing the media during the 1980 election eventually backfired, making Carter appear weak and indecisive rather than concerned, forceful, and presidential. The failed hostage rescue raid and the challenge by Senator Ted Kennedy drove nails into the coffin of Carter's negative media image and sealed his dismal 1980 electoral fate.

Ronald Reagan has been among the most effective of modern presidents in managing and using the media for his own purposes. Dubbed the "great communicator," his passive-positive personality, cheerful disposition, acting skills, and simplistic message facilitated his ability to sell his programs through the media. Despite this image as a skillful media communicator, Reagan has received more negative news coverage than any recent president (Smoller, 1986, p. 43). One example of his lapse in press relations was his visit to Bitsburg, West Germany, when his homage at a German cemetery where Nazi soldiers were buried was controversial and perceived inappropriate. Because of his various factual blunders, political misjudgment, and the increasing skepticism of his mastery of the content of complicated issues by the Washington press corps, he ranks medium on his selling skills to the press.

Reagan has been most effective when he can control the environment in which he interacts with members of the media. When this control is missing, he does less well, lapsing into factual errors and misleading generalizations. He has been able to overcome negative coverage and maintain extraordinarily high popular support as a result of his expert control of electronic media, including presidential addresses, radio speeches, the White House news service, and political advertisements.

Typically, modern presidents experience a three to six month "honeymoon" with the media during which relationships between the press and the president are quite positive. Reagan enjoyed an eighteen-month honeymoon, benefiting from favorable press relations far longer than other presidents. This extended honeymoon resulted from his wooing and charming the Washington establishment. His friendly and open manner and his enormous success in achieving legislative goals within Congress impressed even skeptical and cynical journalists and scholars.

However, seasoned journalists, such as David Broder and Lou Cannon, expressed repeated concerns about Reagan's mastery of policy and details, his frequent factual errors in press conferences, and his ignorance of world affairs. Broder, at one point, exasperated with Reagan's waffling of details about South Africa, expressed sympathy for the White House aides charged with "watering the arid desert between Reagan's ears." Although the most popular of modern presidents with the public, Reagan's professional reputation with the press and the media is much more mixed than with the public at large. As the Iran-Contra affair began to unravel during 1987, Reagan's reputation suffered even more.

SELLING TO THE PUBLIC

The public is the second major audience to whom presidents must sell their programs, ideas, and philosophy. Abraham Lincoln, considered the greatest president of the nineteenth century and one of the greatest in the history of the nation, succinctly expressed this thought: "Public sentiment is everything. With public sentiment nothing can fail; without it, nothing can succeed." Journalist Emmet John Hughes identifies the dependence of presidential authority on popular support as the one unchallengeable truth in history. Presidential scholar George C. Edwards, III agrees that "the greatest source of influence for the president is public approval." (Edwards, 1983, p. 1).

Why is public approval so important to the modern presidency? Public popularity is a necessary but not sufficient condition to overall selling ability in the White House, for the public is only one of the four critical audiences a successful president must persuade. However, a popular president with high ratings in public-opinion polls has much greater leverage. With it the president can more easily capture the attention, if not the respect, of the media, the Congress, and world leaders. Research has shown a positive correlation between the levels of public approval of a president and the support his programs receive. This positive linkage is especially true among representatives and senators (Edwards, 1983, pp. 2, 211). While the public is only one presidential audience, it is the first audience among equals. President's who fail to sell their programs and ideas to the public will not have an opportunity to sell their policies to other audiences for very long.

Hoover to Kennedy

Entering the White House during the last days of the Roaring Twenties, Herbert Hoover's initial public reputation was extraordinarily high. Well respected as a internationally known mining engineer, a dedicated humanitarian, and an experienced cabinet member, he enjoyed considerable approval and acclaim. But his failure to cope with the aftermath of the stock market crash in 1929 and the agonizing throes of the Great Depression soured his public image, ranking him low on his ability to sell his programs to the public. His inflexibility and dogmatism, and his dedication to the principles of a free market and government nonintervention into the economy, froze his capacity to respond to public needs, which the public noticed. By the 1932 election, most observers agreed that the demise of Hoover's presidency was a foregone conclusion.

Franklin Roosevelt arrived at the White House in the midst of the Great Depression with overwhelming electoral and public support. In spite of his inability to pull the country out of the Depression until World War II, he nevertheless managed to hold the trust and esteem of his fellow citizens. As the only four-term president in the history of the Republic, Roosevelt demonstrated a superb mastery of public relations that has seldom if ever been surpassed by any other president. But the country became deeply divided over the New Deal and Roosevelt's plan to "pack" the Supreme Court. Opponents considered him "that man in the White House" and "a traitor to his class." But a strong majority in the country looked to him as a great leader who restored faith in the system and later led the war effort against the Axis.

Harry Truman had much goodwill at the beginning of his presidency, following the death of one of the most popular occupants of the Oval Office. From this upbeat beginning, Truman's popularity declined as his problems grew, so much so that leading Democrats sought to replace him as the Democratic nominee in 1948 with Dwight Eisenhower. Despite some notable successes, including his nationwide whistlestop campaign in 1948 and a high post-election public-opinion rating, Truman had difficulty maintaining approval, ranking him as low in his ability to sell his programs to the public. His failure to run for reelection in 1952 reflected his mixed response from the public. Many who admired his feisty courage were distressed at the same time over his capacity to govern. Although Truman left office with low public approval, his decision not to run eased the popular anguish about mounting domestic scandal and the stalemate in Korea. However, Truman had the lowest average public approval rating (41 percent) of any modern president (Tatalovich and Daynes, 1984, p. 103).

In sharp contrast to President Harry Truman, Dwight David Eisenhower maintained remarkably high approval ratings throughout the eight years of his presidency. According to John Mueller's analysis (Mueller, 1970), Eisenhower was able to maintain his consistently high levels of public approval because of his role in ending the Korean War, as well as the fact that his presidency was relatively inactive, thus offending a small segment of the "coalition of minorities" that make up a president's electoral majority. Eisenhower is the most popular president in the postwar period, with the possible exception of Ronald Reagan. His percentage approval with the general public ranged from a high of 79 percent to a low of 48 percent, with an average of 64 percent. The fact that the country enjoyed economic prosperity and the absence of any major conflict no doubt contributed greatly to the high esteem in which he was held. That Eisenhower was a popular general and war hero who pursued a bipartisan political strategy contributed to his public appeal. He clearly rated high on his ability to sell to the public.

Like Eisenhower, President Kennedy maintained a high level of public acceptance throughout the three short years of his tenure in the Oval Office. Kennedy's approval reading actually went as high as 83 percent; his low was 56 percent, while his average Gallup Poll rating was 70 percent. Kennedy's approval ratings did show some ups and downs, and there is evidence that his approval was declining at the time of his assassination, although it still remained remarkably high, compared to Presidents Truman, Nixon, and Carter. Kennedy captured the collective American imagination with his youth, vigor, good looks, and charm, and he captivated large segments of the population. He also clearly ranked high on his ability to sell to the public.

Johnson to Reagan

Lyndon Baines Johnson is a peculiar case of a man who came into office with very high public support, enabling him to push through some of the most extensive programs in the twentieth century. Johnson enacted the Kennedy legislative program. After his landslide election in 1964, a substantial working majority in Congress allowed him to put his Great Society in place. His strong support in public opinion polls facilitated his legislative victories in Congress.

Johnson ranks moderate on his ability to sell to the public because he was popular in domestic policy but grew progressively less popular in foreign policy. His increasing obsession with the Vietnam War precipitously dropped his public esteem as his White House term wore on. After the Americanization of the Vietnam War and the Tet offensive—actually a military victory but a massive political defeat because the American embassy in Saigon was attacked—Johnson's public-opinion approval rating dropped dramatically. He ended his presidency a virtual prisoner in the White House. Antiwar demonstrations were widespread and the middle class began to desert his leadership of the war. Johnson increasingly assumed a bunker mentality. He chose not to seek renomination in 1968 and did not even attend the Democratic convention in Chicago.

In spite of a constructive first term, especially in the field of foreign policy, Richard Nixon ranks low in his relations with the public. This is attributable to the massive and thorough loss of confidence in his administration after the Watergate coverup when things began to unravel. His approval rating sank to the lows of Hoover and Truman. Nixon's public-opinion ratings were customarily stronger than his popularity with the working press. But when the public grew disillusioned with his coverup of Watergate wrongdoings, his mandate evaporated. At the time of his resignation from the presidency, after articles of impeachment were drawn up by the House Judiciary Committee, Nixon's public standing was at an all-time low.

While Johnson also suffered a loss of support in public opinion, Johnson withdrew voluntarily from presidential politics. Nixon was removed coercively. Johnson's public-opinion losses were due to a failure of policy; Nixon's were due to a failure of character and reflected not just on the presidential incumbent but also on the institution of the presidency itself.

Gerald Ford's short tenure as president began on a public-opinion high. Ford was popularly perceived as restoring legitimacy, decency, and openness to the office. There was widespread acceptance of Ford by both the Congress and the public. However, his popularity declined dramatically following his pardon of his predecessor—Nixon. That single incident dropped his positive rating thirty points in the polls, and he was never again able to recapture his former high approval level. With time he regained ten to fifteen points, ranking him moderate in his ability to sell to the public. This gain was due in part to his feisty vetoes of Congressional legislation, which were so numerous his administration was said to be governed by veto. His *Mayaguez* caper and his talks with Soviet leader Leonid Brezhnev in Vladivostok were favorably received. However, if Roosevelt was the Mercedes of public relations and Johnson was the Cadillac, Ford, aptly named, remained a Ford—capable, competent, and, compared to flashier counterparts, bland.

Jimmy Carter's relations with the public were volatile. As do most presidents, he assumed office on a high note. However, his was higher than most. He was viewed as an outsider who would reinject moral fiber into a flabby executive branch. There was a sharp but uneven decline soon after the traditional honeymoon period. Surrounded on all sides by seemingly intractable problems, buffeted by inflation, recession, growing unemployment, and Soviet aggression in Afghanistan, Carter was viewed as weak and indecisive. Nor did his loyalty to administration members in trouble, such as Bert Lance, improve his public image. The Camp David accords between Israel and Egypt and the initial rally-'round-the-flag mentality after the beginning of the Iran hostage crisis briefly improved his public standing. Carter's failure to generate a quick solution to the hostage crisis, the aborted rescue effort, and mounting economic problems killed this brief interlude of more favorable public approval. By the middle of 1980, his approval ratings had declined below 30 percent, ranking him low on his ability to sell to the public.

By contrast to his predecessor, Ronald Reagan exhibited a high ability to sell himself to the public. In spite of disagreements with large parts of Reagan's programs, the public retained its faith in his competence and goodwill, believing that prosperity was imminent and the quality of life would improve. Reagan's approval ratings have seldom fallen below 50 percent, rebounding in the spring and summer of 1985 after his cancer operation and rising to a high of 65 percent at the time of the Geneva summit with Soviet leader Mikhail Gorbachev. In 1986, Reagan tied with Johnson as having the best job rating after the first twelve months of his second term, and his general approval ratings were above those of F.D.R. and Eisenhower at comparable points in their presidencies. The "Irangate" scandal of late 1986 and 1987 deeply dented Reagan's popularity, however, and as the administration floundered to find its way, Reagan's leadership was widely questioned for the first time. It was unlikely that he would regain his previous high ratings during the remainder of his second term.

SELLING TO THE CONGRESS

In today's environment, presidents are catalysts in the legislative process. Increasingly, presidents are expected to provide leadership in presenting legislative programs to the Congress. As Stephen J. Wayne (1978: viii) has observed, "Congress' seeming inability to provide comprehensive legislative programming and until recently, comprehensive budgeting, has literally forced the president and his staff to develop mechanisms and processes for legislative policy making." As a result of this situation, the president's ability to sell Congress on legislative agenda and programs has become crucially important for the success of the president's administration. The development of the Congressional Liaison Office reflects the heightened importance of presidential-congressional relations.

Often frustrated by the decentralization and chaotic nature of the legislative process, modern presidents may prefer unilateral action. In foreign policy, presidents have increased freedom and maneuverability with higher prospects of success. However, much of a president's time is spent dealing with Congress and special interests over domestic economic issues. One of the biggest obstacles to the successful operation of the American governmental system of separation of powers occurs when the president and Congress are at loggerheads.

As both domestic policy and foreign policy become increasingly interwoven and more complicated at the end of the twentieth century, a president's ability to sell programs to Congress becomes more important. The failure of some recent presidents to establish comity with Congress has proven catastrophic to the enactment of their legislative programs and the achievement of their goals for the nation. The success of other presidents in selling their programs and agenda to Congress has assured their place in history.

Hoover to Kennedy

Overall, President Hoover had a difficult and contentious time in trying to sell to Congress his strategies for dealing with the Great Depression, thus ranking him low on this dimension. However, at the beginning of his administration in 1928, the country was experiencing an economic boom despite threats that the stock market was acting erratically, and the Republicans controlled both houses of Congress. Hoover's reputation as "the great engineer" created a base for interacting with Congress. But the 1929 stock market crash and the Republican loss of control of Congress in the 1930 elections signaled the beginning of his time of troubles.

Although Hoover and the Congress frequently agreed on policies concerning aid to business, they increasingly disagreed about aid to distressed individuals. Hoover was obsessively concerned with maintaining a balanced budget, even to the point of demanding a tax increase in the midst of the Depression, whereas the Democratic leadership in both the House and the Senate increasingly favored stronger spending measures to cope with the economic disaster. As unemployment rose, production dropped and social misery increased, Hoover's reputation dropped precipitously and his well-meaning and earnest efforts to cope with the crisis misfired. Hoover's legislative successes were minor compared to the magnitude of the nation's problems. By 1931 and 1932, Hoover became isolated from both the Congress and the public.

President Roosevelt did not get everything he wanted out of Congress, but he did get most of what he wanted, especially during the first 100 days. John Nance Garner, Roosevelt's first vice-president, was a former Democratic leader in the House, and he facilitated Roosevelt's relations with Congress. Secretary of State Cordell Hull, Postmaster General Jim Farley, and Louis Howe, a Roosevelt advisor, were also influential in fostering White House–congressional relations. Roosevelt enjoyed an effective working majority in both houses of Congress during much of his presidential tenure. His personal and political style was so strong that he was able to mobilize public opinion as an effective form of congressional leverage.

After 1936 and until America's entry into World War II, Roosevelt encountered mounting congressional opposition over the more radical of his New Deal proposals. Many conservative Democrats joined with Republicans in opposition to his programs, including the Supreme Court packing plan. However, his legislative successes in both peace and war are almost unparalleled in the twentieth century, rivaled only by Woodrow Wilson's New Freedom and Lyndon Johnson's Great Society. Among these were the Wagner Act, Social Security, the Agricultural Adjustment Act, the Works Progress Administration, the Civilian Conservation Corps, the Tennessee Valley Authority, a reinstitution of the draft, and price controls during the war. For these reasons we rate him high on his ability to sell his programs to Congress.

Harry Truman exhibited a moderate amount of skill in selling his agenda to Congress. His style was combative and competitive and he sought majorities rather than consensus. He was more successful in foreign policy than in domestic policy. His foreign-policy proposals benefited from a strong element of bipartisanship in Congress. Working with Arthur Vandenberg, a senator from Michigan and chairman of the Senate Foreign Relations Committee, Truman was able to accomplish a number of major achievements in foreign affairs, including the Truman Doctrine, the containment of communism by sending aid to Greece and Turkey, the enactment of emergency assistance for Europe (and later the Marshall Plan), the North Atlantic Treaty Organization, the United Nations Treaty, the Japanese Peace Treaty, the Point-Four program of aid to developing countries, and the reorganization of the U.S. defense structure.

Truman lacked both the charm Roosevelt exhibited and the support F.D.R. commanded, but he is credited with initiating the formulation of a well-constructed presidential legislative package at the beginning of each congressional term (Shull, 1979, p. 75).

Although Truman ran successfully against what he labeled a "do-nothing" Congress in 1948, his intense partisanship in domestic affairs, his narrow majorities in Congress after 1948, and his involvement in the Korean War all handicapped his relations with Congress and the enactment of his Fair Deal. But in foreign policy his achievements with Congress are truly remarkable. Overall we see his success rate with Congress as a mixed bag and therefore rank him as medium.

Like Truman, Eisenhower had an adequate but not extraordinarily successful relationship with Congress. His bipartisan approach is acknowledged as consolidating the New Deal while exercising fiscal restraint in government spending. He proposed modest programs for federal aid to education and civil rights, thoroughly preparing his presentation of each. Eisenhower was able to bring Republican congressional leaders to his middle-of-the-road views and to cooperate with the Democratic leadership, which ran Congress for six of his eight years as president (Hargrove and Nelson, 1984, p. 97).

Eisenhower, however, was not very innovative in proposing new legislation. Rossiter calls him an "earth smoother" rather than an "earth mover." Effective at promoting the legislation he proposed, compared to other modern presidents, Eisenhower proposed very little. His string of vetoes in his last year showed that he could use presidential power to defend programs against assault. However, he did not use his legislative authority to promote change.

In contrast to Eisenhower, who proposed little and accomplished most of it, President Kennedy proposed much to Congress and accomplished little. Critics have argued that Kennedy was less innovative than originally seemed. His New Frontier was cautiously innovative but initially ignored civil rights. His legislative liaisons devised a strategy of dramatizing issues for which majority congressional support was not present, including federal aid to schools, college building construction, medical care for the aged, and a department of urban affairs. Kennedy tried to achieve legislative victories on a few important policies, a strategy which worked well on noncontroversial issues and less well on centerpieces of his New Frontier. Koenig (1981, p. 176) contends that Kennedy employed a buckshot approach to congressional relations. Kennedy has been called a "president of preparation" by Hargrove and Nelson, and had he lived and won a second term by a comfortable margin, Kennedy may have achieved great legislative success. Cut short before the close of his first term, his ability to sell to Congress is rated low.

Johnson to Reagan

Lyndon Johnson had one of the most extraordinarily successful records with Congress in the enactment of domestic legislation, comparable to that attained by Franklin Roosevelt and Woodrow Wilson. Johnson enjoyed a strong working majority in both houses of Congress and used his well-developed powers of persuasion acquired as Senate majority leader to apply the "Johnson treatment" to his former legislative colleagues. While many of his early proposals originated with the Kennedy administration, he developed his own agenda after the 1964 election, especially concentrating on civil rights and aid to the disadvantaged.

Johnson's extraordinary legislative skills were honored by long years in the Senate. He was a protege of Speaker Sam Rayburn and of Franklin Roosevelt. He became one of the most effective majority leaders in the twentieth century. Johnson continued to employ these skills when he became president, maintaining close and intimate relations with members of Congress, especially its leadership. His powers of persuasion and his effective use of the telephone are legends in Washington. Although Johnson, as well as Kennedy, had activist legislative programs and both displayed parity on favorable roll-call counts in Congress, Johnson must be judged "the more skilled and effective legislative leader" because of his ability to get his agenda passed (Renka, 1985, p. 820).

President Nixon's relations with Congress were more contentious than that of any other modern president. He confronted Congress often and sharply, and he disdained the role of legislative coalition builder (Watson and Thomas, 1983, p. 266). Nixon held a plebiscitary view of the presidency, interpreting his election victories as popular mandates and deserving of automatic congressional support. His legislative agenda included "the New American Revolution," through which he sought to rationalize and improve the management of the Great Society. His main domestic initiatives were economic controls, revenue sharing, drug-abuse legislation, and welfare reform. Critics have suggested that he had no real policy other than retrenching and cutting the programs of his predecessors. His attempt to dismantle low-income housing programs in the Office of Economic Opportunity demonstrated his attitude toward social legislation, according to Shull (1979, p. 75). When Watergate intervened, Nixon was already headed toward a crisis with Congress over the implementation of his "administrative presidency" after he impounded huge amounts of congressionally appropriated monies.

Most of Nixon's energy and interest were devoted to foreign policy, and it is here that he obtained his greatest legislative successes, causing him to rank moderate as a salesman to Congress. As he negotiated the laborious, lengthy, and painful U.S. troop withdrawal from Vietnam, he reconfigured American foreign policy to increase the share of the burden among America's allies. This "Nixon Doctrine" strategy gradually relieved the United States from the sole responsibility of providing regional defenses. Congress was supportive of these initiatives to cut back America's police-keeping role and to seek détente with the Soviet Union. Although distrustful of the backdoor diplomacy of both Nixon and Secretary of State Henry Kissinger and their tendency to bypass Congress, the legislative branch was supportive of the end results. Had Nixon avoided the excesses of Watergate and been more attentive to the details of domestic policy, he might have ranked with Lyndon Johnson in his ability to sell programs and issues to Congress.

Gerald Ford's relationship with Congress was colored by his previous twenty-five-year service in the House prior to being appointed vice-president and succeeding to the presidency. Wide distrust of presidential power and Democratic control of the Congress by a substantial margin did not make his job of selling to Congress easier. Ford did not have many new policy proposals, and the ones he did develop emerged slowly, were conservative, and bereft of innovation. He did seek to cut back government spending and undertook numerous fiscal reforms. However, his chief legislative weapon was the veto, which he used frequently and effectively to wield influence with Congress. In all, Ford vetoed sixty-one bills and only twelve were overridden, giving him an 80 percent average at sustaining vetoes. Ten to twenty bills were reshaped to meet Ford's objections after he threatened to veto them. This clout, in addition to his prior congressional history, ranks Ford as moderate in his ability to sell to Congress.

Jimmy Carter entered office with Democratic majorities in both houses of Congress and a full agenda of what he hoped to accomplish. Domestically, he wanted a major energy-conservation bill, government reorganization, a series of privacy acts, energy deregulation, welfare reform, and new departments of energy and education. In foreign policy, Carter fought for a Panama Canal treaty, SALT II, normalization of relations with China, foreign aid tied to the protection of human rights, and a comprehensive political settlement in the Middle East. But his scattergun approach overloaded the agenda and failed to set priorities. As a result, congressional leadership, in spite of being sympathetic to many of his initiatives, experienced difficulties in sorting out the important from the less important issues. His relations with Congress were also uneven because of poor congressional liaison and lack of White House staff rapport with leadership on Capitol Hill.

Carter's first year in office was by no means a failure, but the traffic direction of legislative issues could have been a good deal better. His performance with Congress in 1978 was considerably improved in terms of tough bargaining and setting priorities. But his sense of self-righteousness and moral certitude kept his relations with Congress from being maximally effective. Fishel (1985, p. 196) rightly argues that Carter paid dearly for underestimating the prerogatives and power of Congress.

Carter succeeded on issues that had a coalition of Republican moderates and Democrats, such as environmental and conservation matters. Final passage of the Alaska National Interest Lands Conservation Act and the Panama Canal Treaty occurred during his administration. Successes such as these are enough to rank him as moderate on his ability to sell programs and policies to Congress. However, Carter floundered in such areas as energy policy, national health insurance, a guaranteed income policy, and management of the economy.

In its relations with Congress, the Carter administration left with a whimper whereas Reagan came in with a bang. Reagan moved with the Washington power structure and took pains to establish amicable relations with congressional leaders. He was able to win over "boll weevils"—conservative Democrats—in the House. He combined this conservative dominance in the House with Republican control of the Senate to establish working majorities in both houses. In the first year, Reagan was helped in his dealings with Congress by Max Friedersdorf, an experienced and capable legislative liaison.

These fortuitous circumstances at the outset of his administration, in addition to the sympathy generated by an assassination attempt on his life, produced for Reagan "a series of legislative victories unmatched since Johnson's first year" (Fishel, 1985, p. 204). The crowning achievement of this period was the Economic Recovery Tax Act of 1981, the most massive single reduction in personal income taxes in U.S. history. The first eighteen months of the Reagan administration were a resounding success. Thereafter both his efforts and his successes to redeem his campaign promises of 1980 were more sporadic. But Reagan's extended honeymoon with Congress, coupled with his extraordinary success in convincing Congress to engage in the largest military defense buildup in peacetime in the face of mounting federal deficits, ranks his legislative selling abilities high. Most of his accomplishments came during his first term. His second term was a far cry from the first. When Democrats regained control of both houses of Congress in 1986, his success rate dropped dramatically.

Part of the slowdown in Reagan's congressional success stemmed from the 1982 midterm elections, which resulted in an increase in the number of Democrats in the House. Both Congress and the president interpreted these results as a signal to not fundamentally alter but to slow down the thrust of Reagan's congressional initiatives. The president adopted a strategy of pressing for the maximum legislative outcome but settling for less if Congress was less generous. His use of this style in his dealings with Congress over the MX missile, tax reform, and Social Security reform contrasted directly with Eisenhower's style of asking for little from Congress and getting much. Reagan asked for a full legislative loaf and often settled for half. His ideological convictions gave way to pragmatism when he felt he could win no more concessions from Congress by further negotiation and hard dealing.

SELLING TO WORLD LEADERS

Selling to world leaders is a fourth arena in which presidential communications and persuasive skills are tested. As the United States has become more involved in world affairs, the ability of presidents to sell to world leaders has become more crucial.

Hoover to Kennedy

Herbert Hoover, who ranks low on his ability to sell to world leaders, was basically an isolationist in his view of the role of the United States in world politics. American involvement in World War I was an aberration to Hoover, one not likely to be repeated. America's role was to contribute moral force, not military force, to the maintenance of peace. Hoover inaugurated the Good Neighbor policy with Latin America and put his official stamp on the Clark memorandum, which repudiated the interventionist policy of the Roosevelt Corollary.

Hoover delegated a great deal of power to Secretary of State Henry L. Stimson, who tried valiantly but often unsuccessfully to lead the Hoover administration into a more active world posture. Stimson persuaded Hoover to push for joining the World Court but Hoover's efforts were unsuccessful. Stimson also wanted to cancel World War I war debts and reparations, but Hoover announced a moratorium for only one year. Both Hoover and Stimson supported the Nine-Power Treaty of 1930 to give teeth to the Kellogg-Briand Pact by limiting the size of major navies. However, Hoover's ineffectual response to the Japanese invasion of Manchuria in 1931 was all too typical of his timid international policy after the stock market crash of 1929. While Stimson advocated a nonrecognition policy as a first step toward more forceful action, Hoover was unwilling to take any further action, other than moral protest.

Hoover also proved ineffectual in dealing with the devastating effects of the Hawley-Smoot Tariff Act, which closed American markets to foreign imports and drastically crippled the economies of European and South American countries. The rigidity and inflexibility that characterized Hoover's domestic policy were also reflected in his foreign policy and his dealings with world leaders. As Sidney Warren (1964, p. 163) has written, "Both in domestic and world affairs during a critical period in the nation's history, Hoover's leadership was inadequate."

Franklin Delano Roosevelt led the United States to victory in the greatest war of the twentieth century. He laid the conditions for postwar peace before he died early in the fourth term of his presidency. His noteworthy foreign policy initiatives, such as the Good Neighbor policy, Lend-Lease, the Four Freedoms, the Atlantic Charter, and the United Nations Declaration, are all associated with his administration. In addition, he carried on extensive and important diplomatic communications with world leaders such as Churchill, Stalin, DeGaulle, and Chiang Kai-shek during World War II. In wartime conferences with these world leaders and others, at Quebec, Casablanca, Cairo, Teheran, and Yalta as well as Washington, Roosevelt demonstrated strong leadership. As a member of the "big three," Roosevelt was a major architect of the Allied victory against Hitler, Mussolini, and Tojo.

Roosevelt was instrumental in the policy of unconditional surrender, the construction of the atomic bomb, the postwar settlements in Europe, and of laying the foundation for a new international organization to keep the peace after the conclusion of hostilities. Elmer Plischke (1985, p. 739), a distinguished student of diplomacy, has placed him in the "Summit Hall of Fame," along with Theodore Roosevelt, Woodrow Wilson, Dwight Eisenhower, Harry Truman, and Richard Nixon. Sumner Wells once said, "One man and one man alone made it possible for us to have a working United Nations before the end of the Second World War. That man was Franklin Roosevelt" (Warren, 1964, p. 269).

The comments of these experts, in addition to the record of his achievements, clearly place Roosevelt in the high category of salesmanship to world leaders. As the commander-in-chief of the largest army in U.S. history, he made major decisions that affected the outcome of the war. Admiral Leahy, his personal chief of staff, commented that Franklin Roosevelt and Winston Churchill ran the war (Warren, 1964, p. 284). Historians agree that Woodrow Wilson took the United States to the center of international politics, but he lacked historical perspective, especially of European politics, and failed to shore up his domestic support. His foray there was brief and tentative. Roosevelt restored the American presidency to the center of the world stage and cemented America's role as a permanent player in the all-important game of world politics.

As Franklin Roosevelt's successor, Harry Truman assumed office under the burden of succeeding an acknowledged world leader. The burdens of office at first crushed him, but as he grew accustomed to the onus of responsibility, Truman developed his own personal style in foreign policy and made his mark in history with some of the most momentous decisions in the postwar era. Because of his insecure base as Roosevelt's successor, Truman sought bipartisanship in foreign policy and reached his decisions on the basis of recommendations of such outstanding advisors as George

Marshall, Clark Clifford, and Dean Acheson. Observers have noted that Truman had a penchant for being wrong on the small issues and right on the big issues. His leadership in redirecting the course of American foreign policy from the Stalin-Roosevelt collaboration of World War II to a policy that sought to contain the expansion of the Soviet Union in the postwar period was a major contribution.

The year 1945 proved to be a "baptism of fire" for Harry Truman. He began negotiations with Stalin on the postwar settlement by sending Harry Hopkins to Moscow and later informed Stalin that American scientists had detonated the first atomic bomb, which was used against the Japanese cities of Hiroshima and Nagasaki. Truman conferred at the Potsdam Conference with Stalin and Clement Attlee. It was there that Truman negotiated such questions as the occupation of Germany, procedures for writing the peace treaties, ways to implement the Yalta Declaration on Liberated Europe, German reparations, and Russian participation in the Pacific war. In 1945, President Truman also addressed the final session of the United Nations plenary session on international organization, and he witnessed the surrender of Japan on August 14.

In 1946, Truman invited Winston Churchill to speak at a college in Fulton, Missouri, where the British leader delivered his famous "Iron Curtain" speech. One of the greatest international achievements of the Truman administration was the European recovery program—the Marshall Plan, a four-year effort to rescue Western Europe from starvation and bankruptcy—which involved extensive negotiations with America's European allies. Truman also engineered aid to Greece and Turkey under the Truman Doctrine, recognized the independence of Israel, and initiated negotiations for the formation of the North Atlantic Treaty Organization (NATO). Perhaps Truman's greatest challenge in dealing with world leaders began with his decision to send troops to South Korea in 1950 to oppose invading North Korean forces. The resulting United Nations joint command required inter-ally diplomacy of a high order. During his seven years in office Truman met with most of the world leaders of his time, and was able to more than hold his own in talks and negotiations. Truman literally believed that the buck stopped with him and was able to make firm decisions persuasive to prominent world figures on the basis of his own experience, knowledge of history, and the guidance of first-rate advisers. Amazingly, a relatively inexperienced vice-president and amateur in world affairs, succeeding one of the great world leaders of the twentieth century, Truman was able to follow closely in his predecessor's footsteps.

In sharp contrast to Harry Truman, Dwight Eisenhower as a lifelong soldier rose to be the Supreme Commander of Allied troops in Europe and to become a hero of World War II. He was a thorough professional in his knowledge of both military and foreign policy. Although not a great strategist, Eisenhower is rightly recognized as a superb leader in coalition diplomacy while he was in Europe. When he became president, he was already familiar with many of the world leaders, some of whom had been his comrades-in-arms in World War II. This facilitated his negotiations with contemporary world leaders and his conduct of foreign policy during his administration, an astounding eight-year period of peace and prosperity.

Campaigning on a promise to end the war in Korea, Eisenhower went to that country to survey the situation and then negotiated an armistice. Although he delegated much of the authority for foreign policy to Secretary of State John Foster Dulles, Eisenhower's charisma and persona were such that he carried great prestige and influence in dealing with both America's allies and enemies. When Stalin died in 1953, Eisenhower had to deal with the Soviet leader's successors, including Nikolai Bulganin and later Nikita Khrushchev. In 1957, Eisenhower announced his famous doctrine pledging aid to Middle Eastern countries resisting communist takeovers. He met with British Prime Minister Harold Macmillan at the Bermuda Conference, dealt with the Suez crisis, announced the Atoms for Peace Program, and sent U.S. marines to Lebanon in 1958. Like Roosevelt and Truman before him, Eisenhower ranks high on his ability to sell his foreign policy initiatives to fellow world leaders. In relations with his peers, Eisenhower was a quintessential soldier-statesman by long experience, well-honed expertise, and a conciliatory temperament. Although he left office smarting over the failure of the Geneva Conference of 1960 when Khrushchev walked out over the U-2 spy incident, Eisenhower's worldwide reputation was largely unblemished.

President Kennedy's election signaled the beginning of a period of new energy and transformation in foreign policy. One of the first things he tried to accomplish was to strengthen the U.S. military to enable him to negotiate with world leaders from a position of strength. Among his early initiatives was his proposal for the Alliance for Progress in Latin America. His negotiations with the Soviet Union for a cease-fire in Laos was the result of his calling the Southeast Asian Treaty Organization (SEATO) into action on this front. In response to Sputnik, Kennedy also announced a project to place a man on the moon, which heightened U.S. prestige abroad. These events contributed to Kennedy's high rank when it came to selling to world leaders.

The failure of the Cuban Bay of Pigs invasion weakened Kennedy's reputation and allowed Khrushchev to bully him at the Vienna Summit Conference in 1961. But Kennedy's leadership in opposing the construction of the Berlin Wall and his speech to the people of Berlin raised his reputation to one of worldwide acclaim. The Peace Corps and the Trade Expansion Act signaled to many countries that the United States was willing to use its vast power and resources to help build a more stable and humane international order. Kennedy's image as a youthful, vigorous world leader was further enhanced by his attractive wife, Jacqueline, whose flair and culture appealed greatly to the Europeans, especially the French. Undoubtedly, Kennedy's handling of the Cuban missile crisis redeemed his reputation from the Bay of Pigs disaster and added tremendously to his reputation as a pragmatic leader.

Following the Cuban missile crisis, Kennedy negotiated a hotline with the Soviet Union, establishing a direct communications link between the two countries. He negotiated the Limited Test Ban Treaty, which for the first time banned nuclear tests in the atmosphere, in outer space, and under water. His cancellation of the Skybolt missile project with Great Britain did not endear him to Prime Minister Macmillan. His sending 10,000 additional U.S. advisors to Vietnam strengthened the American role there but created misgivings at home and abroad about the course of U.S. policy in Southeast Asia. However, at the time of his death, Kennedy's reputation was well established, especially among third-world leaders who regarded him as sympathetic to their cause and among the best and brightest of American leaders. His untimely and violent death dealt a crushing blow to the high hopes of many of these heads of state for enlightened and energetic U.S. leadership.

Johnson to Reagan

Lyndon Johnson was a paradoxical figure in foreign policy. Inheriting the Kennedy legacy, he enthusiastically supported an American role of benign leadership in such projects as the Peace Corps, the Great Society exported abroad in the Mekong River Delta project in Vietnam, and a mounting concern for human rights. But his escalation and Americanization of the war in Vietnam clouded this image, causing him to rank medium on international salesmanship. As he sank deeper and deeper in the Southeast Asian quagmire, Johnson was forced to rely upon a declining number of allies in this questionable cause. But he was able to limit overt Soviet and Chinese intervention by avoiding direct threats to their territory. What marred his international reputation, as Stoessinger (1985, p. 202) observed, was his worldview that "Vietnam must be defended" in spite of "abundant evidence for the claim that he could have kept that defense at a modest and relatively low-key level." Stoessinger concludes that "the compulsions of his enormous and yet fragile ego made him deceive the Congress, escalate the war by stealth, and finally turn Vietnam into one of the most terrible and self-destructive conflicts in American history."

In the Dominican Republic uprising of April 1965, Lyndon Johnson's decision to intervene with 20,000 marines was, for him, "just like the Alamo" (Geyelin, 1966, p. 237). For others, it was massive overkill; however, the invasion accomplished its purposes and the marines were quickly withdrawn. This invasion produced the lowest ebb in Johnson's standing as a world statesman. This adventure, along with the Vietnam

War, demonstrated the astuteness of Lady Bird Johnson's observation, "I just hope foreign problems do not keep mounting. They do not represent Lyndon's kind of presidency" (Barber, 1985, p. 43).

In spite of the Dominican Republic intervention and Vietnam, Johnson demonstrated a moderate amount of skill in selling his ideas to world leaders. One of the complexities confronting Johnson was the changing nature of Soviet political leadership. In 1964, Aleksei Kosygin replaced Khrushchev as Soviet premier and Leonid Brezhnev replaced Khrushchev as Communist Party secretary. Later on, Johnson met with Kosygin at the Glassboro summit meeting in 1967 and showed that he was able to deal with the Soviet leadership.

During Johnson's term, the United States, along with sixty other nations, signed a treaty governing the exploration and uses of outer space. At the same time that Johnson was Americanizing Vietnam, he was also negotiating with the Soviet Union to increase commercial and cultural exchanges, was discussing arms limitations, and was dealing with the North Vietnamese in negotiations to release the U.S. intelligence vessel *Pueblo*. Johnson dealt with world leaders like Harold Wilson, Ho Chi Minh, Ayub Khan, and Charles DeGaulle, sometimes applying his well-known and persuasive style to his international negotiations.

A narrow popular-vote majority in 1968 brought to power a man who was both well versed and interested in foreign affairs. Richard Nixon's eight years as vice-president under Eisenhower prepared him for dealing with a variety of national political leaders. During his tenure in office, Nixon met with most of the world's most powerful figures and more than held his own in negotiations with them. Nixon's real love was international diplomacy, and with the help and expertise of Henry Kissinger he was able to establish himself as a major world statesman. Nixon met and negotiated with South Vietnamese President Nguyen Van Thieu; with Chinese leaders Chou En-lai and Mao Tse-tung; and with Soviet leaders Brezhnev, Kosygin, and Andrei Gromyko. Nixon has written in his book *Leaders* (1982) about his dealings with Churchill, DeGaulle, MacArthur, and Konrad Adenauer, and he indicates that he was not only their equal in power and prominence but often felt superior in wisdom and insight.

Nixon was able to accomplish much in his dealings with foreign leaders, including the reopening of diplomatic intercourse with China, winding down the Vietnamese War, détente with the Soviet Union, and commencement of SALT I talks. In comparison to his increasingly deteriorating image at home, he remained popular abroad. He used his popularity among world leaders in the final months of his administration to visit Egypt, Saudi Arabia, Syria, Israel, and the Soviet Union to bolster his sagging political fortunes at home. Foreign leaders from the Soviet Union, China, and France were unable to comprehend why a man of Nixon's international stature could ever be forced from office over what they regarded as the trivial malfeasances of Watergate. In selling his philosophy and programs to world leaders, Nixon was clearly one of the most able, if not the most able, of post-World War II presidents.

Gerald R. Ford had a tough act to follow as a foreign-policy leader when he succeeded Richard Nixon as president. He was not well versed in foreign policy, but fortunately for him he had Henry Kissinger on the job as both Secretary of State and as Special Assistant to the President for National Security Policy. Although Ford was president for less than a full term, he traveled to foreign countries, especially to the Far East, where he consulted with Emperor Hirohito and other Japanese leaders.

Ford also traveled to Seoul, Korea, and was met by an enthusiastic crowd of more than two million people. His most important stop on this Far Eastern trip was Vladivostok, where he and Soviet leader Leonid Brezhnev held discussions that resulted in the Vladivostok Agreement, which set new ceilings on the number of nuclear weapons and the number of multiple independently targeted reentry vehicles (MIRVs) each country could possess. Unfortunately, the agreements later were aborted. Technical negotiations at the later Geneva conference were unable to resolve complicated issues surrounding arms control. The Vladivostok Agreement was not converted into a SALT II treaty during the remainder of the Ford presidency.

In the summer of 1975, Ford went to Europe to meet with the leaders of Britain, France, and West Germany in Helsinki, Finland. Here he discussed international economic problems. Nothing significant came of the meeting, but the Helsinki summit accords were signed at the final session of the CSCE (the European security conference), which dealt with the banning of environmental warfare, foregoing a second ABM site, and drafting a treaty to stop underground nuclear tests over a specified threshold of nuclear power (Kissinger, 1982, p. 1165). Ford also met with Yugoslavian President Tito in the summer of 1975. In December 1975, President Ford flew to China and consulted with Mao Tse-tung and Chou En-lai. As a result of disagreement over the Taiwan question, little of concrete substance was accomplished. China did promise to return the remains of two airmen shot down during the Vietnam War and to provide information on other Americans missing in action.

Ford tried to follow in Nixon's footsteps but fell short. Although Ford had some accomplishments and held his own in negotiations with Brezhnev, the short length of his time in office and his very heavy reliance on Kissinger rank Ford as low in selling to world leaders. His accomplishments pale in comparison to his predecessor.

Jimmy Carter came into the presidency determined to restore human rights to the center of American foreign policy and to treat the Soviet Union as an ordinary world power, not a major international menace. His implementation of a human rights policy propelled him to a poor start in relations with Brezhnev, other communist leaders, and some third-world leaders who were less dedicated to human rights. The Soviets did not appreciate Carter's reception of Soviet activist Vladimir Bukovsky and his open letter to Andrei Sakharov, the foremost Soviet dissident. Argentina, Brazil, El Salvador, and Guatamala also rejected U.S. efforts to tie military aid to their human rights practices.

Carter and Panamanian President Torrijos were able to negotiate a new Panama Canal Treaty, which was eventually accepted after substantial reservations. Plainly, Carter's negotiations with Israeli Prime Minister Menachem Begin and Egyptian President Anwar Sadat at Camp David over a Middle East settlement must rank as a high point in his relations with foreign leaders, although according to William B. Quandt (1986), Sadat and Carter were not fond of Begin and had to continually make concessions to the Israelis to achieve the agreement.

Carter's obvious hard work, mastery of details, and negotiating persistence impressed his peers in Europe, but Germany's Helmut Schmidt, probably the most brilliant of the Western European leaders, was particularly upset at Carter's decision to defer production of the ERW (Enhanced Radiation Weapon, or neutron bomb). This permanently soured relations between the two men. Carter successfully negotiated a SALT II agreement at a summit meeting with Brezhnev in Vienna in 1979, but was unable to secure approval of the treaty by Congress because of lack of Senate support and the Soviet invasion of Afghanistan. When Carter cancelled U.S. participation in the 1980 Olympics, which were hosted by the Soviet Union, and imposed a grain embargo on shipments to that country, relations with the Soviet Union rapidly deteriorated.

Carter's support of a more evenhanded policy in the Middle East was favored by moderate leaders in that region, especially by the Saudis who benefited from Carter's support of sending sophisticated weapons, including AWACs and late-model jet aircraft. Until the Shah of Iran fell from power, his chief supporter was President Carter, but his successor, the Ayatollah Khomeini, precipitated the Iranian hostage crisis, which drove the last nail in the casket of Carter's presidency. Despite an image of high morality and purpose, a willingness to accommodate change, the acceptance of the Soviet Union as a diplomatic equal, and the formal diplomatic recognition of Communist China, Carter's diplomacy must be judged to represent a marked drop from that of Kissinger and Nixon. For that reason, his success in selling to foreign leaders is ranked moderate.

Although Ronald Reagan is very popular at home, he is less popular abroad. He ranks only moderate on his ability to sell programs and ideas to world leaders. Reagan started his first term in office with an acute intensification of ideological warfare against the Soviets. As a result, relations between the two countries became so hostile that many observers believed his intention was to inaugurate a new cold war. To the Soviet leaders, Reagan appeared to be a crusader, particularly compared to the more businesslike approach of Nixon and Kissinger. Relations between the two superpowers had deteriorated so badly that by 1983, George Arbatov, the leading Soviet expert on America, accused Reagan of behaving like Hitler.

Although in 1981 Reagan lifted the grain embargo originally imposed by Carter and communicated by personal letter to Leonid Brezhnev, he avoided proposed summit meetings during Brezhnev's tenure, which ended in 1982. Reagan failed to attend the funerals of Brezhnev, his successors Uri Andropov and Konstantin Chernenko, and did not meet with any Soviet leaders until the summit meeting in Geneva with Mikhail Gorbachev in November 1985. Until Gorbachev's ascendancy, the Reagan administration frequently felt that there was no one in charge in the Soviet Union. With Gorbachev's rise, a new relationship between Soviet and U.S. leadership was established, and Reagan found a worthy competitor for the title of The Great Communicator. In Geneva, Reagan and Gorbachev established what appeared to be a good working relationship, although subsequent events dashed early hopes for comprehensive arms control agreements.

With Western European leaders, Reagan's relations were often uneasy at best. Many perceived him to be "ill equipped for the responsibility that he bears, a kind of cowboy figure, bellicose, ignorant, with a simplistic view of the world pieced together from journals of right wing opinion and old Hollywood movies" (Watt, 1984, p. 521). He did manage to relate reasonably well with Great Britain's Margaret Thatcher, a fellow conservative, and with West Germany's Helmut Kohl. But many others found themselves at odds with him over Soviet policy, trade, and the Nicaraguan situation.

Early administration policy toward China went very poorly until "a combination of domestic pressures, alliance insistence, and diplomatic realism compelled the administration to pull back from early policy changes" (Maynes, 1986, p. 513). As Teng Hsiao-ping encouraged private initiative in China, President Reagan became increasingly sympathetic to a man who he believed agreed with his supply-side economic views. Reagan's standing with such leaders as Lybia's Quadafi, Cuba's Fidel Castro, and Nicaragua's Daniel Ortega was naturally very low. But with such leaders as Menachem Begin of Israel, President Zia of Pakistan, Edward Seaga of Jamaica, and Hosé Lopez Portillo of Mexico, Reagan's standing was considerably better than that of Jimmy Carter. American influence in the Middle East declined under Reagan's administration and such allies as King Hussein of Jordan and Hosni Mubarak of Egypt experienced increased difficulties in relating to the White House. The enunciation of the Reagan Doctrine through which the United States favored aid to insurgents against communist governments brought Reagan great influence and prestige with the insurgency leaders, but most governments throughout the world regarded these efforts with profound skepticism. The decrease in ideological diplomacy in the beginning of Reagan's second term, coupled with a new effort directed toward U.S.-Soviet arms control negotiations, gave many world leaders hope that the United States would exercise more responsible world leadership. New U.S. initiatives proposed by Secretary of the Treasury James A. Baker to ease the debt problems of third-world nations favorably impressed financial leaders in a number of countries. These initiatives indicated that the United States would not stand idly by and allow massive debt failures to occur. Reagan has been a very fortunate president in taking advantage of forces and trends outside of his control and using them to his personal benefit. While some presidents are gifted in their relations with world leaders, Ronald Reagan has been lucky; however, his luck may have run out at the Reykjavik summit and in the Iran-Contra scandal. Whether he has been as lucky as Mandelbaum (1986) asserts, or a president who has lost opportunities to come to grips with the nuclear problem, the trade deficit, and world debt as Maynes (1986) argues, is still open to the verdict of history.

ASSESSING PRESIDENTIAL SELLING ABILITIES

In assessing presidential selling abilities, presidents range from high to low. Not only can presidents be evaluated for their selling skills to specific audiences but these specific skills also may be used to derive overall scores for presidential salesmanship. If numerical ratings are assigned for skills to specific audiences, these ratings may be averaged to derive a total selling ability score for each president. The numerical ratings of 1 for low skills, 2 for moderate skills, and 3 for high skills were used (see Table 3–1).

Of modern presidents, only Roosevelt received high rankings in all four categories of selling to the public, the media, the Congress, and to world leaders. Only Hoover received all low rankings. The other presidents show a variation in skills, good in some areas and less than good in others. Both Truman and Nixon illustrate the wide variability a president may exhibit, running the gamut from low skills to high skills before various audiences. Truman proved inept at selling to the public, but excelled at selling to world leaders. Nixon was low on selling to both the media and the public, but, like Truman, ranked high on selling to world leaders (see Table 3–2).

The overall numerical selling scores, resulting from calculating numerical averages for each president across specific audiences, may be used to distinguish presidents with high selling skills from those with low selling skills. Several presidents exhibited high selling skills: Roosevelt,

TABLE 3–1 Presidential Selling Skills

	SELLING SKILLS			
	MEDIA	PUBLIC	CONGRESS	WORLD LEADERS
Reagan	Medium	High	High	Medium
Carter	Low	Low	Low	Medium
Ford	Medium	Medium	Medium	Low
Nixon	Low	Low	Medium	High
Johnson	Medium	Medium	High	Medium
Kennedy	High	High	Low	High
Eisenhower	Medium	High	Medium	High
Truman	Medium	Low	Medium	High
Franklin Roosevelt	High	High	High	High
Hoover	Low	Low	Low	Low

Reagan, Eisenhower, Johnson, and Kennedy. The highest score, 3.00, was obtained by Roosevelt, who excelled in selling to all audiences. Closely behind Roosevelt is Kennedy, who, with a 2.50, ranked high on selling to the media, the public and world leaders, but was low at selling to the Congress. Eisenhower was high on selling to the public and world leaders but medium on selling to the media and Congress. Johnson also ranks high on salesmanship, but his overall score of 2.25 is lower than that of other presidents in this category, except Truman, who ranks 2.00. Johnson excelled at selling to Congress, but was moderate at selling to other audiences. Truman ranges from low in selling to the public to high in selling to world leaders, receiving medium scores for selling to the media and to Congress.

Several presidents rank low on overall selling skills: Nixon, Ford, Carter, and Hoover. Hoover's overall score, 1.00, reflects a low selling rating to every presidential audience. Carter, with 1.25, achieved a moderate rating for only one audience—world leaders, while scoring low on his selling to the media, the public and Congress. Both Ford and Nixon

TABLE 3–2 Presidential Selling Ratings

	PRESIDENT	OVERALL SELLING SCORE
High Selling Ability	Roosevelt	3.00
	Kennedy	2.50
	Reagan	2.50
	Eisenhower	2.50
	Johnson	2.25
Low Selling Ability	Truman	2.00
	Nixon	1.75
	Ford	1.75
	Carter	1.25
	Hoover	1.00

received overall scores of 1.75. Ford was medium in three of the four categories, but ranked low on selling to world leaders. Nixon, on the other hand, scored high with world leaders, medium with Congress, and low with the media and the public.

Presidential salesmanship is not the same as presidential greatness. Presidential greatness is far broader and more encompassing than salesmanship alone. Nonetheless, the ability to sell is an important component of greatness. Without great skills in communicating effectively to important audiences, presidents experience difficulty in achieving greatness, especially in the latter part of the twentieth century.

REFERENCES

BAILEY, THOMAS A., *Presidential Greatness*. New York: Appleton-Century-Crofts, 1966.

BARBER, JAMES DAVID, *The Presidential Character: Predicting Performance in the White House*, 3rd edition. Englewood Cliffs, N. J.: Prentice-Hall, 1985.

Congressional Quarterly Almanac, 1981. Washington, D.C.: Congressional Quarterly Press.

EDWARDS, GEORGE C., *The Public Presidency: The Pursuit of Popular Support*. New York: St. Martin's Press, 1983.

FAUSOLD, MARTIN L., *The Presidency of Herbert C. Hoover*. Lawrence, Kansas: University of Kansas Press, 1985.

FISHEL, JEFF, *Presidents and Promises*. Washington, D.C.: Congressional Quarterly Press, 1985.

GEYELIN, PHILIP, *Lyndon B. Johnson and the World*. New York: Frederick A. Praeger Publishers, 1966.

HARGROVE, ERWIN C., and MICHAEL NELSON, *Presidents, Politics, and Policy*. New York: Knopf, 1984.

HOXIE, R. GORDON, "About This Issue," *Presidential Studies Quarterly*, 16 (1986), 7–10.

KERBEL, MATTHEW R., "Against the Odds: Media Access in the Administration of President Gerald Ford," *Presidential Studies Quarterly*, 16 (1986), 76–91.

KISSINGER, HENRY, *Years of Upheaval*. Boston: Little, Brown, 1982.

KOENIG, LOUIS W., *The Chief Executive*, 4th edition. New York: Harcourt Brace Jovanovich, 1981.

MANDELBAUM, MICHAEL, "The Luck of the President," *Foreign Affairs*, 64 (1986), 393–412.

MAYNES, CHARLES WILLIAM, "Lost Opportunities," *Foreign Affairs*, 64 (1986), 413–434.

MUELLER, JOHN E., "Presidential Popularity from Truman to Johnson," *American Political Science Review* (March 1970), 136–148.

NIXON, RICHARD M., *Leaders*. New York: Warner Books, 1982.

PETERS, THOMAS J., and ROBERT H. WATERMAN, *In Search of Excellence*. New York: Warner Books, 1982.

PLISCHKE, ELMER, "Rating Presidents and Diplomats in Chief," *Presidential Studies Quarterly*, 15 (1985), 725—742.

QUANDT, W. B., *Camp David: Peacemaking and Politics*. Washington, D.C.: The Brookings Institution, 1986.

RENKA, RUSSELL D., "Comparing Presidents Kennedy and Johnson as Legislative Leaders," *Presidential Studies Quarterly*, 15 (1985), 806—825.

RUBIN, RICHARD, *Press, Party, and Presidency*. New York: W. W. Norton & Co., Inc., 1981.

SCHLESINGER, ARTHUR M., Jr., *The Crisis of the Old Order, 1919–1933*. Boston: Houghton-Mifflin, 1957.

SHULL, STEVEN A., *Presidential Policy Making: An Analysis*. Brunswick, Ohio: King's Court Communications, Inc., 1979.

SMOLLER, FRED, "The Six O'clock Presidency: Patterns of Network News Coverage of the President," *Presidential Studies Quarterly*, 16 (1986), 31—49.

STOESSINGER, JOHN, *Crusaders and Pragmatists*, 2nd edition. New York: W. W. Norton & Co., Inc., 1985.

TATALOVICH, RAYMOND, and BYRON W. DAYNES, *Presidential Power in the United States*. Monterey, Calif.: Brooks/Cole, 1984.

WARREN, SIDNEY, *The President as World Leader*. Philadelphia: Lippincott, 1964.

WATSON, R. A., and N. C. THOMAS, *The Politics of the Presidency*. New York: John Wiley, 1983.

WATT, DAVID, "As a European Saw It," *Foreign Affairs: America and the World, 1983*, 62 (1984), 521—532.

WAYNE, STEPHEN J., *The Legislative Presidency*. New York: Harper & Row, 1978.

CHAPTER FOUR
THE NONPERSUASIVE PRESIDENCY:
When Presidents Can't Sell

WHEN PRESIDENTS CAN'T SELL

Richard Neustadt has highlighted the importance of the power of persuasion in the American presidency. By making persuasion one of the main themes of his classic book on the presidency, *Presidential Power*, Neustadt argues that "the essence of a president's persuasive task is to convince. . . men that what the White House wants of them is what they ought to do for their own sake and on their own authority" (Neustadt, 1960, p. 34).

But what happens when presidents do not have this persuasive ability or fail to exercise it? If the president fails to exercise forceful salesmanship, followers may miss the cues needed to prompt them into desired action. Without clear-cut cues, staffers may become confused about the president's intentions. The result is stagnation and inaction. The result of nonpersuasion is ineffectual presidential leadership and the loss of presidential power. Nonpersuasion has the most serious policy consequences when a president fails to communicate effectively with and persuade one of the four crucial audiences of the presidency: the media, the public, the Congress, and world leaders.

Failure to Sell to the Media

Perhaps failure to sell policies and ideas to the media is the most serious breach in presidential communications because the media are intermediaries between the president and the president's followers. Increasingly with the development of a mass culture and growing reliance upon modern communication networks, presidents reach citizens through the media. Columnists, network television anchors, editorialists, and leading reporters are all influential members of the communications elite who crucially affect how people think and feel about the president and the president's administration.

Congress, as a crucial part of the Washington establishment, is a consumer of political information via the media. Members of Congress are even more informed and interested than the average consumer of media information. The interaction between members of Congress and the communication elite is frequent and intense in the close confines of the nation's capital, which is essentially a one-industry town where the industry is government.

Presidents even use the media to communicate indirectly with world leaders. In this interface of world leaders through the media, leading editors and television anchors interview world leaders and act as power brokers or actors in the unfolding political process. The prestige press, such as the *London Times* and the *New York Times*, becomes the chronological record of interactions between the presidency and other world leaders.

In contrast to Lyndon Johnson's success in selling his Great Society to the Congress, the media, and the public was his inability to convince all three sectors, and especially the media, of the wisdom of his Vietnam policy. As U.S. involvement increased and casualty figures rose with the Americanization of the war, media coverage of the conflict brought home vivid pictures of Americans in bloody combat, which was far removed from the glamorized view of war that military recruiting posters and television advertisements portrayed. Newspaper reports from the front daily showed the difficulties and dangers that befell American troops in a far-off land of jungle, heat, sickness, and death. Television cameras recorded the awful aspects of GIs bogged down in a guerrilla war in a foreign country fighting unseen enemies. These continual, stark, realistic, and bloody reports began to color middle-class perceptions of the Vietnam War, especially as student demonstrations grew in number and fervor and draft evaders fled north to Canada. Reporters like David Halberstam, Max Frankel, Stanley Karnow, and Seymour Hersh and television correspondents such as Dan Rather and Walter Cronkite grew more critical of U.S. strategy and deployment of troops and weapons in a war that seemingly could not be won. After the Tet offensive of early 1968, the United States slowly disengaged itself from Vietnam, but as Paul Kattenburg observes, the war itself "continued, and was. . . broadened to the whole of Indochina." (Kattenburg, 1980, p. 107). Thereafter, more and more criticism mounted in the media against Johnson's policy and he himself admitted that the loss of support by Walter Cronkite, "the most trusted man in America," symbolized the loss of the support of the nation as a whole.

Failure to Sell to the Public

The failure to sell ideas, programs, and policies to the public is usually fatal for presidents. Without wide and deep public support, no president can expect to accomplish much in the long run. Strong public approval in a democratic society is the equivalent of a mandate from heaven in classical Chinese society, and once it is lost or withdrawn, it is difficult to regain or retrieve. Presidents who lose popular support fail to get reelected if they are in their first term, and they suffer from early political paralysis in their second term. They also find it more difficult to get their programs enacted by a skeptical Congress, which is equally, if not more, sensitive to the barometer of public opinion.

Franklin Roosevelt's attempted purge of conservative Democrats from the Congress in the 1938 midterm elections was precipitated by Congress' defeat of his Supreme Court "packing plan" in 1937. This defeat was caused by several Democrats who had consistently opposed Roosevelt. In one of his famous fireside chats, Roosevelt announced his intention to influence the outcome of Democratic primary contests in 1938. He crisscrossed the country several times on behalf of his political allies and against Democratic opponents. Roosevelt's strategy was a massive failure, so much so that, with only one exception, every senator and representative that he had targeted for defeat won election. His failure to succeed in this famous purge set a precedent which no president has ventured to follow in succeeding years.

Failure to Sell to Congress

Presidents who fail to sell to Congress are not successful in implementing their national programs. They can, for a while, maintain their reputation and public image, but only for a while. Eventually, failure to communicate with Congress is translated to the public via the media and affects a president's reputation with both of these audiences. Perhaps more than any other factor, effective communication with Congress and the persuasion of Congress are important to a president's place in history.

One example of presidential failure to persuade Congress was Jimmy Carter's inability in 1979 to win over the Senate to ratify SALT II. This treaty proposed additional limitations on strategic nuclear weapons for the United States and the Soviet Union. Among other things, the treaty set a ceiling of 2,400 missiles and bombers, a number that was to be reduced to 2,250 after 1982.

Carter has admitted that the failure to surmount this legislative hurdle was his single biggest disappointment in office. His inability to persuade even some members of his own party led him to withdraw the treaty from consideration after the Soviet invasion of Afghanistan gave him a good excuse to do so. Indicative of the importance of this proposed treaty was the fact that both the Soviet Union and the United States continued to observe its provisions without formal ratification until 1986 when the Reagan administration announced that it would discontinue informal observance in response to alleged Soviet violations. The fact that a conservative Reagan administration could live with this treaty for six years, albeit uneasily, makes Carter's failure to persuade the Senate to ratify SALT II even more poignant.

Failure to Sell to World Leaders

The consequences of presidential failure to sell ideas and policies to world leaders range from the trivial to major issues of life and death. Failure to persuade presidential peers increases the risk of having to go forth without allies and be isolated from the world community. Many examples illustrate this danger, including Ronald Reagan's failure to enlist the support of his Western European allies in U.S. cessation of observance of SALT II. This created hostility and antagonism that extended even to Canada, the best and closest friend of the United States. The Soviets also were outraged, not only because of U.S. accusations of Soviet violations of the agreement but also because America's unilateral decision stymied Soviet desires for a second summit and renewal of arms control talks.

Other Reagan actions also reflected his inability to persuade various world leaders to support his lead and his willingness to act even in the absence of that support, thereby isolating America. Among these were Reagan's support of the so-called freedom fighters in Nicaragua, his blockading of Nicaraguan ports, and his long reluctance to enact sanctions against the government of South Africa.

TYPOLOGY OF NONPERSUASION

This chapter develops a framework for looking at failures in presidential selling ability. The central importance of selling ability for a successful presidency in the late twentieth century implies that understanding failures in selling ability is critical for understanding instances of poor presidential performance. Some presidents clearly were not as effective in selling their programs and ideas as were others.

Presidents differ in whether they hold strongly held internal value systems developed from early childhood, or whether they reflect the prevailing external values of the times. Accordingly, they vary in how susceptible they are to the external environment. Their adaptive behavior to environmental pressures may err by being too flexible or too rigid. Both are nonpersuasive. Crossing these two dimensions creates four types of nonpersuasive leadership (see Table 4–1).

TABLE 4–1 Types of Nonpersuasion

		VALUES PREDOMINANTLY GENERATED	
		INTERNALLY	EXTERNALLY
Nonpersuasive Weakness	*Too Flexible*	Milquetoast	Vacillator
	Too Rigid	True Believer	Godfather

The Milquetoast: Milquetoasts have value systems that remain relatively constant and do not change with the political mood of the country. Rather, their values are internally generated and held. However, they are very flexible in their approach to implementation of their values. Fearing conflict, they often give in to opposition, giving the appearance of collapse and sacrificing the very values they hold dear. Instead of compromising to advance their principles, they compromise their principles.

The Vacillator: Unlike the Milquetoast, the Vacillator adopts prevailing values of the times. The Vacillator is akin to Riesman's other-directed person who takes cues from others and external events. When the Vacillator errs in judgment it is in being too flexible. Not having an internal gyroscope of one's own, the Vacillator is subject to buffeting by crosscurrents of opinions and events.

The True Believer: The True Believer is like Riesman's inner-directed person who has deeply held internal values derived from childhood and other salient socialization experiences. However, the True Believer is too rigid and inflexible to implement those values successfully in a highly charged political environment where politics is a compromise between the desirable and the possible. True Believers find it difficult to adjust to the give-and-take of partisan politics, the legislative process, and the ebb and flow of public opinion.

The Godfather: Godfathers have value systems that are influenced by external events and changing norms. They adopt rather than reject prevailing values. Godfathers are prone to maximize values of wealth, status, and power. Other values are secondary and may shift. Godfathers, however, sometimes err by being too rigid. They are often convinced that they are right and that if they persist, others will be persuaded by the wisdom of their policies. At their worst, Godfathers manifest a perverted form of charismatic leadership that has degenerated into destructive egocentricities. The Godfather often demands blind, unswerving loyalty from subordinates.

All presidents since and including Hoover will be classified by nonpersuasive tendencies. This classification indicates tendency rather than degree. Some presidents have been good communicators and salespersons much of the time, but not all of the time, for all presidents occasionally fail to persuade (see Table 4–2).

TABLE 4–2 Classification of Modern Presidents by Nonpersuasion

MILQUETOAST	*VACILLATOR*	*TRUE BELIEVER*	*GODFATHER*
Ford	Eisenhower	Hoover	Roosevelt
Carter	Kennedy	Truman	Johnson
	Reagan		Nixon

FORD AS A MILQUETOAST

The category of Milquetoast is not a natural one for presidents whose job calls for sensitivity to the political mood of the country, which changes often with opinion swings. Of modern presidents, Gerald Ford comes the closest to the Milquetoast category, but even his fit is a loose one. Ford's value system was the product of his all-American midwestern upbringing in the nation's heartland. His long political career exhibited a consistent pattern of Republican conservatism that closely reflected the values of the constituencies he served. His rise to a leadership position in the House of Representatives was the result of long, consistent, and safe service to his Republican colleagues. His sudden ascension to the presidency did not radically change his views, but the circumstances in which those views found expression were radically different.

Ford was confronted with a new set of problems and uncertainty about how to deal with them. One problem he faced in 1974 and 1975 was the deteriorating state of the economy, which was suffering a 12 percent inflation rate. One way that Ford responded to this situation was his Whip Inflation Now (WIN) program, which was based upon the simplistic notion that the average American could help combat price and wage escalation. Ford had WIN badges made and enlistment forms printed for citizens to sign and thereby "enlist" in the battle against inflation. Prominent journalists, such as columnist Sylvia Porter, were recruited to lend impetus and respectability to the WIN campaign.

Because the WIN campaign was based on voluntary action, it was probably doomed to fail from the beginning. Only a few months passed before the program lost its thrust and failed to win the continuing support of the American people. The WIN campaign inspired comedians, cartoonists, and political opponents to laugh at both the program and the president. According to Nessen (1978, p. 75), "I never found out who was responsible for dreaming up the WIN program. Nobody claimed credit."

Although Ford was an experienced politician who did call for other measures to combat inflation, such as a surtax on corporations and upper-income individuals, the WIN program was more hope than reality. The resort to volunteerism was a feeble and underwhelming attempt to cope with a pressing problem. Without some degree of legal coercion, it was unrealistic for Ford to expect that the broad cross section of American public opinion would respond positively to such preachments. The resort to volunteerism is usually the last refuge of weak leadership. Ford's failure to persuade the American people to rally around the WIN button was all too indicative of his ineffectiveness, which was caused by too great a flexibility in approach rather than inconsistency in values. It is difficult to imagine that a Franklin Roosevelt or a Harry Truman would allow themselves to be persuaded that such a program could succeed.

CARTER AS A MILQUETOAST

Like Ford, Carter was a Milquetoast who exhibited internally developed and strongly held values from his childhood and Christian upbringing. Privately, Carter was driven, ambitious, and a very self-disciplined person, but publicly he was remarkably flexible while trying to accommodate himself to public attitudes and external pressures. While campaigning for the presidency, Carter was noted for his attempts to be all things to all people and to tailor his views and his speeches to the audiences to whom he spoke.

Whereas Carter held deep convictions about the need to treat the Soviet Union as an ordinary power and to place more emphasis on human rights, he was flexible enough to readjust his policy goals in the face of external pressures. Certainly after Soviet actions in Angola and Afghanistan, Carter belatedly appreciated the need to be firm with the Soviets and to initiate a major new defense program.

Carter initially planned to pull U.S. troops out of Korea, pursue normalization of relations with Cuba and Vietnam, and put conservative regimes at arm's length. Encountering considerable resistance from Congress and the public, Carter reversed himself on all counts. Despite public proclamations of intentions to the contrary, he failed to balance the budget, halt inflation, or curtail oil imports. Nor was he successful in obtaining hospital-cost containment, in developing national health insurance, and in getting authority for standby gasoline rationing.

Perhaps Carter's greatest failure to persuade was his inability to win over the Congress to many of his legislative proposals. Carter's strongly held internal convictions and intentions were never in question, but he often overloaded the legislative agenda to such a point that his priorities were not clearly communicated and he appeared to shift from one emphasis to another. As Carter himself wrote in his personal diary of January 28, 1977, "Everybody has warned me not to take on too many projects so early in the administration, but it is almost impossible for me to delay something I see needs to be done." Failing to target key issues and agencies, he proceeded with a comprehensive approach and often both he and his staff failed to appreciate the complexities and the congressional and bureaucratic constraints involved.

EISENHOWER AS A VACILLATOR

Especially during his tenure in the Oval Office, Eisenhower displayed at times the characteristics of a Vacillator—of having externally generated values and of being too flexible on public issues. Because of his long and active military career, Eisenhower never developed well-defined public-policy positions. When both Democrats and Republicans approached him to be their presidential candidate in 1948, neither side was sure where Eisenhower stood regarding party affiliation or public issues. Once in office, he frequently exhibited indecision. One example of his indecisiveness occurred during his first term when Senator Joseph McCarthy attacked the patriotism and integrity of General George Marshall. Eisenhower deleted a paragraph from a Wisconsin speech that defended Marshall against McCarthy's slanderous accusations, and because the president said nothing, it was widely assumed he approved.

In the Little Rock incident of 1957, Eisenhower sent troops enforcing the court-ordered desegregation of a southern public school system. In Neustadt's famous case study of the events surrounding the incident, he quotes Eisenhower as saying:

> I can't imagine any set of circumstances that would ever induce me to send federal troops. . .into any areas to enforce the order of a Federal Court, because I believe the common sense of Americans would never require it. Now there may be that kind of authority resting somewhere, but certainly I am not seeking any additional authority of that kind, and I never would believe it would be a wise thing to do in this country. (Neustadt, 1980, p. 22)

Eisenhower's comments reveal a reluctance to use force to carry out court policy, but he capitulated under pressure to do what he implied he would not do. Eisenhower vacillated on this issue, swinging between the pole of enforcement and the opposite pole of states' rights.

Unlike some successive presidents, Eisenhower held no strong internal convictions on civil rights and, indeed, opposed the 1954 Supreme Court ruling of *Brown* v. *Board of Education,* even trying to influence the outcome of that case, according to Chief Justice Earl Warren. Warren later declared that he always believed that Eisenhower resented the 1954 decision and the subsequent cases and actions that it spawned (Warren, 1977). His stand on civil rights illustrates both Eisenhower's lack of strongly held internal values on many social issues and his vacillation on policies under external pressure. Warren also wrote that had Eisenhower used his great popularity to stress enforcement of the *Brown* decision, much of the racial strife the nation confronted soon after could have been avoided. Yet Eisenhower never stated publicly that he supported the *Brown* decision until after he left office.

KENNEDY AS A VACILLATOR

Like Eisenhower, John Kennedy also exhibited Vacillator tendencies on occasion. His values sometimes appeared more externally than internally driven, and he was often excessively flexible on public policy. One striking example, called a "perfect failure" by Irving L. Janis (1982, p. 14), was the Bay of Pigs decision to invade Cuba using a small brigade of Cuban exiles. In this circumstance, Kennedy inherited a dubious invasion plan from his predecessor, first suggested to Eisenhower by Richard M. Nixon. Kennedy's ambivalence about the plan was only belatedly overcome when he was given assurances that it could succeed without overt American intervention. By the time the invasion actually took place, it was so crippled by restrictions that it was doomed to failure without U.S. support and air cover. Having made the decision to allow the invasion, Kennedy vacillated and refused to authorize American air support on the day of the invasion, thus causing the enterprise to collapse into ignominious failure.

Another example of Kennedy's lack of strongly held internal values and his willingness to be excessively flexible on policy issues was his failure to publicly oppose the activities of fellow Senator Joseph McCarthy when Kennedy was in the Senate. In spite of McCarthy's obvious violations of ethical and moral standards, and his defaming attacks on outstanding Democratic leaders, John Kennedy straddled the issue because of the strong support that McCarthy had among Massachusetts Catholics. Perhaps Kennedy's lack of strongly held internal values may be attributed to a conflict between his sense of democratic political values—nurtured in the fertile intellectual milieu of Cambridge and Harvard—and his desire not to displease his conservative Catholic constituency in Massachusetts. By opposing McCarthy's demagoguery he would have jeopardized his own local power base.

Kennedy's susceptibility to external pressure is also illustrated by his stand on civil rights. In spite of his intellectual sympathy for the civil rights struggles of blacks in America, as a pragmatic politician, Kennedy was slow to move into the fray until forced to do so by events. Kennedy was concerned about his narrow margin of victory in the 1960 presidential race and his lack of strong support in the Congress. As a result he was a reluctant dragon in the civil rights battle, but when civil rights marchers were killed in Mississippi, when James Meredith was denied entry into the University of Mississippi, and when fire hoses were turned on demonstrators, Kennedy responded to national outrage and the urgent pleas of Martin Luther King, Jr., with the full force of the Justice Department. Herbert S. Parmet (1983, p. 354), a leading expert on the Kennedy presidency, observed that Kennedy withheld the full force of the Executive Office of the President too long with too many reasons for delay. According to Parmet, "He had to be pressed too hard, but when the time came, he provided the leadership that the struggle for equality had always needed from the White House."

REAGAN AS A VACILLATOR

Ronald Reagan talked dogmatically but played a pragmatic political game. His values shifted considerably across his various careers and were influenced considerably by external forces. Early in his film career, he espoused liberal Democratic views, was an active union member, and eventually became president of the Screen Actors Guild. He was even a founding member of the California branch of the Americans for Democratic

Action (ADA) and later served on the ADA national board. Supporting the Labor League of Hollywood Actors for Truman in 1948, he also backed Helen Gahagan Douglas, a liberal Democrat, against Richard M. Nixon for a California Senate seat in 1950.

By 1952 Reagan was a Democrat for Eisenhower, and as his Hollywood career faded he became the host of television's "General Electric Theater," setting the stage for him to become a spokesperson for that company. In time, Reagan became even more outspoken for business interests. Barber (1985, p. 477) illustrates Reagan's willingness to compromise his values for self-interest in a story about Reagan's attacks on the Tennessee Valley Authority (TVA) while he was a spokesperson for General Electric (GE), not knowing that GE sold about $50 million worth of goods to the TVA annually. Even though Reagan was guaranteed free speech by the president of the company, Ralph Cordiner, when Reagan learned of complaints about his public statements he deleted subsequent attacks on the TVA until he was no longer employed by GE. Reagan actually shifted so far to the right ideologically that he became too conservative for GE and was let go.

Reagan also exhibited considerable flexibility on policy positions to the point of vacillation. His acceptance and then rejection of observance of the unratified SALT II treaty is one example, as was his commitment to "constructive engagement" regarding apartheid in South Africa. During the intense debates in 1986 in Congress over South African policy, Reagan continued to oppose sanctions but nevertheless proceeded to modify his opposition by making concessions to his opponents. He proposed sending a black ambassador to that country and tightening the reins on South African airline landing rights and South African investment in the United States. But Reagan's concessions only spurred on his critics and did not gain new supporters to his positions.

On summitry and arms control, Reagan was unwilling to meet the Soviet leaders during his first term, and little progress was made on arms control during that time. He did not offer decisive leadership to his own administration and even, when in his second term, he decided to meet Soviet leader Gorbachev and engage in serious arms control talks, he found it difficult to unify the quarreling executive departments behind a single policy. For every positive reason that Secretary of State George Shultz could find for summitry and arms control negotiation, it seemed that Secretary of Defense Casper Weinberger could produce a countering negative reason.

On three core issues, however, Reagan remained adamant. He would not raise taxes, would not reduce defense spending, and would not add any new social programs. But he was singularly unsuccessful in persuading his Republican colleagues in the Senate and the House, let alone his

Democratic opposition, that such hard policy stances were desirable. In fact, Republican leaders such as Robert Dole, Peter Domenici, and Robert Packwood repeatedly expressed the need for smaller deficits, higher taxes, and lower defense expenditures. Richard Lugar and Nancy Landon Kasselbaum, Republican members of the Senate Foreign Relations Committee, consistently opposed Reagan's South African policy. In these two areas, Reagan's notable persuasive powers failed.

In spite of his remarkable selling powers, Reagan was unsuccessful, especially in his second term, in persuading both the Congress and the public about the correctness of his policies toward the Contra "freedom fighters," South Africa, defense spending, and the budget. Although the Congress and the public continued to like President Reagan, they did not necessarily like his policies.

HOOVER AS A TRUE BELIEVER

True Believers have strongly held and internally developed values and convictions, and they rigidly adhere to policies, often refusing to compromise or change their positions. Herbert Hoover was a True Believer. In the face of the deepest depression the country had ever known, Hoover would not surrender his beliefs about how the country should be run, refusing to take the politically expedient action. His successor, Franklin Roosevelt, was as conservative and almost as economically orthodox as Hoover, but he was willing to experiment with innovative solutions.

Hoover's deep and sincere convictions about American individualism and free enterprise made it inordinately difficult for him to bend in the political winds of crisis and to break out of his mind-set. His belief in the balanced budget and his aversion to deficit spending continued almost intact to the end of his term. Even as late as 1931, when the Roaring Twenties' bubble had burst, Hoover was pressing for a tax increase. The angry cries of the unemployed left him unmoved.

To the very end of his administration, Hoover remained convinced that his policy was correct and to change would be to take the easy way out. He believed that his austere programs had to be maintained to see the crisis through. For Hoover, Roosevelt represented a radical breaking with precedent and tradition that would undermine the very form of government under which the country had grown and prospered. Hoover's rigid character and mentality in the face of growing threats at home and abroad represent the True Believer in its purest form. Ultimately, events and reality overcame his best efforts to persuade the American people of the rightness of his cause.

TRUMAN AS A TRUE BELIEVER

Like Hoover, Harry Truman also exhibited many of the characteristics of a True Believer, but he was not nearly as rigid in either his actions or his point of view. Truman was an experienced politician familiar with the compromises of politics between the desirable and the possible, but he showed great self-confidence and belief in himself and was hard to move when he believed a cause was just. His belief in the American system and the American people were rooted in small-town Missouri. His service in World War I as an artillery captain solidified his basic beliefs in both the destiny of the United States and the efficacy of firm decisionmaking.

Truman's stubborn fight for his Fair Deal program against the Eightieth Congress and his uphill battle for reelection in 1948 exemplify his feisty intransigence in both beliefs and policy positions. Although Truman delayed both his removal of General Douglas MacArthur as commander-in-chief of American forces in the Far East and his defense of Secretary of State Dean Acheson against the slanderous charges of Senator Joseph McCarthy, when Truman did finally bite the bullet he was forceful and decisive. He agonized initially over these decisions, but once deciding upon his course of action he fought with the passion of a True Believer. MacArthur was dismissed and Truman took the heat. He defended Acheson and took McCarthy's abuse.

In spite of Truman's courage, conviction, and wisdom in dismissing General MacArthur and resisting the general's plan to expand the Korean War by crossing the Yalu River into China, Truman was unable to persuade the American people of the foresight of his actions. He progressively lost public support for a stalemated war increasingly symbolized in the public mind as a war of attrition with mounting casualties and inconclusive battles. Thus far, history has been kind to Truman as a president who upheld civilian supremacy over the military and resisted pressures to widen an already bloody and costly war. His combativeness and stubbornness undercut his ability to persuade the American people, and these traits compelled him to pursue policies that he felt were right. Although he was unable to persuade the nation, he was able to persuade most historians that his actions benefited the long-term interests of the country.

ROOSEVELT AS A GODFATHER

Godfathers, as a nonpersuasive presidential type, have values that are subject to great influence by external events and prevailing public opinion. Despite the impact of external forces on their values and goals, Godfathers are often rigid in their pursuit of those goals, once adopted. Godfathers are very concerned about personal power and status, and they demand intense loyalty from those around them. Three modern twentieth-century presidents have exhibited characteristics of Godfathers. The first of those examined here is Franklin Roosevelt.

Franklin Roosevelt is a prime example of a man holding conventional views on society, politics, and economics who came to power as president in unconventional times. Contrary to his present image, Roosevelt was conservative, but because of his character structure his values were changed by the external forces operating in his enlarged environment. He learned to use his administration as a vehicle for social experimentation in order to cope with the myriad problems created by the Great Depression.

On foreign affairs Roosevelt evolved from being an isolationist in the early years of his presidency to one increasingly concerned with the mounting conflicts in Europe and Asia. His metamorphosis from insularity to world cosmopolitanism demonstrates vividly his capacity to absorb new information, new ideas, and new perspectives. By the end of his tenure, Roosevelt was a first-rate world statesman who was concerned about the structure of the postwar world and the future of world government.

Throughout his presidency, Roosevelt demanded fierce loyalty of his subordinates and often chose to work through people like Harry Hopkins, Averell Harriman, and Sumner Welles, rather than ranking cabinet officials. Like underworld Godfathers, Roosevelt was always surrounded by a crowd of trusted lieutenants. He could dispense many favors and punish offenders.

Overall, Roosevelt was a superb salesman and a very persuasive president, but when he failed to persuade, his rigid adherence to goals even in the face of overwhelming obstacles contributed to his failures. He was unable to convince several of his close associates about the wisdom of running for a third term. Vice-President John Garner, economic advisor Raymond Moley, Postmaster General James Farley, and others broke with the president over this issue, just as Roosevelt broke with the two-term tradition.

Both in economic and foreign policy, Roosevelt had increasing difficulty in persuading Congress to follow his lead after the 1938 congressional elections. He was forced to back down after his "quarantine speech" of October 5, 1937, in which he warned of growing world lawlessness that could not be averted by isolation or neutrality. There was a notable lack of public and congressional support. These failings forced Roosevelt to slow down his attempts to bring a greater awareness to Americans of the dangers of the deteriorating international situation. In spite of Roosevelt's clear perception that Hitler, Mussolini, and Tojo represented a major threat to U.S.

security, the isolationist-interventionist debate was never fully resolved until the Japanese attack on Pearl Harbor unified the country behind his leadership.

Roosevelt's charismatic leadership degenerated into destructive egocentrism in both his aborted Supreme Court-packing plan and subsequent political purge. His ill-considered decision to run for a fourth term in 1944 also has been judged by many historians to have pushed his health to the breaking point, bringing on his death soon after his reelection. Roosevelt's enormous ego, stubbornness, and ruthlessness had both a negative and positive side. Fortunately, he was elected during a time of crisis when such characteristics were more often in demand than not. As someone once observed, "Friends come and go, but enemies just accumulate." Roosevelt accumulated his share of enemies—enough so that the Twenty-second Amendment was soon enacted as a barrier to any future president emulating Roosevelt's unprecedented election to a third and fourth term.

JOHNSON AS A GODFATHER

Lyndon Johnson is a classic Godfather. His ambitious ascent to power, as chronicled by Caro (1982), exhibited a great drive for political status, aided and abetted by the use of money. Johnson's passionate demand for almost servile loyalty by his associates has been attested to by George Reedy (1970) and Joseph Califano (1975). To Johnson, other values were subservient to his passion for money and power and shifted with the political winds. Not unlike an underworld Godfather, Johnson, throughout his political career, always had rich and powerful men in his corner, including Speaker of the House Sam Rayburn, Oklahoma Senator Robert Kerr, and even President Franklin Roosevelt.

Johnson's Godfather characteristics bear a strong resemblance to James David Barber's active-negative classification. His penchant for persisting in a wrong course of action until disaster struck was all too evident in his unswerving belief that the next increment of American power in Vietnam would bring victory. In spite of mounting evidence to the contrary, Johnson remained convinced to the end that his course was correct, even when colleagues such as Robert McNamara and Clark Clifford tried to persuade him otherwise. He was certainly nonpersuasive of his own defense secretaries, other subordinates, and large segments of the American public that his policies in the Far East were beneficial to longterm U.S. interests. The victory that was always in his mind as being "just around the corner" never arrived, and his dreams both for a Great Society at home and in Southeast Asia were victims of that "bitch of a war."

Johnson also had great difficulties in shedding the image of a Texas wheeler-dealer. His long and intimate relationship with Bobby Baker, his senatorial assistant, created problems for Johnson as president when Baker was indicted and convicted on charges of financial chicanery. His wife's ownership of a Texas television station raised questions about conflict of interest. He was never fully able to persuade the public that he was aboveboard in these endeavors. He used J. Edgar Hoover and the FBI to obtain derogatory information about his political enemies, and even the famed "Johnson treatment" suggested willingness to use whatever means were necessary to achieve his goals. No matter what Johnson did on behalf of blacks and Chicanos, for the poor and underprivileged, and in behalf of education and culture, he was never able to persuade the American public that he was free of the taint of political corruption. His singleminded ruthlessness in pursuit of his domestic policy goals and dogged wrong-headedness in foreign policy remained a political albatross throughout his presidency.

NIXON AS A GODFATHER

Nixon, like Johnson, was a political Godfather with many of the same characteristics that Johnson held, including externally driven values and rigid adherence to public-policy positions. Nixon was secretive, power-seeking, and demanding of strong loyalty by his subordinates. He also was an egomaniac who represented a distorted form of charismatic leadership with dangerous and destructive overtones. Nixon, a man of mercurial values, was often willing to say what was necessary to save his political career, as, for example, his famous "Checkers" speech. Vehemently anticommunist as a member of the House Committee on Unamerican Activities early in his career, Nixon shifted to a position of moderation in dealing with communist nations while president, paving the way for official relations with China and an era of détente with the Soviet Union.

The greatest example of Nixon's failure to persuade was his losing campaign with the Congress, the courts, and the American public that he was innocent of wrongdoing in the Watergate case. No matter what he tried or what explanations he gave, the situation only deepened and worsened until even a conservative U.S. Supreme Court, led by his own appointee Warren Burger, admonished him to turn over the White House tapes to the House Judiciary Committee.

In yet another example of nonpersuasion, Nixon was unable to persuade the Congress to continue backing the Vietnam War. In spite of announcing the signing of the Paris Peace Accords ending the war in 1973, he undertook the bombing of Cambodia without any legislative authorization after the Gulf of Tonkin Resolution had been repealed by Congress in

1970. Congress was not convinced by Nixon's justifications about the need to shift $750 million within the Defense Department to finance Cambodian raids, after Nixon and his adminstrative officials failed to inform the various appropriations committees. Congress then passed an amendment banning all similar trust transfers and forbade the use of any Department of Defense funds for combat use in Cambodia. Other congressional fund cutoffs occurred during 1974 and 1975, which systematically reduced the level of appropriations available for military and economic aid to both Laos and Cambodia. For all practical purposes, Congress forced Nixon to end the Vietnam War by cutting off funds to continue the war.

Following his resignation from office, Nixon was unable to persuade historians and political scientists that his presidency could be judged without reference to Watergate. No matter how considerable his accomplishments were in foreign policy, he was not able to purge the memory of his willingness to subvert democratic values to his own political ends. When Nixon failed to persuade, he rigidly adhered to goals that others deemed unobtainable or unworthy.

NONPERSUASION AND THE PRESIDENCY

If selling ability is an essential ingredient of a modern successful presidency, then the absence of it must necessarily harm the performance of the president and the president's administration. This chapter has attempted to show what happens to modern presidents when they fail to persuade. Obviously they do not fail all the time. Neither do they succeed all the time. Whether they succeed or fail is in part due to the caliber of skills they possess as salespeople and the type of personality they bring to the job of selling their policies to the four audiences they play to. The caliber of presidential skills was examined in the last chapter. The personal proclivities that affect their ability to sell or not sell have been classified, discussed, and applied in this chapter. The case has been made that the nonpersuasive attributes of modern presidents, whether Milquetoast, Vacillator, True Believer, or Godfather, are important aspects of their presidencies. Even the greatest of presidents can fail at times and exhibit the characteristics that lead to nonpersuasion. The failure to sell and persuade can be a fatal flaw for a modern president. Johnson, Nixon, and Carter all had major flaws in this area and Roosevelt, Kennedy, and Truman were not immune to the problem. To recognize the symptoms and understand the problem is the beginning of the cure. While a complete cure is impossible, it is not beyond hope that nonpersuasive tendencies can be reduced, contained, and managed. How good management can help is the subject of the next chapter.

REFERENCES

BARBER, JAMES DAVID, *The Presidential Character: Predicting Performance in the White House*, 3rd Edition, Englewood Cliffs, N.J., Prentice-Hall, 1985.

CALIFANO, JOSEPH A., *A Presidential Nation*. New York: W.W. Norton & Co., Inc., 1975.

CARO, ROBERT A., *The Path to Power: The Years of Lyndon Johnson*. New York: Knopf, 1982.

JANIS, IRVING L., *Groupthink*. Boston: Houghton Mifflin, 1982.

KATTENBURG, PAUL M., *The Vietnam Trauma in American Foreign Policy, 1945–75*. New Brunswick, N.J.: Transaction Books, 1980.

NESSEN, RON, *It Looks Different from the Inside*. Chicago: Playboy Press, 1978.

NEUSTADT, RICHARD, *Presidential Power*. New York: John Wiley, 1960, 1980.

PARMET, HERBERT S., *JFK: The Presidency of John F. Kennedy*. New York: Penguin, 1983.

REEDY, GEORGE E., *The Twilight of the Presidency*. New York: New American Library, 1970.

RIESMAN, DAVID, *The Lonely Crowd*. New Haven, Conn.: Yale University Press, 1950.

WARREN, EARL, *The Memoirs of Earl Warren*. New York: Doubleday, 1977.

CHAPTER FIVE
PRESIDENTS AS MANAGERS:
Chairpersons of the Board

This chapter explores presidents as managers. The increasing institutionalization of the White House, the growth in the scope of federal policy, and the expansion of the federal bureaucracy all dictate that modern presidents be managers as well as salespeople. Presidents must manage policies and bureaucracies in four critical areas: defense, foreign affairs, social policy, and economic policy. Each area will be discussed, including the expansion of federal responsibility, and the tools presidents employ to manage policy. As in the previous chapters, presidents will be rated according to their demonstrated abilities to manage policies in different areas. Numerical scores will be assigned and overall management scores will be computed. These overall management scores will be used to distinguish between presidents with high and low management skills.

To help our search for the characteristics of successful managers, we will examine the findings of recent studies of successful management techniques in the corporate world, and note their applicability to the public sector, particularly the presidency.

WHAT IS MANAGEMENT?

Most people, including managers themselves, do not agree on the essence of management. Sometimes the functions of management have been identified by the acronym POSDCORB. Mangers are involved in planning, organizing, staffing, directing, coordinating, reporting, and budgeting (Graham and Hays, 1986). Views of how to carry out these management functions vary across different schools of thought.

Beginning with the scientific management school espoused by Frederick Taylor, in the second decade of the twentieth century, different views of appropriate managerial styles and activities have emerged. This school employed several principles, including the necessity of gathering large quantities of data prior to decisionmaking, selection of individual workers by merit, employing known scientific and behavioral information and laws, and clear-cut divisions of responsibility between management and labor. Scientific management employed Theory X—a view of workers as inherently disinterested in their jobs and in work, constantly needing either a reward or carrot, or a stick or punishment, to perform the work.

In the 1930s, the emergence of the Hawthorne school, or behavioral approach, reflected a shift to Theory Y, which viewed humans as inherently and intrinsically motivated to work and perform, rather than requiring external incentives as under Theory X. Initially created as tests of the effects of lighting upon worker productivity at a Western Electric plant, the Hawthorne studies provided several results that illustrate that social effects, including peer opinion and attention from outside reviewers, outweighed illumination changes. Out of this grew a view of the role of managers as providing incentives to workers that allowed them to achieve their own personal and organizational goals simultaneously.

In more recent times, Theory Z has stormed management circles. The development of this school is often attributed to the Japanese. Under Theory Y, managers work to reduce conflict between the worker and the organization. Theory Z pushes this conflict reduction to include a minimization of confrontation among individual workers as well. Theory Z managers are adept at providing incentives for cooperation and for promoting harmony within the organization.

All schools of management agree that the twentieth century has witnessed the rise of management as a function and task from either direct labor or from creative invention. In modern organizations, managers are supposed to oversee the invention process and the completion of tasks rather than perform either one directly. However, in government, unlike business, professional management never quite developed the status of a separate discipline. Moreover, as Robert B. Reich (1983, pp. 76–77) has observed, "Just as professional managers in business came to preempt the authority of inventors—promoters by virtue of their special knowledge, so professional managers in government came to preempt legislators and elected officials by virtue of their technical understanding of the public interest."

The president's duties as manager begin with the president's role as chief executive, which is grounded in Article II of the Constitution. This article vests the president with "the executive power" and empowers the president "to take care that the laws be faithfully executed." Moreover, presidents receive substantial managerial power from their role as "commander in chief of the army and navy." In addition to these two powers, presidents have been broad constructionists of their delegated powers, especially in times of war and crises. Both past and present presidents have received broad delegations of powers by statutes passed by Congress.

Despite considerable formal authority, the president's constitutional and statutory powers frequently are less than those implied by the classic "textbook presidency." A close student of the president's role as manager, Richard Rose (1980, p. 339) has observed that "the President's title of chief executive is a misnomer; he can more accurately be described as a non-executive chief." Rose argues that the president's power to command is limited and that the ability to achieve objectives as an administrator depend upon skills at persuading others. The stronger the president's authority, the more the president is likely to rely upon formal command power. The weaker the president's authority, the more the president will rely upon persuasion, political skills, and reputation.

Cronin (1980, p. 155) has sketched the president's job description to include three subpresidencies dealing with foreign policy and national security, aggregate economics, and domestic policy and programs. Within each of these subpresidencies, the nation's chief executive performs a variety of activities: crisis management, symbolic and morale-building leadership, priority setting and program design, recruitment leadership, legislative and political coalition building, and program implementation and evaluation. Additional functions in each of the subpresidencies are oversight of government routines and the establishment of an early warning system for future problem areas.

Stephen Hess (1976, p. 9) argues that four factors contribute greatly to the management problems of the modern presidency. The first is the prodigious growth of the presidency in terms of sheer size of presidential staff. A second characteristic is the increasing influence of White House staff members as presidential advisors with an accompanying decline in cabinet influence. This diminishes the ability of cabinet officers to control their own departments and clouds the lines of authority. A third characteristic is increasing suspicion by modern presidents of permanent government, which leads to a proliferation of functional offices within the Executive Office of the White House. Presidential assistants have increasingly become "special pleaders," a fourth trend, which has complicated presidential management. As presidential assistants become White House representatives for a variety of interest groups, including specific industries, minorities, governors and mayors, labor, religious groups, etc., the role of the White House has shifted from mediating different interests to collecting interests.

Watson and Thomas (1983, pp. 283–284) also discuss the impact of bureaucratic power on presidential management and suggest that several factors are important. They identify the growth in the size, complexity, and dispersion of the executive branch as increasing the number of programs to be administered and the number of employees to be supervised. Bureaucratic inertia and momentum are contradictory forces that influence presidential management. According to a famous law of organizational governance, bureaucracies at rest tend to stay at rest, whereas bureaucracies in motion tend to stay in motion (Rourke, 1976, p. 29).

Although in theory, a large number of political appointees to the executive branch gives the president greater control of the bureaucracy, the reality is often to the contrary. Political appointees, particularly at subcabinet levels, are often unknown to the president and to each other. Not all political appointees have their primary loyalty to the president. "Departmentalists" may be distinguished from "presidentialists" by their loyalty to presidential programs. While presidentialists predominantly identify with the president personally and professionally, departmentalists protect parochial department interests foremost.

The independent legal status of departments and agencies further complicates presidential management of the bureaucracy. Congress not only establishes the departments and agencies through statutes but also allocates the funds and establishes appropriate personnel levels for continuing operations. The president's subordinates, not the president, enter into contracts and make grants. Although the Constitution makes the president the chief executive, Congress delegates power and imposes duties on many administrative officials.

The susceptibility of the executive branch to external political influence is also a factor influencing modern presidential management of the bureaucracy. According to Watson and Thomas, the decline of American political parties into impotency has left a power vacuum filled by special interest groups. The classic "iron triangle" in American national politics illustrates the crucial linkages of the bureaucracy with special interest groups and congressional committees, not political parties.

Given the considerable administrative complications in the modern presidency and impediments to presidential management of the bureaucratic policy initiatives, what are the ingredients of a sound presidential administrative strategy? Richard Nathan discusses five components that astute presidents should include in their managerial plans (Nathan, 1983, p. 88). These include selecting cabinet secretaries whose views are closely in line with the president's, selecting subcabinet officials who also agree with presidential policy initiatives, motivating cabinet and subcabinet officers to give their attention to the operations and administrative processes of their agencies, using the budget process as the main organizing framework for policy making, and, finally, avoiding overreliance on highly centralized White House control and clearance systems.

Presidents must overcome defects in the civil service to achieve effective management (Malek, 1978, pp. 95–117). Adversarial attitudes by career bureaucrats toward political leadership result in resistance to change and innovation. Career bureaucrats are sometimes inadequately trained as managers and fail to develop skills to overcome training deficiencies. They also frequently suffer from narrow perspectives due to narrowly focused career patterns in only one or two agencies. Nor do the poor pay practices employed by Congress, which limits the upper-level salaries for the career service, contribute to effective management. The Senior Executive Service, created by the Civil Service Reform Act of 1978, attempted to provide presidents with greater flexibility and incentives in motivating and rewarding career bureaucrats, but whether this legislation leads to significantly greater managerial expertise and less parochialism by career bureaucrats remains to be seen.

In addition to defects in the civil service, the lack of institutional memory concerning management practices in the Executive Office of the President has proved troublesome for effective presidential administration and oversight. Can the country continue to afford the luxury of a *de novo* presidential administrative educational process every time a new president assumes office? Price and Siciliano (1982, pp. 305–307)have argued no, although they contend that the nation needs a general framework for the organization of the Executive Office of the President, not a detailed blueprint. Among their recommendations is greater appreciation for a diversity of organizational approaches, thus allowing the use of both chiefs of staff and alternate forms of organization depending on the needs of the president in office. Moreover, presidents should collaborate with both the executive branch and the Congress; rely on nonpartisan, unbiased, professional advice; develop systems to sort out, organize, and give priority to issues; and recruit high quality personnel, especially in the Senior Executive Service. Further, presidential staffs should remain small. Operating responsibilities belong in the executive departments and agencies, not in the Executive Office of the President, except in national emergencies. The Executive Office of the President should only intervene selectively, and then to promote central perspectives. Special interests represented elsewhere should not be mirrored in the Executive Office of the President; presidents speak for national interests not special interests. Continuity and planning are essential. Price and Siciliano recommend that the president employ three professional staffs on international, domestic, and economic matters, in addition to a small coordinating staff for processing information for decisionmaking and a director for long-term policy research and analysis.

Other suggestions on how to increase the effectiveness of presidential managerial capacities have been proposed by Paul C. Light, who contends that four steps are needed to overcome "the no-win presidency" (Light, 1983, pp. 225–233). Presidents first need to plan ahead by scanning the environment and anticipating upcoming problems. Second, occupants of the Oval Office should hire expertise, especially in the Congressional Liaison Office and the Office of Management and Budget. A third need is to set priorities rather than taking a shotgun approach to policy development and management. Finally, Light agrees with and reiterates Neustadt's admonition that the presidency is no place for amateurs, and he extends this beyond the president to include the president's advisors.

In their efforts to overcome "the no-win presidency" described by Light, modern presidents have employed different managerial styles. Herbert Hoover, when he was Secretary of Commerce in the Coolidge administration, viewed the nation as a single industrial organism oriented toward the single goal of maximizing profits. He sought to implement the ideas of Arthur Eddy to stabilize production by eliminating wasteful competition. Hoover's Department of Commerce was a center of innovative activity. Hoover tried to carry his ideals to rationalize American business activities into his presidency, but external events overwhelmed his efforts to apply scientific-management techniques to government.

In managerial style, Franklin Roosevelt contrasted sharply with Hoover. Rather than rationalize bureaucratic arrangements, Roosevelt created an atmosphere of administrative competition among aides and officials. He allowed areas of specialization to overlap, relied on oral not written reports, delegated the same duties to competing advisors, and kept a balance of opposites in his cabinet and staff. A "hands on" administrator, he was his own secretary of state. He dominated his government in the early years, but as his health declined and he became increasingly preoccupied with World War II, greater power shifted to his staff. When he took the oath of office as president in March 1933, his staff consisted of only thirty-seven people, nine of professional rank. The Reorganization Act of 1939, resulting from the famous Louis Brownlow report on methods to create greater efficiency in government, gave Roosevelt the authority to reshape his staff to suit his own aggressive and innovative managerial style.

Unlike Franklin Roosevelt, Harry Truman was an orderly and tidy man who objected to Roosevelt's style of confusion and innovation. Truman believed in orderly government and a strong cabinet, and he placed great emphasis on loyalty as a principle of management. As Hess has observed, "Truman's method of running the government was almost midpoint between the designed chaos of his predecessor and the structural purity of his successor" (Hess, 1976, p. 45). Truman generally picked superbly qualified people for the most important jobs and ordinary and sometimes unqualified people for positions of less importance. During his administration, two major institutional additions to the presidency were created—the National Security Council and the Council of Economic Advisors.

The chief of staff system, derived from his military experiences, was the bulwark of the Eisenhower administrative presidency. His was a highly structured presidential staff that increased both in size and in congressional funding. Eisenhower used his cabinet for collective advice, and he initiated both a cabinet secretariat and National Security Council secretariat, giving both of those organizations institutional memory or a record of what transpired. His managerial techniques have been blamed for the lack of creative proposals generated by his administration to deal with domestic problems.

The institutionalized arrangements of the Eisenhower administration were rejected by his successor, John F. Kennedy, who showed little interest in the organization and operations of the executive branch. Kennedy had a disdain for routine and a disrespect for tradition and the "old boy" system. He emphasized crisis management and made the presidency the focal point of government. He attracted many young, energetic, intelligent, and creative people into government service. His personalized administrative style was in the spirit of Franklin Roosevelt, but the size and complexity of the government had grown drastically during the time between the New Deal and the New Frontier. While a personalized presidency worked for Roosevelt, it proved less effective in the Kennedy era because of the growth of both presidential and governmental responsibilities.

Kennedy's successor, Lyndon Johnson, was an unpredictable manager who was very idiosyncratic in style. His unhealthy insecurity produced great strain and tension among his staff, and led to a high personnel turnover in his administration. Personal loyalty became an overriding issue in his governmental style. At first, he made heavy use of Kennedy holdovers but gradually replaced them with his own people. A great many new agencies were created by Great Society legislation in his administration. Johnson often staffed them with people close at hand, strongly loyal to him personally.

As vice-president under Eisenhower for eight years, Richard Nixon emulated the chief of staff system of presidential management with which he became familiar under Eisenhower. He was particularly enthusiastic about Eisenhower's use of the National Security Council, and revived its staff system, placing Henry Kissinger in charge of directing the flow of foreign policy. Nixon proposed some of the most ambitious reorganization plans in the history of the modern presidency. According to Louis Koenig (1981, p. 206), no other president presented such sweeping reorganization plans so rapidly. His reforms reflected the philosophy of the Ash Council, which proposed four super departments—community development, economic affairs, human resources, and natural resources. Under this scheme, the departments of state, defense, treasury, and justice would remain, making a total of eight departments instead of the then existing eleven. Nixon's managerial style was one of boldness toward the goal of administrative efficiency. However, Nixon's ambitious plans for reorganization were broken by Watergate.

Coming to office on the heels of Nixon's resignation, Gerald Ford was not in a good position to exercise aggressive leadership over the federal government. Unlike some presidents who have been governors or who held administrative appointments, Ford had been a congressman for most of his adult life, a career path that did not provide him with extensive experience managing large scale organizations. Ford's administration was noted for the intensity of staff infighting. His tenure as president was brief and did not permit him to make a strong impact on the federal bureaucracy. Like Eisenhower, Ford wanted to restore the cabinet as a meaningful advisory body. He did make strides toward this goal by reactivating the cabinet secretariat and making his cabinet meetings meaningful. As Gordon Hoxie (1980, p. 50) points out, "More than any other post-World War II president, with the exception of Eisenhower, Ford did establish a collegial system and restore a sense of purpose to the Cabinet, as a deliberative, meaningful advisory and administrative body." However, his overall managerial style was ineffectual compared to many of his predecessors and successors, and his greatest contribution was not administrative but rather the restoration of public faith in the open presidency.

Jimmy Carter, too, was a believer in the cabinet-style of government, especially as propounded by Hess (1976) in his book *Organizing the Presidency*. However, in spite of Carter's attempt to implement Hess's suggestions, the noble experiment gradually faded into the realm of lip service, particularly after the Carter cabinet was purged of Joseph A. Califano and Michael Blumenthal. Jimmy Carter, the engineer, saw government as a machine to be well designed and maintained. He advocated the establishment of new departments of energy and education. Although the Reorganization Act of 1977 prohibited Carter from abolishing or creating departments or independent agencies mandated by statute, Carter did manage a series of reforms in the civil service that Congress enacted as the Civil Service Reform Act of 1978, which replaced the Civil Service Commission with the Office of Personnel Management and the Merit Systems Protection Board. Carter delegated very little and sought to have a White House staff without a chief of staff. When he finally appointed one, he named the wrong person, Hamilton Jordan, to that position. Carter's managerial style lacked effectiveness as a top executive administrator, and he was often accused of failing to see the forest for the trees.

Ronald Reagan brought to his White House a philosophy that viewed the appropriate managerial role for the president as the equivalent of the head of a large corporation. He believed the president should only provide oversight for the executive branch. Reagan delegated much responsibility to trusted subordinates, and he was not overly concerned with the daily details of policy implementation. In theory, this allowed him to retain a big-picture perspective. In practice, it caused him to lose a tight grasp of the nuts and bolts of his policies and administration. Like other presidents before him, Reagan was a devoted believer in cabinet government and tried hard to make it work, even to the extent of establishing cabinet councils that handled policies on a functional basis. While his close associates continued to pay lip service to the validity of the cabinet government experiment, critics were skeptical of its past record and performance. Reagan's loose managerial style at the very pinnacle of government engendered much staff antagonism during his first term although the infighting did not disrupt the political effectiveness of his administration. In the second term, chief of staff Donald Regan brought structure and discipline to the White House staff, but he lowered appreciably the degree of political sophistication displayed by his predecessor, James Baker. Reagan made a determined effort to place people of his own conservative persuasion in agencies, departments, and regulatory commissions within the federal government.

MANAGING DEFENSE POLICY

Because the first order of business for any country is survival, the management of national defense policy is of primary importance to modern presidents. Such considerations as the size and readiness of the armed forces, the size and composition of the defense budget, the selection and development of new weapon systems, and the state of morale in the military are of great concern. How well a president is able to manage defense resources not only can affect the security and survival of the country but also the effectiveness of the country's diplomacy, for military preparedness is the strong right hand of effective foreign policy.

Hoover to Kennedy

During Hoover's presidency from 1929 to 1933, the international environment in Europe and Asia was beginning to disintegrate. One of his first moves was to reach an understanding with British Prime Minister Ramsay MacDonald to end Anglo-American naval rivalry. The London Naval Conference of 1930 was the last successful effort to limit the size and number of great power navies by international agreement. After the Japanese aggression in Manchuria in 1931, Hoover asked the British to join the United States in sanctions against the Japanese, but a new British government refused. Thereafter, Hoover did restore funds that had previously been cut from U.S. naval appropriations. After the Japanese bombing of Shanghai in 1932, Hoover, acting as commander in chief, sent American ships and troops to that Chinese city, and strengthened both Hawaiian and Philippine military bases. He also moved the battleship fleet to the Pacific. In January 1933, just before leaving office, Hoover requested congressional authority for an arms embargo against foreign states that the president designated. The House agreed to his proposal, but the Senate added so many qualifications that the act was never passed. Although Hoover clearly recognized the nature of the problem of Japanese aggression, the effectiveness of his responses was moderated by his hesitancy to take bold actions without British support. However, his attempts to bolster U.S. military strength in a period of increasing international restlessness and armed buildup ranks him medium on management of defense policy.

When Franklin Roosevelt succeeded Hoover, threats from Germany, Italy, and Japan mounted, and although Roosevelt was fully cognizant of the situation, American public opinion turned inward and isolationism was rampant. Inhibited by such public opinion, Roosevelt was reluctant to take overt action until after hostilities in Europe began. He did seek the repeal of the American arms embargo and the restoration of the draft. After June 22, 1940, when France capitulated to Germany, Roosevelt began taking bold steps toward U.S. rearmament. He proposed a "destroyer for bases" deal with Britain by way of an executive agreement which bypassed Congress, a Lend-Lease Act, and began joint military planning with the British.

After the Japanese attack Pearl Harbor in 1941, Roosevelt assumed full powers as commander in chief. According to Hoxie (1977, p. 48), "Once the war fully came, Roosevelt proved himself a consummate Commander in Chief. He envisioned an alliance on a grand and glorious scale." Roosevelt took the lead in January 1942 for a Declaration of the United Nations, which was originally signed by twenty-six nations and, by war's end, had been signed by forty-six states. The declaration affirmed the principles of the Atlantic Charter, pledged wholehearted support for the war effort, and promised no separate peace settlement. During World War II, Roosevelt exercised commander-in-chief powers more assertively than had Woodrow Wilson during World War I. He was able to appoint and effectively utilize three superb U.S. generals in Dwight Eisenhower, named Supreme Allied Commander in Europe; George Marshall, Chief of Staff; and Douglas MacArthur, U.S. Far East Commander. Roosevelt ranks high on management of defense policy, especially during the biggest and most devastating war that either the United States or the world had ever seen. He was able to maintain high morale for the war effort and helped craft a winning strategy.

On military and defense policy, Harry Truman is a paradox. Truman presided over the dismantling of U.S. forces in Europe after the close of

World War II, which created a massive power vacuum that enabled the Soviets to consolidate their positions in Eastern Europe. On the other hand, Truman also presided over the rearmament of the United States at the beginning of the cold war. He was instrumental in the formation of the North Atlantic Treaty Organization (NATO) in 1949 and fought a costly and protracted war with the North Koreans in the early 1950s. He upheld the principle of civilian supremacy over the military by removing General MacArthur from his command, which may have prevented the spread of the Korean War by aborting MacArthur's strategic goal of invading the mainland of China.

Truman inaugurated the Atomic Age by his decision in 1945 to use nuclear weapons against the Japanese cities of Hiroshima and Nagasaki in the closing days of World War II. Truman's reorganization of the Department of Defense in 1947 was a genuine postwar revolution that created not only a unified defense establishment but also the National Security Council (NSC), the Central Intelligence Agency (CIA), and the Joint Chiefs of Staff. He also racially integrated the armed forces of the United States. In spite of some legitimate questions about Truman's campaign to "bring the boys home" from World War II and his use of atomic weapons, Truman's achievements in the area of defense-policy management far outweigh his shortcomings. As a result, he is ranked high in this area.

Among modern presidents, Dwight Eisenhower was undoubtedly the best-qualified defense manager by virtue of his long and distinguished career as a professional military officer. His experience ranged from being a successful Allied commander in World War II, Chief of Staff of the Army, and Supreme Commander of NATO. Eisenhower knew more about the defense establishment than did any other president or politician of his era. He successfully terminated the Korean War, kept the defense budget under tight and effective control, and was innovative in his approach to integrating new weapon systems into the military. Eisenhower also was responsible for the adoption of Reorganization Plan Number 6, which became effective in June 1953. This plan strengthened the authority of the Secretary of Defense, reorganized the Department of Defense by eliminating a number of superfluous boards and committees, and established clearer lines of authority for both better civilian control of the military and improved planning capabilities. Eisenhower institutionalized a secretariat for the National Security Council and, in the closing days of his presidency, warned the nation against the dangers of militarizing society through the growth of a military-industrial complex. Eisenhower, though often low-keyed in his managerial approach, ranks high on management of defense policy because of his deep knowledge of the complexities of the military budget, interservice rivalries, and national security policy.

As is the case with so many presidents, John F. Kennedy tried to undo what he regarded as the stultification of defense planning and policy under his predecessor. For example, he undid many of the reforms that Eisenhower had achieved in the operation of the National Security Council (NSC) and he discontinued its staff organization and frequent meetings. Only after the Bay of Pigs disaster did he restore to the NSC some of prestige it enjoyed in the Eisenhower administration. Kennedy also sought a major reorganization of the Department of Defense by the installation of Robert McNamara as its Secretary of Defense. Decision-making power in the department was centralized under the secretary. A systems-analysis staff was attached to McNamara's office, that utilized the techniques of cost-effectiveness and strategic analysis, in reviewing the proposals of the professional military staff. As a result, the role of the uniformed chiefs of staff of the armed services was downgraded. These reforms tended to depress interservice rivalries and strengthened civilian policymakers, but the acid test of Vietnam lessened the credibility and viability of many of these reforms.

Kennedy's "missile gap," alleged during the 1960 campaign, was found to be nonexistent after he took office, but he sought to upgrade the quality of U.S. weaponry, started the army's elite Green Beret program, and created a new Strike Command that sought to transport American troops any place in the world at a moment's notice. Kennedy was willing to spend more money on defense than Eisenhower to support his activist foreign policy. Although the Bay of Pigs invasion was an unmitigated failure, Kennedy's conduct of the Cuban missile crisis was almost exemplary in the cautious use of military force in support of diplomacy. Kennedy's willingness to launch new initiatives caused him to respond to the Soviet launching of Sputnik by calling for an expanded space program and landing a man on the moon within the decade. Unfortunately, his activist defense policy also escalated American involvement in Vietnam and set the stage for the agonizing decisions that Lyndon Johnson faced in that military arena. Kennedy ranks medium on defense management. Although his intentions were admirable, he did not carefully calculate the military consequences of implementing his sometimes overly ambitious goals.

Johnson to Reagan

Lyndon Johnson inherited Kennedy's defense organization and policies, and he had the difficult job of following a popular and charismatic leader. At first, he tried to carry out Kennedy's programs, both at home and overseas, and pledged that the United States would honor its defense commitments, from South Vietnam to West Berlin. Johnson's decision to increase America's involvement in Vietnam was a particularly crucial one because it expanded his role and duties as commander in chief. As the shadows of that conflict lengthened and cast a pall over the White House,

Johnson became more and more involved in the details of daily management of the war, even to the point of selecting bombing targets.

Johnson's step-by-step escalation of the conflict bogged him down in a defense-policy quagmire from which he never fully extricated himself. In spite of his efforts to complete a nuclear nonproliferation treaty with the Soviets and to lay the foundation for Strategic Arms Limitation talks at Glassboro, N.J., Johnson became profoundly disturbed about his inability to secure an armistice for Vietnam or to lessen tensions in the Middle East, which resulted from the Six-Day War in 1967. In the final analysis, Johnson ranks low on defense policy management. His judgment about America's ability to win the war in Vietnam was flawed. Constrained by both domestic and world opinion from using nuclear weapons and allied only by a corrupt puppet government in the south, the United States was faced with the awesome military task of winning a guerrilla war as an outsider. Johnson's failure to finance the war by new taxes laid the foundation for major economic stagflation and dislocations in the 1970s.

A notable achievement of Richard Nixon's management of defense policy was his reorganization of the National Security Council under Henry Kissinger. Not only did he restore it to the place of prominence it held under the Eisenhower administration, but he gave it a role of even greater importance because Nixon, unlike Eisenhower, was his own secretary of state. Under Secretary of Defense Melvin Laird, Nixon also returned the uniformed services to their earlier major role. Nixon and Laird were far more respectful of the military opinions of their uniformed chiefs than were the "whiz kids" of the Kennedy era. While Nixon's management of the Vietnam War has been criticized for its failure to end that conflict earlier, his command decisions to mine the harbor at Haiphong and to bomb North Vietnamese military targets, accompanied by political overtures, helped bring about the agreement that ended the war in January 1973. Nixon's summitry with the Soviet Union laid the conditions for detente and lessened the risk of nuclear conflict. The Nixon administration engaged in seven rounds of arms limitation talks before concluding SALT I, and it then began discussions on SALT II. In 1971, the United States reached an agreement with the Soviet Union on measures to take in case of nuclear accidents. A Biological Weapons Convention was signed in 1972. In 1974, Nixon signed a Protocol Treaty on limiting antiballistic missile systems and also the Threshold Test Ban Treaty.

However, Nixon's management of defense policy was not uniformly sagacious, causing him to rank medium on this dimension. In 1971, he violated Cambodian neutrality by ordering a U.S. invasion, which eventually spread the war throughout that beleaguered country. In the same year, fighting in Indochina spread throughout the region, and the United States conducted secret bombing raids against Laos. The American public was not informed about the role of the U.S. military in that country. While some observers believe that Nixon brought about a timely end to the Vietnam War with a culmination in the Paris Peace Accords of 1973, many others are severely critical of Nixon for prolonging the war four long years beyond the time he assumed his position as commander in chief.

Gerald Ford was in office for only a short period and failed to have the prolonged impact on defense policy that many other modern presidents have achieved. However, during his presidential tenure, Greece withdrew its military from the NATO integrated structure and the U.S. suspended arms shipments to Turkey over its involvement in Cyprus. Ford's meeting with Brezhnev in 1974 resulted in a new arms level agreement. Ford also lifted a ten year old embargo on arms sales to Pakistan and India and presided over the tragic and chaotic exodus of American forces from South Vietnam and the fall of Saigon to the North Vietnamese and the Viet Cong.

In 1975, relying primarily upon the National Security Council, Ford devised a strategy to rescue the crew of the American ship *Mayaguez*, which had been captured by the Cambodian navy on May 12. Within three hours after U.S. Marines landed in Cambodia, the crew of the *Mayaguez* was released, although thirty-eight Americans were killed in this operation. Ford's administration also supported "Operation Feature" to recruit mercenaries to fight insurgents in Angola. The mission failed as Angola fell the following year to Cuban military forces and Angolan insurgents. Ford also signed an Underground Nuclear Test Accord in 1976.

Ford was not an outstanding or even good manager of defense policy, but neither was he a unmitigated disaster. He was not innovative, but rather continued the policies of the Nixon-Kissinger era. However, his inability to manage infighting among competing national security and defense interests led to considerable upheaval in top personnel, including the dismissal of Secretary of Defense James Schlesinger and CIA Director William Colby. This mismanagement and his lack of direction ranks Ford low on defense-policy management.

The final evaluation of Jimmy Carter's management of defense policy is difficult and may depend upon the evaluator's ideological perspective. As Phil Williams points out, "The accepted wisdom among conservative commentators and officials is that Carter seriously neglected America's defenses, that he was soft on the Soviet Union, and that he did not take measures commensurate with the threat posed by Moscow" (Williams, 1984, pp. 84–85). However, these same critics accept the fact that after Afghanistan, Carter redeemed himself by adopting a harder line and initiating a rearmament program that was accelerated later by the Reagan administration.

Carter began his administration with the idealist goal of supporting human rights around the world by coupling arms and foreign aid with the internal human rights policies of recipient countries. Carter intended to end preoccupation of U.S. defense policy with the Soviet Union and to replace it with a more global approach to world problems. Carter initially sought to reduce defense spending by $7 billion. His commitment to strategic arms control was deep and abiding, but because of external events triggered by the role of the Soviet Union in Angola and Afghanistan, Carter found himself reverting to the cold war policies of Nixon and Kissinger. For liberals, Carter's later record represents a retreat from his earlier strong stance in support of human rights and his pledge to cut the U.S. defense budget. To liberals, Carter appeared to give in to expediency and too quickly forfeit his ideals by returning to a hard line policy against the Soviet Union.

Carter personally thought his successful conclusion of negotiations with the Soviet Union over SALT II was one of his most important accomplishments, and the failure to have the treaty ratified by the Senate was one of his greatest disappointments. Some of Carter's problems in defense management were similar to his problems in other policy areas. He had difficulty grasping the reality of bureaucratic and congressional politics. Carter frequently appeared indecisive, an image enhanced by his cautious handling of the Iranian hostage crisis and his failure to provide clear leadership to his quarreling advisors, Zbigniew Brezezinski and Cyrus Vance. Carter was bold and innovative in his attempt to redirect defense policy but was ultimately unable to achieve this major reorientation. Because of his failure to recognize "the centrality of force in world affairs," as Brezinski phrased it, we rank Carter medium on defense policy.

Although Ronald Reagan vigorously criticized Carter in practically all policy areas, Reagan's own record on defense expenditures was similar to the last two years of the Carter administration. Reagan essentially continued a policy of defense buildup but made a virtue of the policy that Carter reluctantly adopted. Reagan's hard line on anticommunism went hand in hand with his call for a trillion-and-a-half-dollar increase in defense expenditures over five years. His pro-military stance endeared him both to the armed forces and domestic defense industries. Reagan's successful deployment of military forces in Grenada and the air strikes in Libya against Khadaffi strengthened his reputation as a foreign-policy activist who was willing to use military force. His support of so-called freedom fighters against Marxist regimes in Nicaragua, Angola, and Afghanistan was rationalized in the Reagan Doctrine.

All of this created the strong image that Reagan was in control of defense policy. However, his shortcomings in this area rank him medium on defense policy management. He reactivated a cold-war mentality and reoriented defense policy into a superpower struggle with the Soviet Union, calling that country an "evil empire." Reagan's defense secretary, Caspar Weinberger, contradicted his earlier title of "Cap the Knife" in matters of budgetary cuts and became an almost uncritical advocate of a massive increase in defense spending—the largest peacetime increase since World War II. Weinberger's management of the Department of Defense came under increasing fire for faulty procurement policies and poor staff work by the Joint Chiefs. Demands for reforms of defense department organization and procurement policies escalated in the second term of the Reagan administration.

During his first term, Reagan was very reluctant to enter into arms negotiations with the Soviet Union, and only in response to strong political pressure by America's allies did he begin serious arms negotiations after his reelection in 1984. Reagan did provide decisive leadership in reducing squabbling between the Department of State, which supported both arms control and continued unofficial observance of SALT II, and the Department of Defense, which opposed both those policies. These and other failures, especially in the Iran-Contra affair where certain members of the National Security Council ran amok, result in a gap between Reagan's public pronouncements and actual performance on defense policy management.

MANAGING FOREIGN POLICY

More than any other areas, modern presidents are expected to provide national leadership in the areas of foreign policy and defense policy. Many evaluators couple these two areas into a single dimension. However, changes in the international economy and political arena have heightened the importance of international trade policy, global environmental issues, and the management of scarce world resources all of which fall in the domain of foreign policy. According to the U.S. Constitution and the courts, the president is the single authority for articulation of foreign policy. Foreign policy in a nuclear age is now even more than a matter of winning and losing national face and national standing. It has become an arena in which basic questions of species survival are addressed. Neustadt's shibboleth that the presidency is no place for amateurs has never been more true than in the area of modern foreign policy.

Hoover to Kennedy

The dominant factor impinging on Herbert Hoover's conduct of foreign relations was the economic depression that struck the country after the stock market crash of 1929. The Great Depression caused a turning inward and a preoccupation with domestic problems. In spite of Hoover having a very able secretary of state in Henry L. Stimson, Hoover was very reluctant to take firm actions outside of the United States despite the rapidly deteriorating situation in Europe and the Far East. The United States did not belong to the League of Nations and would only extend limited cooperation.

Hoover abhorred taking strong actions, such as economic sanctions, believing they would lead to war. Five days after the Mukden incident in Manchuria by the Japanese in September 1931, Hoover declared he would "never support any scheme of peace based upon the use of force" (Leopold, 1962, p. 499). The failure of both the League of Nations and the Hoover administration to take more forceful action against Japanese incursions into Manchuria undermined the Pacific treaty system, the Kellogg-Briand Pact, the limitation on armaments, and the limited U.S. cooperation with the League of Nations. The Hoover-Stimson Doctrine of nonrecognition of Japanese conquests failed to arrest the Japanese advances. Because Hoover would not back Stimson's plea for stronger actions, American protests proved ineffectual. The Kellogg-Briand Pact of 1928 outlawing war was also violated, but because it lacked machinery for punishing violators, it too proved an ineffective deterrent. In Europe, the United States generally followed a policy that it would not enter into any agreement that might lead to military consequences.

Hoover's proposals of June 22, 1932, which placed arms limitations into mathematical formulae, ignored French concern for security and hardly recognized Germany's need for equality. When this dramatic gesture failed to win French, English, or Japanese support, a two-month recess in negotiations was voted. The reaction in Europe was devastating. German elections gave the Nazis 230 seats in the Reichstag and toppled the von Papen government. On January 30, 1933, Hitler became German chancellor and quickly dismantled the Weimar Republic. Japan also withdrew from the League of Nations. Hoover's management of foreign policy ranks low. Although it was well-intentioned, it was ineffectual. Not only did it not deter but it eventually encouraged foreign aggression. The Hawley-Smoot Tariff Act of 1930, which Hoover signed with six gold pens, turned the United States inward economically as well as politically and hastened the collapse of the international trading system.

Franklin Roosevelt's conduct of foreign policy is a matter of great controversy among diplomatic historians. Many have, of course, rated him very highly because of his leadership of the United States and its allies in World War II, winning against the formidable Axis powers in Europe and Asia. His wartime conferences and leadership in proposing such policies as the Atlantic Charter, United Nations, and unconditional surrender of the Axis powers certainly are important diplomatic achievements.

On the other hand, a respectable body of opinion contends that Roosevelt's prewar policies toward the Japanese were provocative and ill-conceived. His early isolationism and torpedoing of the London Economic Conference of 1933 exacerbated a deteriorating situation. His policy of providing protection by "shoot on sight" orders to U.S. merchant ships carrying contraband of war to Britain during a period when the U.S. was supposedly neutral is seen as unduly provocative to Germany. Roosevelt agreed to provide protection to British freighters between Newfoundland and Iceland, if the freighters joined U.S. and Icelandic cargo carriers under escort. He used deception to hide the facts of a 1941 incident involving the American destroyer Greer and a German submarine, making it appear that the destroyer had been deliberately assaulted in American waters, which was blatantly untrue. Roosevelt is also criticized for his failure to see the strategic and postwar political implications of military actions often directed to battlefield victory alone. He failed to heed the Clausewitzian injunction that war is the continuation of state policy by other means. Churchill and Stalin exhibited a superior perception of the political consequences of military actions. Because of his shortcomings, Roosevelt ranks medium on the management of foreign policy, but as a result of the industrial and military might of the United States, he accomplished historic triumphs that sometimes disguised his limitations.

Harry Truman came to power with Roosevelt's wartime and postwar policies yet unfulfilled. Although ill-prepared and uninformed by F.D.R. about the details of his policies, Truman nevertheless was a quick and able student. He rapidly came to the conclusion that the Soviets were not living up to the agreements they had made with Roosevelt, and his growing disillusionment with the Soviets let him to take a far firmer stand against the Russians than had Roosevelt. Truman was the architect of most of postwar American foreign policy through such programs as aid to Greece and Turkey, the Truman Doctrine of containment, the Marshall Plan to restore Europe to economic health, and NATO to protect it from Soviet aggression. During his administration, the United States was established as the world's leading nuclear power. Truman's postwar policy of occupying Japan under General MacArthur's remarkably successful command must be counted as a considerable triumph. His decision to oppose the North Korean invasion of South Korea was a controversial but courageous decision, as was his attempt to bring some international control to atomic weapons under the Baruch proposals submitted to the United Nations.

Truman has often been described as being right on the big issues and more frequently wrong on the small issues. Most of the big issues of his day concerned his conduct of American foreign policy, which was widely and bitterly criticized during his tenure, but which many now see as successfully dealing with problems of historic proportions. While some revisionist critics hold him responsible for the start of the cold war, the use of atomic diplomacy against the Soviets, and the globalization of containment policy, his achievements nonetheless rank him high.

During the presidential campaign of 1952, conducted in the midst of the Korean War, candidate Dwight Eisenhower promised to go to Korea if it served the cause of peace. As Stephen Ambrose has observed, "The nation's number-one hero, her greatest soldier, and most experienced statesman, was promising to give his personal attention to the nation's number one problem." (Ambrose, 1983, p. 570) Public response was enthusiastic and overwhelming. Eisenhower's landslide victory in the 1952 election reinforced the conviction that perhaps no previous president had been better qualified by temperament and experience to lead the nation in international affairs. Ambrose noted: "The man who had organized and commanded Overlord was confident that he could organize and run the United States as it faced the challenges of the Cold War." (Ambrose, 1983, p. 572) Few dispute that Eisenhower was eminently well prepared in the field of international relations and that his management of America's defenses was competent and perhaps outstanding, but whether his conduct of foreign relations was comparable to his management of defense is highly questionable. Eisenhower's appointment of John Foster Dulles as secretary of state reinforced his own expertise. However, Ike's generous delegation of authority to Dulles created an image of his own presidency as a figurehead, with Dulles the architect of foreign policy. Dulles's penchant for extravagant phraseology and provocative, often belligerent similes—"liberating" Eastern Europe, "rolling back" the Iron Curtain, and "massive retaliation"—created great anxieties within the country and with America's allies. In spite of the fact that Dulles's "brinkmanship" rhetoric was usually unaccompanied by provocative action, his language created a widespread image that the administration was reckless and enjoyed saber rattling.

Eisenhower's unleashing of Chiang Kai-shek to attack the Chinese mainland in 1953, and his suggested use of nuclear weapons to fill personnel gaps in European rearmament, punctured the euphoria surrounding his assumption of office. Furthermore, Dulles's threat to resume the Korean War with nuclear weapons after an armistice was reached in July 1953 sent the British Prime Minister to Washington to quiet European fears. These and other adventures, including American support of the Shah's overthrow of Iranian Premier Mossadegh and the petulent withdrawal of American assistance to Egypt's Nasser for the construction of the Aswan Dam, thus precipitating the Suez Canal crisis of 1956, rank him medium in the management of foreign affairs.

However, Eisenhower was not without some accomplishments in foreign affairs, for during his eight years in office, the United States was not engaged in any major conflicts, although it was involved in several diplomatic crises. Eisenhoweer did manage an armistice in Korea, proposed an imaginative "Plans for Peace" proposal in the United Nations, cemented a defense agreement with Japan in 1954, and helped stabilize Europe with a pledge to maintain U.S. forces there as long as necessary. Still controversial today are his policies which (1) created SEATO

(Southeast Asia Treaty Organization), (2) sent U.S. military advisors to the South Vietnamese, (3) sided with Egypt and the United Nations against Britain and France in the Suez Canal crisis, and (4) the Eisenhower Doctrine pledging U.S. aid to Middle Eastern countries resisting communist takeovers. Eisenhower's reemergence as his own secretary of state after the death of John Foster Dulles symbolizes the mixed record of his administration.

Like his immediate predecessor in the Oval Office, John Kennedy was average in his management of foreign policy, but for totally different reasons. Although Kennedy entered office proclaiming the need to strengthen the military establishment and to bring vigor and innovation to what he regarded as the stagnant policies of the Eisenhower administration, Kennedy's good intentions were not always fulfilled. As noted previously, the Bay of Pigs invasion was policy run amok. His 1961 summit conference with Khrushchev left the Soviet leader with an image of Kennedy as too young and soft to fight. United States commitment in Vietnam increased from 500 military advisors in 1961 to 10,000 additional advisors in 1963. The U.S. role in the assassinations of Rafael Trujillo, a Dominican Republic dictator, and President Ngo Dinh Diem of South Vietnam was severely criticized.

Kennedy's record in foreign policy was not all negative by any means. He had a number of innovative ideas that found fruition in such programs as the Alliance for Progress in Latin America; the Peace Corps, which became a permanent U.S. agency under his administration; and the "man on the moon" project, which resulted in Alan Shepard becoming the first American in space in 1961. A "hot-line" agreement in 1963 established a direct communications link between the United States and the Soviet Union. In the same year, a limited test ban treaty was signed, which prohibited nuclear tests in the atmosphere, in outer space, and under water. The Cuban missile crisis was successful crisis management, and Kennedy's speech at American University in 1963 is widely acknowledged as a precursor of detente. Kennedy's short thousand days in office saw successes as well as failures in the area of foreign affairs. Younger and less experienced than many other presidents in this area, he was clearly learning his job and was putting his considerable talents to use in foreign policy when his life was cut short in Dallas.

Johnson to Reagan

Lyndon Johnson was comparatively inexperienced in foreign policy. His main field of expertise was domestic politics and policy, although as vice-president he did have some exposure to foreign policy as a member of the National Security Council. As vice president, he also headed an oversight committee on the space program, and he made frequent overeseas trips at the behest of the president. Johnson tried at first to keep the Kennedy diplomatic team intact, including Secretary of State Dean Rusk, who played a more significant role under Johnson than under Kennedy. Johnson's relative inexperience in foreign affairs was thought by many to have allowed him to become almost totally immersed in the Vietnam War, which became the dominant focus of both his foreign policy and defense policy concerns. Johnson's escalation of the Vietnam War turned out to be a tragic blunder and undermined his dream of a Great Society, not only at home but also through the Mekong Delta Project in Southeast Asia. Despite his good intentions, Johnson lied to the American public about American actions in Vietnam and demonstrated ignorance of the history and culture of the region. Although his advisors were frequently brilliant intellectuals, they too were often ignorant about Asian affairs and based their historical analogies and judgments on European experiences.

While Johnson's Vietnam policy seemed an exercise in futility, he did at least limit conflict with the Soviets to the extent that the Soviets did not intervene militarily in Vietnam. As a result, while the United States fought in Asia, it did continue to negotiate with the Soviets in other areas, including the uses of outer space, arms limitations, and cultural and commercial exchanges. Johnson had a moderately successful summit meeting with Soviet Premier Aleksei Kosygin in Glassboro, N.J., and a nuclear nonproliferation treaty was signed with the Soviets in the last year of Johnson's presidency. He gained release by North Vietnam of the crew of the *Pueblo*. Despite these successes, Johnson's rigid orientation and abysmal record in Vietnam contaminated his management of both foreign policy and defense policy, thus ranking him low in this area. As John Stoessinger (1985, p. 202) observes, "The compulsions of his enormous and yet fragile ego made him deceive the Congress, escalate the war by stealth, and finally turn Vietnam into one of the most terrible and self destructive conflicts in American history."

Richard Nixon ranks high on management of foreign policy, which presents a political paradox: one of the biggest rascals in the history of the presidency ranks as one of the most competent, experienced, and far-seeing administrators of U.S. relations with other nations. The answer to this paradox lies in the nature of foreign affairs—a field where the moral constraints of domestic politics do not apply as rigorously and sometimes not at all. In the post–World War II history of the Oval Office, perhaps only Harry Truman was a peer to Nixon as a successful foreign policy manager. Truman, as we have already stated, was often right on the big issues and wrong on the little ones. Similarly, Nixon was more often right than wrong on issues of war and peace but, unfortunately, more wrong than right on legal and moral issues in domestic affairs.

Despite taking four years to end the Vietnam War, Nixon conducted businesslike, competent, and realistic relations with the Eastern Bloc nations. He broke the stronghold that Taiwan held over U.S. relations with China, and he personally inaugurated a new era of Chinese-American rapprochement. This one initiative alone would have stamped Nixon's foreign policy as outstanding, but he was able to couple this opening of relations with a nation that contained one-fourth of the world's population with the beginning of détente with the Soviet Union. Strategic arms limitations talks were not only begun but culminated in the agreements of SALT I, a momentous first step toward the limitation and control of nuclear weapons. Nixon had the intelligence and judgment to work closely and productively with his national security advisor and later secretary of state, Henry Kissinger, who was unquestionably one of the most competent and knowledgeable holders of these offices in recent American history. Unlike Kennedy, Nixon downplayed issues involving "have" and "have not" nations and did not place great emphasis upon the economic development of less developed countries. His prime concern was great power relations, and in that area he excelled.

Gerald Ford's handling of foreign policy can be characterized as short in duration and nondescript. He did not exercise strong leadership in this area, but depended upon Henry Kissinger, a Nixon carryover, for guidance. Although Kissinger tried to continue the policies of the previous administration, doing so became increasingly difficult. The United States and the Soviet Union clashed over the Middle East, and the oil embargo of 1974 imposed new hardships on U.S. relations with the Arabs. Congress began asserting itself in opposition to Kissinger's policies on the Turkish-Greek-Cyprus dispute of 1974. Congress also disagreed with Kissinger's opposition to the Jackson amendment to the USSR trade bill, which mandated that the Soviets permit Jewish immigration, mostly to Israel. Events in Angola and Rhodesia were other points of dispute between Kissinger and Congress, and negotiations on SALT II faltered while second thoughts arose about detente, even to the extent of Ford's purging the word from his election campaign. Increasingly, the Ford administration paid attention, mostly ineffectually, to global problems, including the world economy, energy, seabeds, health, and international law. The increasing complications in international affairs, the fallout from Watergate that weakened the presidency and aroused the Congress, and Ford's lesser knowledge of foreign affairs compared to Nixon precluded the creative leadership and close partnership that Kissinger had had with Nixon. Nonetheless, Ford did conduct moderately successful summit meetings with Brezhnev and avoided any major disasters in foreign affairs, thus earning him a moderate and average performance in foreign policy management.

When Jimmy Carter became president of the United States, he was confronted by the legacy of the Nixon and Ford administrations, called, not without reason, the Kissinger era. As the *New York Times* remarked on his departure, "Henry Kissinger has not been president of the United States for the last eight years. It only seemed that way much of the time" (January 16, 1977). Carter was determined to change the style and substance of the Nixon-Ford-Kissinger foreign policies and he attacked them as tarnished because of Machiavellian tactics. He also felt the United States had become a status quo power, that human rights had been neglected for realpolitik, and that third world countries had been ignored in the pursuit of an East-West condominium. Carter installed a new foreign affairs team, composed of Secretary of State Cyrus Vance, National Security Advisor Zbigniew Brzezinski and Secretary of Defense Harold Brown. For the first two years they worked in reasonable harmony with Carter, who took an active interest in foreign policy.

The Carter administration's effort to downplay the communist threat, to emphasize human rights violations, and to push for new arms control agreements with the Soviet Union all moved forward with some degree of success. Carter also wanted to weave a worldwide web of closer relations among Western Europe, Japan, and other advanced democracies. He wanted to develop more accommodating relations between developed and underdeveloped nations, normalize U.S.-Chinese relations, obtain a comprehensive Middle East settlement, and set in motion a progressive and peaceful transformation of South Africa toward a biracial democracy.

In spite of Carter's many good intentions, he experienced difficulties achieving his goals but obtained partial success in several of these areas. In human rights, Carter was reasonably successful with African and South American countries, but less successful with nations in the communist bloc. His views on the Soviet Union were sharply challenged by Soviet actions in Ethiopia, Zaire, and Afghanistan. Internally, his administration began to experience strains and stresses as disagreements between Vance and Brzezinski magnified, and Carter reversed himself on such issues as the neutron bomb and troop withdrawal from South Korea. His handling of the Iranian hostage crisis during the last year of his administration did ultimately succeed in bringing all the hostages home alive, but his "Rose Garden" strategy was a political disaster in his 1980 campaign for reelection. However, on the positive side, Carter was successful in negotiating a new Panama Canal Treaty, in achieving a limited peace agreement in the Middle East through the Camp David Accords, in formally recognizing Communist China, and in negotiating SALT II with the Soviets, thus ranking him moderate on management of foreign policy.

Ronald Reagan exhibited a simplistic view of the world during his presidency, which did not serve him well in foreign policy, a realm filled with complexities and nuances. His previous careers as movie actor and governor of California provided him no experience in world affairs. His White House staff appointments did not fill this experience gap in foreign policy, except for Richard Allen, Reagan's first National Security Advisor. Reagan's original choice for secretary of state was Alexander Haig, a man of long and vast experience in international relations who wanted to be the "vicar" of American foreign policy but who, unfortunately for himself, was unable to overcome his rivals in turf battles at the White House and in the defense department. The result was great confusion in the management of foreign policy, especially in Reagan's first year. Haig's replacement, George Shultz, provided continuity and competence, but whether or not he provided wisdom and sound direction to foreign policy is a matter of continuing controversy. His leadership was frequently contested by Secretary of Defense Caspar Weinberger and by Reagan loyalists in the White House.

Reagan's management of foreign affairs seemed to have been general and distant, rather than daily and specific, in contrast to both Nixon and Carter. The outward belligerence of adminstrative policy was often belied by more circumspect actions by his top officials. It is, perhaps, indicative of the uneven record of the Reagan administration in foreign affairs that it claimed as great victories its quick military strikes against Grenada and Libya. However, any success in these two incidents was more than offset by the deaths of hundreds of U.S. Marines in a militarily indefensible compound in Beirut, Lebanon when terrorists drove a truck loaded with explosives into the compound and blew up the installation. Reagan made small progress in easing tensions with the Soviets, and to an outcry of protests in both Europe and at home, he decided to permit the lapse of informal recognition of SALT II. Reagan opposed the Sandinistas in Nicaragua, followed a policy of "constructive engagement" rather than a more stringent position of economic sanctions toward the apartheid government in South Africa, and supported "freedom fighters" battling the Marxist government in Angola. He rekindled the cold war with the Soviets, especially in his first term, and dragged his feet on arms control negotiations, making little progress in the goal of limiting the danger of thermonuclear war until late in his second term. Nor was little if any progress made toward a Middle East settlement, and volatile situations in Central America and Africa continued to boil. While all of these cannot be construed as disasters, most cannot be construed as successes either. Reagan's lackluster performance, coupled with his lack of detailed information and his simplistic worldview, ranks him low in the management of foreign policy.

MANAGING SOCIAL POLICY

If foreign policy is the outer reflection of the soul of the nation, social policy is the inner reflection. Social policy covers a large number of issue areas, including civil rights, health, education, transportation, welfare, employment training, agriculture, labor relations, energy and environmental concerns. Presidents set a social agenda by making selections and setting priorities from among a broad number of social issues. What issues the president selects for the presidential agenda are an indication of what the president believes to be important and personal values. The president's commitment to the realization of these key domestic policies, coupled with the president's managerial skills, determine how well these personal values are stamped upon the nation.

Hoover to Kennedy

Wedded rigidly to a philosophy of individualism and an unregulated profit system, Herbert Hoover developed an inflexible approach when dealing with domestic problems. Throughout his term, his rigidity increased, contributing to his low ranking on social policy management. Hoover's engineering orientation solidified and caused him to value efficiency and economy as goals in themselves. He cared more about the achievement of these goals than more people-oriented goals, and cared as much about how a job was done as what was done.

When Hoover entered office his philosophy of keeping the activities of the national government at a reasonable minimum was popular and viewed as appropriate against the backdrop of the prosperity of the Roaring Twenties. After 1929, according to Hofstadter, "Hoover ceased to be the philosopher of prosperity and turned to the unexpected and melancholy task of rationalizing failure" (Hofstadter, 1974, p. 389). He blamed the Great Depression on both incidental and accidental influences, mostly from abroad. He continued to espouse the soundness of the American social system, despite rapidly mounting evidence of great misery. Although he kept speaking of prosperity as just around the corner, he nevertheless began to cope reluctantly with the social crisis that followed the 1929 stock market crash. One idea he attempted was the Reconstruction Finance Corporation to shore up the financial structure—through government credits—to keep banks, mortgage companies, and life insurance companies, where the savings of millions of Americans were deposited, from collapsing. Most of his actions to alleviate social distress were directed toward maintaining the status quo. Many of his policies were detrimental to labor and further reduced the purchasing power of the average citizen. Despite a 25 percent unemployment rate and an even greater percent underemployed, Hoover advanced no innovative welfare, employment, or health programs. Even when severe depression hit the agricultural and manufacturing sectors of the country and social distress was widespread, Hoover, who had gained a worldwide reputation for successfully distributing relief to over 150 million people in the Western world, as president of his own country was profoundly reluctant to use any mechanism other than voluntary agencies, together with local and state governments, to distribute relief. He did not use his presidential powers or enlist the help of the central government to enlarge and administer such programs.

Franklin Roosevelt, the patrician, launched one of the most fundamental expansions in social policy in this century, making him "a traitor to his class" to many and "that man in the White House" to others. Unlike his predecessor, Franklin Roosevelt was willing to engage in large scale experimental programs to alleviate the suffering of the time. He was also willing to use the apparatus of the central government to accomplish many of these reforms. In spite of what many conservative critics have said in the 1970s and 1980s about the New Deal reforms of the 1930s, these reforms were regarded by many people of the time as the salvation of the country.

Many of Roosevelt's domestic policy reforms have become a permanent part of the social fabric of the country, and even Ronald Reagan found political danger in proposals to change radically the Social Security program. Roosevelt's reforms are well known to historians and students of politics. They include relief for the jobless, unemployment insurance, old age pensions, help for labor to organize, aid to the farmer, protection against discrimination for blacks in employment, the regulation of stocks and bonds and financial markets, and the Tennessee Valley Authority, among others. Although critics believe that some of these programs have outlived their usefulness, they revolutionized domestic policy for much of the century, ranking Roosevelt high in the management of social policy.

Harry Truman's Fair Deal was less comprehensive than Roosevelt's New Deal, but Truman did embrace wide-sweeping changes, including Oscar Ewing's proposal for national health insurance. Foreign policy and national security concerns for the most part dominated the Truman presidency, but his Fair Deal social program was a modest success, ranking Truman moderate on the management of social policy. His greater success in foreign policy is paradoxical because he came to the presidency well versed in domestic issues and lacking experience and expertise in foreign affairs. During his presidency, the major problems confronting the nation were in the realm of foreign policy.

During the first two years of Truman's administration, both houses of Congress were controlled by Republicans, making it difficult for Truman to enact major portions of his Fair Deal program. Even after his astounding victory of 1948 when he ran against a "do-nothing" Congress, bitterness generated in the campaign continued to create difficulty in passing his domestic program. Truman proposed benefits that included low-cost housing, higher social security benefits, and federal aid to education, which he hoped to accomplish with a tax increase and a low military budget to cut the national debt of $252 billion in 1949. Truman also sought repeal of the Taft-Hartley Act, and his victory encouraged Democratic liberals to press for new civil rights reforms. As part of his Fair Deal, Truman proposed antilynching legislation, repeal of the poll tax, a commission on civil rights, a permanent fair employment practices commission, and reforms of voting laws that barred blacks from registering. In addition to Republican bitterness against Truman, the Democratic party was deeply split between its right and left wings. Truman was unable to form a consensus to implement his domestic policy initiatives. A growing Cold War national mentality and obsession with anticommunism on the part of the nation further undercut Truman's social initiatives.

Dwight Eisenhower inherited the results of the Roosevelt social revolution and was unable to dismantle the policies Roosevelt had put into place, but he was also unwilling to extend them. His general inactivity and lack of interest in the area of social policy cause him to rank low on management in this area. His primary goals were to destabilize communism, eradicate New Deal socialism, and globalize American business and values (Cook, 1984, p. xviii). His presidency coincided with one of the most prosperous periods of economic growth in the post–World War II period, a factor which further contributed to the lack of interest in social policy. He had no burning interest in reforming civil rights, nor was he enamored of the activist role of the Supreme Court under Earl Warren, whose appointment Eisenhower regarded as the worst mistake of his presidency. His interest, experience, and expertise as well as his most notable contributions were in the area of foreign affairs. Only with great reluctance did he uphold the Supreme Court decision to desegregate public schools by sending federal troops into Arkansas to maintain public order. Eisenhower adhered to a Whig philosophy of the presidency, which minimized the role of presidential initiatives. He was reluctant to usurp what he understood to be the proper powers of Congress to initiate and enact social policy. His administration, more than any modern president's, is characterized by quiescence in the area of social affairs.

John F. Kennedy stressed a theme of revitalization of social policy after the inattentiveness and inaction of the Eisenhower years. He sought to get the country moving again by building a "New Frontier." Although Barber characterizes Kennedy's administration as expressing an "active positive" commitment, Kennedy's success in implementing and managing policies was not equivalent to his creativity in generating new ideas for programs. He frequently lacked votes in the Congress to pass his legislative proposals, especially in the field of civil rights, which had to go through or around the Rules Committee in the House. However, Kennedy undertook vigorous administrative action on behalf of civil rights when events and when activists such as Martin Luther King, Jr., and others pressured him to act, and when resistance mounted to the implementation of *Brown* v. *Board of Education* and to freedom riders on public bus systems. Kennedy, through the Department of Justice and his brother, Robert, the Attorney General, pushed strongly in this area from the battle of Oxford,

Mississippi, in 1962 when Governor Ross Barnett refused to admit a black student, James Meredith, to the University of Mississippi, to the confrontation with Governor George Wallace over the barring of a black student from the University of Alabama. Kennedy also proposed the first black cabinet member. His brother, Robert, enlarged the number of black attorneys in the Department of Justice from ten to fifty.

Kennedy's major domestic programs when he took office were medical care for the aged, aid to education, aid for housing, a higher minimum wage, and aid to depressed areas. He faced a hostile coalition of southern Democrats and northern Republicans in the Congress, which was able to thwart many of his initiatives and forced Kennedy to withhold civil rights legislation until late in his term. Kennedy's contributions to social issues were in the areas of style and the creation of a new awareness of problems, rather than in tangible achievements. This paved the way for his successor. Had he lived, his social record might have been far different.

Johnson to Reagan

Lyndon Johnson was clearly the beneficiary of much of the spadework in the area of social policy that occurred in the Kennedy administration. As the progenitor of one of the most sweeping social programs of this century, Johnson clearly ranks high on management of social policy. Through a combination of sympathy following Kennedy's assassination and his own landslide electoral victory in 1964, which gave him a working majority in both houses of Congress, Johnson was able to enact one of the largest and most far-reaching social agenda of any U.S. president.

Johnson's Great Society program sought to eliminate both poverty and the social and legal inequities that afflicted the underprivileged in American society. Johnson's commitment to making blacks equal partners with whites in America was full and complete. The Great Society, in Louis Koenig's words, "offered something to everybody, the privileged and underprivileged, by waging intensive drives against disease, crime, and ugliness" (Koenig, 1981, p. 294). The nation was to be beautified by removing billboards from highways, by creating new national park areas, by reducing pollution of the air and water, and by encouraging and supporting the arts and humanities. Laws protecting both consumers and workers were introduced and passed, including higher safety standards in automobiles truth-in-lending laws, and the control of pesticides.

Johnson's War on Poverty intended to eliminate a host of social evils that Americans had borne for generations. A number of these proposals were enacted into law, along with landmark civil rights legislation in 1964 and 1965. However, the pressing demands of the Vietnam War made possible only modest appropriations, which relegated many of these programs more to the realm of promise than practice. Seen from current perspective,

Johnson overloaded the plate of social legislation, and many of his proposals have since been significantly altered or rescinded, but in the long perspective of American history, there is little doubt that his social policy platform was among the most creative and innovative of modern presidents. His management of routine bureaucratic affairs fell short of his conceptualization of the Great Society as well as his management of legislative coalitions to implement it, but his social policy management may be characterized by creative chaos resembling that of Roosevelt's New Deal.

After the herculean efforts of Johnson to create the Great Society, Richard Nixon was confronted with the job of consolidating and rationalizing an almost chaotic creation of program innovations. His task in social policy was to reform the faults in the administrative machinery that managed the social programs of his predecessor. Under the influence of advisor Patrick Moynihan, Nixon proposed an overhaul in the social welfare system to set up a guaranteed income to poor families called the Family Assistance Plan. Nixon retrenched from social policy expansion by reorganizing and reducing funding for the Office of Economic Opportunity, a showcase program for the War on Poverty. Revenue-sharing, which granted funds without strings attached to states and localities, was initiated in 1971. Along with this new source of state and local funds, Nixon relinquished much social policy to the states, a move that pleased conservatives and alarmed liberals. He also brought about cost-of-living adjustments in Social Security payments, eliminated the draft, and generally held down expenditures for social experiments. He used his veto powers on appropriations and frequently, to the dismay of Congress, used executive impoundment to terminate certain social program spending.

In 1972, Nixon proclaimed his "New American Revolution," which consisted of a new national health program, antipollution measures to improve the environment, improved consumer protection laws, and new social welfare proposals and revenue-sharing. However, Nixon ranks moderate on social policy management, which pales by comparison with his foreign policy successes. In many areas, his push for retrenchment not only reformed but also gutted social programs. As Koenig points out, "Typically, after an election, Nixon's ardor for social policy evaporated, and he reverted to his tactics of curtailment" (Koenig, 1981, p. 294).

Gerald Ford's contribution to social policy was consistently low-keyed, ranking his social policy management as low. Although Ford maintained a consistent conservative voting record in Congress, he was uniformly receptive to new social programs. For instance, he supported the Housing Act of 1974, the first comprehensive housing and community development legislation since 1968, and advocated long term mass transit legislation. In spite of his opposition as a congressman, as president he supported the Equal Rights Amendment banning sex discrimination, as well as legislation prohibiting lending corporations from denying credit to women on the basis of sex. Ford urged passage of a national health insurance plan. Ford, however, initiated little himself in the area of social policy. Rather, he endorsed the proposals of others and was not in the forefront of encouraging passage of the policies he sometimes passively endorsed.

By the beginning of the Carter administration, public opinion had turned against massive and sweeping social policy changes and continued to emphasize better and more efficient management of existing programs rather than the inauguration of any new and innovative proposals. Reflecting this public opinion, Carter's social policy focused on reorganizing and streamlining existing bureaucracies and programs, particularly by applying the theme of centralization of responsibilities. Although most students of public administration do not feel there is any special superiority to centralization over decentraliztion, Carter was a true believer in the former.

The rapid increase in inflation to an annual rate of 18.2 percent in February 1979 did more to dampen enthusiasm for new social programs in the Carter administration than perhaps any other factor. Budget reductions and retrenchment became the order of the day. The so-called new realities forced the president to reshape the traditional Democratic social agenda of helping the poor, the elderly, the unemployed and minorities to a new philosophy of "small is better."

Despite these pressures for retrenchment, Carter did create a new Department of Education, and was instrumental in the passage of the Alaska Federal Lands Act, which conserved 100 million acres of Alaska's land from private development. One of Carter's promises of the 1976 campaign was massive welfare reform. He wanted a two track welfare system, with one track providing for further training and job opportunities for unemployed but able-bodied persons, and the other track paying unemployed people a set and livable payment. He endorsed a national health insurance plan, tried to curb soaring medical costs, initiated guaranteed loans to develop distressed areas, and proposed a consolidation of a number of individual welfare programs such as food stamps, Supplemental Security Income, and Aid to Families with Dependent Children, but like other proposals for welfare reform, his became bogged down in Congress. Because of the constraints of the conservative climate of public opinion, high inflation, and an uncooperative Congress, Carter was limited in his ability to implement many of these programs, but he did keep the flame of social reform and compassion alive in an otherwise chilly era. Because of his mixed record, however, he ranks moderate in management of social policy.

Ronald Reagan's election in 1980 embarked the United States on a major new social agenda comparable in significance to the New Deal and the Great Society. Palmer and Sawhill comment that the Reagan administration "raised fundamental questions about the appropriate role of government in national life, and it has been partially successful in implementing a program—one with distinct premises about economic and social behavior—that substantially alters that role" (Palmer and Sawhill, 1984, p. xiii). The Reagan record is difficult to assess and looks better on its own terms than on objective criteria. Whether it is judged to be the Reagan "detour," as Richard Reeves contends, a compromised revolution, as David Stockman argues, or the beginning of a conservative ascendency, as Jack Kemp expects, depends partially upon one's ideological perspective and perhaps remains for historians to ascertain.

In setting his social agenda, Reagan looked to the past, not the future. In the political management of his social revolution, he adopted a policy of radical restoration harkening back to the Coolidge administration. Reagan's own administration emphasized fiscal retrenchment, programmatic cutbacks, and relinquishing social policies to the states. His attacks on big government, an institution in which he was the head manager, were accompanied by a plea for the reassertion of moral imperatives in American life. Although he did achieve some consolidation of categorical intergovernmental grant programs into block grants, reducing funding in most areas by 25 percent as he did, Reagan was unsuccessful in implementing most of the proposals in his New Federalism, including a swap of responsibilities whereby the federal government would assume sole responsibility for Medicaid, while states assumed full responsibility for the food stamp program and Aid to Families with Dependent Children. Nor was he successful in his goal of abolishing the departments of energy and education

To curb rising medical costs in government programs that provided health services for the elderly and the poor, Reagan shifted a greater proportionate burden in those programs to recipients. Advocating greater reliance upon private charity and institutions, he reduced spending for social services for the poor, as well as spending for student loans, housing assistance, and community development and credit programs. He halted the expansion of subsidies to homeowners, proposed a fundamental shift in housing policy away from the poor, and advocated a return to a more pure market system. He vitiated the Equal Employment Opportunity Commission with appointments unsympathetic to affirmative action programs for blacks and minorities, and his cuts in social programs caused the number of homeless and those living below the poverty line to increase substantially, despite an improvement in the economy. Although openly critical of many Supreme Court decisions on such social issues as school prayer, abortion, aid to parochial schools, and defendant's rights, and the Court's lack of judical self-restraint (much to the consternation of the radical right), the Reagan administration achieved only modest headway in causing the nation to reassess these positions. As Salamon and Lund suggest (1984, pp. 2–3),"Serious questions were also being raised about Ronald Reagan's apparent inability to grasp, or take an interest in, much of the substance and detail of the vast government under him." Because most observers agree that Reagan's primary successes in social policy were in his "honeymoon period" (he experienced increasing difficulties with Congress after that period in achieving his proposed budget cuts), and because his policies were a return to traditionalism rather than innovative and imaginative solutions to pressing social concerns, Reagan ranks low on social policy management.

MANAGING ECONOMIC POLICY

The president has less power in managing economic policy than in any other area but is confronted with higher public expectations of performance. Presidents must cope with a pluralistic free enterprise system that decries government interference yet tends to blame government when that system goes awry. Presidents cannot ignore the economic life of the nation, but they are severely handicapped in their ability to regulate and control it. Economic policy, more than any other area, has been a determinant of voting behavior and presidential success.

Hoover to Kennedy

Herbert Hoover, confronted with major economic disaster, proved to be a poor manager of the economy. Hoover shared Calvin Coolidge's idea that the business of government was to help business, and he believed in an activist interventionist role for the government to stabilize the economy by the management of the budget. Hoover did call for increased government expenditures, especially on public works, and even accepted the idea of a small deficit. He supported a reduction of taxes after 1929, in spite of a possible deficit. His problem, according to Herbert Stein in *Presidential Economics*, (1984, p. 32), was that "when these measures failed to stem the decline of the economy, he was left with no theory of how to deal with a deeper and longer lasting depression. . .." Hoover did not reject possible options because they involved too much government activity; he rejected alternatives because he felt they would not work. In the latter days of his administration, Hoover set up the Reconstruction Finance Corporation to make loans to distressed businesses and to state and local governments, but this measure was too little and too late. A second step Hoover took was a proposal in 1932 for a large tax increase. While this decision can be seen in retrospect as almost certainly a mistake, Hoover intended to drive down interest rates, thus inspiring investor confidence, to stop the flight of gold from the country, and to encourage the Federal Reserve Board to increase the money supply. Although Hoover's administration, which followed the

Roaring Twenties, marked the beginning of a more activist interventionist economic policy, the intervention was limited, and compared to the magnitude of the national economic woe, was ineffectual. By the end of his presidential term, the unemployment rate approached 25 percent in a period without national unemployment compensation, welfare, or many two-worker households. Since Hoover's Republican party had reaped the credit for the prosperity of the twenties, he could not easily avoid the blame for the subsequent Great Depression.

With Roosevelt's inauguration, the White House assumed a more vigorous interventionist strategy in the economy. Roosevelt felt that he had a popular mandate to do something about the Great Depression, although what that something should be was unclear. According to Stein (1984, pp. 35–37), Roosevelt believed that economic performance depended heavily upon citizen and business confidence, and that a psychology of confidence rather than fear and pessimism needed to be restored. In his first inaugural address, Roosevelt expressed this thought in his now famous and often quoted line, "We have nothing to fear but fear itself."

Roosevelt at first attacked Hoover's failure to balance the budget and embarked upon a program of economizing government outlays. These early efforts were soon overwhelmed by his New Deal programs. Roosevelt perceived a need for central planning to overcome extremes in the business cycle, and he tried to create institutions to provide that through the National Recovery Act and a variety of planning agencies, such as the National Resources Planning Board. Roosevelt also inaugurated a policy of strict application of antitrust laws to promote private-sector competition.

Roosevelt's contributions to economic policy included the idea that the government should bear responsibility for maintaining full employment, even if deficits resulted, and in interpersonal transfer payments to lower-income individuals financed by higher progressive taxes on high income individuals and corporations. Under Roosevelt, the New Deal brought about an expansion of federal regulation through the development of the Civil Aeronautics Board, the National Labor Relations Act, the Federal Power Commission, the Wage and Hour Act, and other regulatory activities. While the economic success of the New Deal was doubtful, with true recovery not occurring until the buildup of production for World War II, its political success was unquestioned. However, as Hugh S. Norton (1977, pp. 68-69), points out, "Some of FDR's policies would likely have worked if more adequate data or more capable administrators had been available." The contributions made by Roosevelt rank him medium in the management of economic policy.

Harry Truman was both a consolidator of the gains and innovations of the Roosevelt era and the beneficiary of a 77 percent increase in total economic output between 1939 and 1944, an average 12-percent increase a year. Truman was also able to make the transition from a wartime to a peacetime economy, dismantling a sizable government apparatus that administered price controls, rationing, and materiel allocations during World War II. In spite of predictions of a massive postwar recession, Truman was able to reconvert the American economy to peacetime without major dislocations.

Inheriting the Roosevelt legacy, Truman was faced with a federal budget considerably higher in 1945 than it had been in 1939 before the war. Truman's Fair Deal was the product of leftover New Dealers who sought to continue and expand structural changes, especially in labor relations and agriculture. They also wished to expand government programs for housing and health and ensure full employment through the Employment Act of 1946. Under this act, the Bureau of the Budget assumed the responsibility of estimating the size of the government deficit that would be required to achieve full employment. The act also created the Council of Economic Advisors whose appointees required Senate confirmation. Amid much controversy and much to Truman's chagrin, the conservative Taft-Hartley Act, which tilted the balance between labor and business back toward a pro-business position, was passed during Truman's administration. While the economy performed well under Truman, with only a short and mild recession in 1949, much of this success is due to the performance of the private sector rather than bold and creative economic policy initiatives, thus ranking Truman moderate on economic policy management.

Dwight Eisenhower stabilized federal expenditures as a proportion of GNP, so that by 1960, nondefense expenditures were 9.6 percent of GNP, compared to 8.4 percent in 1939. During Eisenhower's eight years, there were mild recessions in 1954, 1958, and 1960, although overall his administration was marked by economic prosperity where total output increased, real disposable income per capita increased, and differences in income between different regions of the economy and between agricultural and nonagricultural sectors declined. Because of the high performance of the private sector, Eisenhower had little incentive to encourage an activist interventionist economic policy. Unemployment in 1958 did reach 7.6 percent, but the economic growth rate was 3 percent a year, an increase considered healthy for the times.

Later liberal administrations would attack Eisenhower on unemployment, economic growth, the quality of life, and poverty, but viewed from the perspective of the 1980s, the economic problems his administration experienced were comparatively mild. One distinctive Eisenhower contribution was the professionalization of the Council of Economic Advisors through the appointment of professional economists. Eisenhower's economic stance was pro-business, and his cabinet and economic advisors reflected this bias. Eisenhower's economic policies were adequate for the times which benefited from a vigorous and prosperous economy, thus ranking his management in this area as moderate.

In spite of the prosperous years of the Eisenhower administration, John Kennedy found a number of economic policies to criticize during his 1960 presidential campaign. Kennedy zeroed in on the economic performance of the Eisenhower years and expressed concern that the U.S. economy fared badly in comparison with the economic growth rates in France, Germany, and Japan. He was also concerned about the ability of the United States to compete with the Soviets in space as a result of the successful launching of Sputnik in 1957.

Kennedy revived activist interventionist economic policies to address the problems of unemployment, economic growth, the quality of life, and poverty and to "get America moving again" after the stolid Eisenhower years. He was an avowed liberal realist who sought to apply pragmatic solutions such as economic "fine-tuning," advocated by Walter Heller, Paul Samuelson, and James Tobin, and a reemphasis upon economic regulation. While the Keynesian philosophy of pump-priming the economy by increased expenditures had been employed by previous administrations, Kennedy, through a proposed tax cut in 1962, was the first president to employ tax reduction to counter a downward spin into recession, despite an existing deficit. He adopted the new notion of a full employment budget, which implied that below full employment, deficit spending would not be inflationary. Although enacted after his death, this tax cut was claimed a success by both Keynesians and, paradoxically, the Republican precursors, of supply side advocates. As predicted, tax revenues rose after the implementation of the tax cut in 1964.

Kennedy established goals for economic performance through his economic report of 1962. Although Kennedy himself lacked a clear economic philosophy, he was willing to embrace the new economic strategies advocated by his neo-Keynesian advisors, and this ranks him medium in this management area.

Johnson to Reagan

Kennedy's tax cut proposals were enacted under Lyndon Johnson and proved successful in the short run. Johnson, however, wanted some monuments of his own. One was a large growth in social expenditures to fund his War on Poverty. The Congress was receptive after the election of 1964, and Johnson felt that his Great Society proposals put him in the company of his role model, Franklin Roosevelt. These programs had a large effect on the federal budget in the coming decades. Although at the time sufficient revenues to finance these policies were available, time proved that Johnson and his chief advisors, including Joseph Califano, had underestimated long-term costs. Many of these programs eventually were financed by inflation, which increased tax revenues by pushing people into higher income brackets. Johnson also had to cope with the mounting expenditures of the Vietnam War, which, unhappily, contributed to yet another monument of his administration—the unleashing of inflationary spirals that grew in his own administration and put pressure on his successors.

Johnson's reluctance to increase taxes and his insistence on both "guns and butter" at the same time drove the inflation rate to 5 percent by the time he left office. Although modest by the standards of the 1980s, this 5 percent inflation rate nonetheless represented a considerable increase over previous rates and was the highest inflation rate experienced in America since the Korean War. Johnson's liberal activism might have survived unscathed if Vietnam and inflationary pressures had not undermined the economic viability of his well intentioned programs. His ideas for programs were often superior to his actual execution of those programs. Because of his mixed record in management of economic policy, Johnson ranks medium.

Richard Nixon's economic advisors were conservative men with liberal ideas. Contrary to conservative expectations, the federal budget, the federal deficit, nondefense spending, and inflation all grew during the Nixon years. Moreover, Nixon's wage and price controls were massive departures from a policy of nonintervention of government in the private economy and were implemented at a time when the inflation rate was 5 percent and the the unemployment rate was 4 percent. His activist orientation toward the management of the economy caused him to take the extreme meausure of wage and price controls, even though these economic measures pale by comparison with the stagflation of the 1970s and 1980s.

Under Nixon, inflation became a key economic issue, but Nixon himself was politically sensitive about the unemployment rate, which he believed had cost him the election of 1960. According to Herbert Stein, one of his chief economic advisors, Nixon "was impatient with the dull, pedestrian, and painful economics of conventional conservatism" (Stein, 1984, p. 135). He even announced in January 1971 that "now I am a Keynesian." Unlike foreign policy, economic policy was not a passion for Nixon. While he was certainly pro-business, he was not particularly pro-big business. During his administration, the economy slowed down significantly, and inflation and unemployment both rose simultaneously. As with Johnson, his disinterest and mixed record rank him medium in management of economic affairs.

Economic turmoil and anxiety characterized both the Ford and Carter administrations. In 1974, inflation soared to the highest annual rate since 1919. Inflation was fueled by a quadrupling in the price of OPEC oil and, by the end of price and wage controls, a drop in the world food supply that was brought about by bad weather. During Gerald Ford's short tenure, unemployment rose to 9.2 percent, 2 percent higher than any other period in the postwar era. Shortages occurred in gasoline and heating oil, and general productivity declined. Ford was an ardent advocate of deregulation and regulatory reform. His response to inflation was to rely predominantly upon voluntary persuasion through his WIN program (Whip Inflation Now). The inflation rate rose in 1974 to between 12 percent but did come down slightly in 1975 and 1976. Because of the poor performance of the economy and his lack of effective innovative measures, Ford ranks low on management of the economy.

When Jimmy Carter took office the economy, while not in the best of condition, was better than when he left office, a point that Reagan repeatedly used to his advantage in the 1980 presidential campaign. The unemployment rate in January 1977 was 7.4 percent. The Carter team believed that this was much too high, but that as long as it did not rise higher, the danger of reviving inflation was low. The administration set an unemployment rate of 4.5 percent as a goal to be reached by 1981, a year when the budget was to be balanced and government outlays reduced to 21 percent of GNP.

Carter, like Kennedy, wanted to get the economy moving again, a feat to be accomplished by fiscal and monetary expansion, cutting taxes, and increasing the growth of the money supply as a way to reduce interest rates. The expectation was that when these expansionist policies threatened the revival of inflation, income policies would be invoked to hold down prices and wages. The administration anticipated a reduction in inflation from 7 percent in 1976 to 6 percent in 1977 and 1978, and 5 percent in 1979 and 1980. These goals were not reached and inflation rose rather than declined during the Carter years. By March 1979, the inflation rate reached 13 percent.

As inflation became a political issue, the administration attempted to cool the economy by inducing a recession before the election season. Inflation remained high, however, and was an issue in the 1980 campaign. The size of the deficits—in retrospect, small compared to the Reagan years but perceived as large at the time—was also an issue. Deficits ranged from $66 billion in 1976 to $60 billion in 1980, dropping $45 billion in the intervening years. Though well-intentioned, and somewhat successful in holding the line on deficits if not lowering them, Carter's management of the economy more than any other factor was his political Waterloo. While subject to tremendous external, uncontrollable factors, the fact remains that his inability to lower inflation or to restore public confidence in the future of the American economy ranks him low in economic policy management.

Ronald Reagan's number-one problem when he assumed office in 1981 was the economy. As Pfiffner (1986, p. 4) notes, "The United States has come to expect leadership from the president in times of crisis, and the economic situation of this decade certainly qualifies as a crisis." Reagan's plan to restore confidence among investors and consumers involved orienting the nation on a fundamentally different path leading to less inflation, more growth, a revival of the economy, improvement in the nation's defense capability, and the transfer of important powers and responsibilities to both the private sector and to state and local governments. Whether or not Reagan succeeded in these efforts without paying a terrible price is a matter of lively controversy. According to Robert Lekachman (1982, p. 3), "Ronald Reagan must be the nicest President who ever destroyed a union, tried to cut school lunch milk rations from six to four ounces, and compelled families in need of public help to first dispose of household goods in excess of $1,000."

Reagan's major innovation in economic policy was supply-side economics, which, in direct opposition to the Keynesian solution, called for a tax reduction to reduce inflation. The logic of supply-side economics was that greater personal disposable income resulting from a tax cut would increase savings and investment, which, in turn, would be invested in new plants and equipment, thus increasing productivity. And as productivity rose, the amount of goods and services would rise, causing prices and, consequently, inflation to fall. Supply-side economics were based on the Laffer curve, which contended that personal taxes could be dramatically cut without a corresponding drop in federal revenues, since, according to Laffer, the relationship between tax revenues and tax rates was curvilinear. Supply-siders argued that there were two tax rates, one high and one low, which would result in the same tax revenues, so that high tax rates could be cut without hurting the federal treasury.

Using supply-side logic, the Kemp-Roth tax cut, which reduced personal tax rates in all brackets by 25 percent, was passed in 1981. By 1982, evidence was mounting that supply-side logic was fallacious. The tax cut resulted in federal deficits of almost $200 billion and drove up the total federal debt. By the beginning of Reagan's second term in 1985, the national debt was approaching $2 trillion, 120 percent higher than when Reagan first assumed office. Record deficits of $58 billion in 1981, $111 billion in 1982, $195 billion in 1983, and $200 billion in 1984 were compiled during his first term.

Nor was Reagan successful in improving the international debt of the United States. In 1985, America became the world's largest debtor nation, surpassing Brazil and Mexico. In just three years, the United States moved from being the largest creditor nation to the largest debtor. According to C. Fred Bergsten (1986), "The pace of the deterioration has been incredibly rapid. We will be vulnerable to foreign withdrawal of funds, and possible foreign pressure on our foreign and economic policies." Trade deficits also rose during the Reagan years, approaching $150 billion annually and exacerbating the international debt position.

Nonetheless, Reagan managed to restore public confidence in the economy. Interest rates dropped from the high teens to below 10 percent, and inflation fell to 4 percent annually in 1985. Industrial production rose, and the value of the overpriced dollar in international markets declined. By juxtaposing the short-run success of economic recovery versus the deterioration of the United States in international markets and mounting federal deficits, Reagan left a mixed economic legacy for his successors. As a result of his economic policies, Reagan retained high popularity, but the cost of his political success will be borne by future presidents and generations.

ASSESSING PRESIDENTIAL MANAGEMENT ABILITIES

Presidents may be ranked on their overall management skills as well as their management of specific policy dimensions. Numerical ratings have been assigned to each president for the management of each policy area so that *low* equals a score of 1, *medium* a score of 2, and *high* a score of 3. The scores are then averaged for each president across the policy areas to derive an overall management score, which ranges between 1 and 3. Presidents with a score of 2 or more are considered to have high management skills, whereas those with a score below 2 have low overall management skills (see Table 5–1).

No president ranked high on management of all four policy areas. The closest were Franklin Roosevelt and Harry Truman, who scored high

TABLE 5–1 Presidential Management Skills

	MANAGEMENT SKILLS			
	DEFENSE POLICY	FOREIGN POLICY	SOCIAL POLICY	ECONOMIC POLICY
Reagan	Medium	Low	Low	Medium
Carter	Medium	Medium	Medium	Low
Ford	Low	Medium	Low	Low
Nixon	Medium	High	Medium	Medium
Johnson	Low	Low	High	Medium
Kennedy	Medium	Medium,	Medium	Medium
Eisenhower	High	Medium	Low	Medium
Truman	High	High	Medium	Medium
Franklin Roosevelt	High	Medium	High	Medium
Hoover	Medium	Low	Low	Low

TABLE 5–2 Presidential Management Ratings

	PRESIDENT	OVERALL MANAGEMENT SCORE
High Management	Roosevelt	2.50
	Truman	2.50
	Nixon	2.25
	Eisenhower	2.00
	Kennedy	2.00
Low Management	Johnson	1.75
	Carter	1.75
	Reagan	1.50
	Ford	1.25
	Hoover	1.25

on two policy management areas. Roosevelt was high in defense and social policy and Truman had highs in managing defense and foreign policy, and medium in social and economic policy. Kennedy, the most youthful of any president, scored medium in all policy areas, a ranking that would have been raised had his life and term not been abruptly terminated. No president, not even Hoover, ranks low in all policy areas. Despite many low scores, Hoover scored medium in defense policy. Ford also scored low in three categories, but placed medium in management of foreign policy. Overall management scores are presented in Table 5–2.

In reality, presidents are spread across almost the entire range, with scores ranging from high of 2.50 for Roosevelt and Truman to low of 1.25 for Hoover and Ford. When presidents are divided into high and low categories, five presidents fall into each. Besides Roosevelt and Truman (2.50), Nixon (2.25), Eisenhower (2.00), and Kennedy (2.00) have high management scores. In addition to Ford and Hoover, Reagan (1.50), Carter (1.75), and Johnson (1.75) have low overall scores.

Managerial skills in the presidency do not equate to presidential greatness but are an important component in successful presidencies. Coupled with selling skills and integrity, high managerial skills can facilitate effective leadership in the Oval Office. Without managerial skills, modern presidents, confronted with increasing complex and numerous policy areas and huge bureaucracies to govern and motivate, will find their efforts crippled. A combination of high skills in both selling and management is a winning combination, leading to presidential greatness.

REFERENCES

AMBROSE, STEPHEN E., *Eisenhower*. New York: Simon & Schuster, 1983.

BERGSTEN, C. FRED., quoted by Martin Crutsinger, Associated Press Dispatch, June 6, 1986.

COOK, BLANCHE WEISEN, *The Declassified Eisenhower*. New York: Penguin Books, 1984.

CRONIN, THOMAS E., *The State of the Presidency*, 2nd edition. Boston, Little, Brown, 1980.

GRAHAM, COLE B., and STEVEN W. HAYS, *Managing the Public Organization*. Washington, D.C.: Congressional Quarterly Press, 1986.

HESS, STEPHEN, *Organizing the Presidency*. Washington, D.C.: The Brookings Institution, 1976.

HOFSTADTER, RICHARD, *The American Political Tradition and the Men Who Made It*. New York: Vintage Books, 1974.

HOXIE, R. GORDON, "About This Issue," *Presidential Studies Quarterly*, 16 (1986), pp. 7–10.

———*Command Decision and the Presidency*. New York, New York: Reader's Digest Press, 1977.

———"Staffing the Ford and Carter Presidencies," in *Organizing and Staffing the Presidency*, Bradley D. Nash, Milton S. Eisenhower, R. Gordon Hoxie, and William C. Spragens, eds. New York: Center for the Study of the Presidency, 1980.

KOENIG, LOUIS W., *The Chief Executive*, 4th edition. New York: Harcourt Brace Jovanovich, 1981.

LEKACHMAN, ROBERT, *Greed Is Not Enough: Reagonomics*. New York: Knopf, 1982.

LEOPOLD, RICHARD, *The Growth of American Foreign Policy*. New York: Alfred A. Knopf, 1962.

LIGHT, PAUL C., *The President's Agenda: Domestic Policy Choice from Kennedy to Carter*. Baltimore: Johns Hopkins University Press, 1983.

MALEK, FREDERICK V., *Washington's Hidden Tragedy*. New York: The Free Press, 1978.

NATHAN, RICHARD P., *The Administrative Presidency*. New York: John Wiley, 1983.

The New York Times, January 16, 1977, p. 20.

NORTON, HUGH S., *The Quest for Economic Stability: Roosevelt to Reagan*. Columbia, South Carolina: University of South Carolina Press, 1985.

OUCHI, WILLIAM G., *Theory Z: How American Business Can Meet the Japanese Challenge*. New York: Avon Books, 1981.

PALMER, JOHN L., and ISABEL V. SAWHILL, eds., *The Reagan Record*. Cambridge, Mass.: Ballinger, 1984.

PFIFFNER, JAMES P., ed., *The President and Economic Policy*. Philadelphia: Institute for Study of Human Issues, 1986.

PETERS, THOMAS J., and Robert H. Waterman, Jr., *In Search of Excellence*. New York: Warner Books, 1982.

PRICE, DON K., and ROCCO C. SICILIANO, "Revitalizing the Executive Office of the President," in *Rethinking the Presidency*, Thomas E. Cronin, ed. Boston: Little, Brown, 1982.

REICH, ROBERT B., *The Next American Frontier*. New York: New York Times Books, 1983.

ROSE, RICHARD, "Government Against Subgovernments: A European Perspective on Washington," in *Presidents and Prime Ministers*, R. Rose and Ezra N. Suleiman, eds. Washington, D.C.: American Enterprise Institute, 1980.

ROURKE, FRANCIS, *Bureaucracy, Politics, and Public Policy*. Boston: Little, Brown, 1976.

SALOMON, LESTER M., and MICHAEL S. LUND, eds., *The Reagan Presidency and the Governing of America*. Washington, D.C.: The Urban Institute Press, 1984.

STEIN, HERBERT, *Presidential Economics: The Making of Economic Policy from Roosevelt to Reagan and Beyond*. New York: Simon & Schuster, 1984.

STOESSINGER, JOHN, *Crusaders and Pragmatists: Movers of Modern American Foreign Policy*. New York: W.W. Norton, 1985.

WATSON, RICHARD A., and NORMAN C. THOMAS, *The Politics of the Presidency*. New York: John Wiley, 1983.

WILLIAMS, PHIL, "Carter's Defence Policy," in *The Carter Years*. Edited by M. Glenn Abernathy, Dilys M. Hill and Phil Williams. New York: St. Martin's Press, 1984.

CHAPTER SIX
NEUROSES IN THE WHITE HOUSE:
Presidential Mismanagement Styles

Neuroses in the White House? Presidential *mis*management styles? Presidents, like any modern managers of large complex organizations, occasionally exhibit tendencies toward excess and aberrant behavior. This chapter will use a typology developed by Kets de Vries and Miller (1984) to examine the impact of aberrant executive behavior on organizational effectiveness. We will apply this typology, previously developed to look at corporate managers, to modern presidents.

As political scientists familiar with the controversy and problems associated with the use of pyschological and psychoanalytic analyses of presidential behavior, the authors approach this subject very carefully. However, we are also aware that such attempts can provide new insights and help us to better understand how presidents behave under duress. Witness the upsurge of interest in presidential character when Barber (1985) borrowed his active-passive and positive-negative categories from the psychology of adaptation. Historically, in the study of the presidency, this was a major new departure. While hardly claiming the same for our approach we nevertheless feel that the classifications that Kets de Vries and Miller use in their book, *The Neurotic Organization,* are rewarding enough to attempt to use their framework, classifying presidents, analyzing their aberrant behavior, and assessing its effect on their administrations.

This application recognizes that, despite the presidential image of infallibility and strength, presidents are human. As such, they are subject to all the human emotions and stresses that confront any high-level executive. As the chief executive of the entire country, carrying the burdens of peace and war, the psychological stress on the president may, indeed, exceed that of most modern managers. The repercussions of presidential stress are far greater than the repercussions of stress upon ordinary citizens, for presidential actions can alter the course of the nation.

Manfred Kets de Vries and Danny Miller bring impressive credentials to their study of *The Neurotic Organization.* While the neurotic styles they discuss are derived from the findings of psychiatrists, clinical psychologists, and psychoanalysts, they themselves are well versed in this literature, as well as that of organizational behavior. Kets de Vries is a professor of organizational behavior at McGill University and the European Institute of Business Administration. He is also a practicing psychoanalyst, a full member of the Canadian Psychoanalytic Society, and has published extensively in both of his fields of interest. Miller is a professor of management policy and organizational theory at McGill University and at the Ecole de Hautes Etudes Commerciales, Montreal. He too has published widely, and his most recent book, with co-author Peter Friesen, is entitled *Organizations: A Quantum View.*

NEUROTIC ORGANIZATIONAL STYLES

Traditionally, three psychological approaches to the study of organizations have been used: the human relations school, the trait or attribute school, and the cognitive constraint theorists. The *human relations school* stresses the importance of crucial social needs of employees and the consequences of those needs on job performance. These theorists showed the importance of considerate treatment of workers and of managerial perceptions that workers are responsible and sensitive human beings. However, this approach has certain shortcomings. It concentrates on workers rather than managers. It does not explain the origin of human needs or the method selected for their expression. Nor does the human relations school examine or explain individual differences.

The second mode of traditional psychological approaches to the study of organizations is the *trait* or *attribute school.* This school looks at the various psychological traits among managers for the purpose of discerning their impact on organizational functioning. Individual personality or cognitive attributes are analyzed to determine how these factors influence decision making, leadership, risk-taking, and crisis management. The focus is on individual differences. The shortcoming of this approach is that individuals are classified along some simple psychological dimension or trait. Many facets of personality and context are left out in this approach.

The *cognitive constraint theorists* look at the overall psychological limitations of individuals working in organizations. The works of Simon (1947), March and Simon (1958), and Cyert and March (1963) have demonstrated how general cognitive limitations affect decision making and limit rationality. Decisions are problem driven rather than opportunity driven. They are incremental and remedial rather than comprehensive and innovative. Like the human relations school, these theories ignore individual idiosyncracies, yet idiosyncratic differences are critical to any understanding of the dysfunctioning of organizations.

Kets de Vries and Miller present a new typology to examine the impact of aberrant leadership styles upon organizations. They concentrate on dysfunctional and neurotic behavior rather than functional and normal behavior, postulating that the difference between neurotic and normal is one of degree rather than intrinsic difference. This method of applying the findings and theory of one field to another field is intellectually risky because the shift in context may alter the usefulness of the framework. However, this cross fertilization also has great potential for providing valuable insights and for preventing increasingly narrow parochialism within a field. The Kets de Vries and Miller framework in particular provides a useful counterpoint to the more commonly used and sometimes misused structural framework.

These authors identify five types of neurotic behavior that executives may exhibit to varying degrees. The five types are paranoid, compulsive, dramatic, depressive, and schizoid behaviors. They examine the impact of neurotic managerial styles upon the organization, arguing that the organizational configurations mirror the neurotic configurations of top executives.

Human behavior is rarely one type or style exclusively, but rather more typically exhibits a mixture of styles, each of which may be triggered in different circumstances. However, one style tends to dominate for many aspects of behavior for a single executive. Any extreme manifestation of a single style can lead to pathological behavior and serious mismanagement. We will examine each of the five neurotic managerial styles and the impact of those styles on organizations. See Tables 6–1, 6–2, and 6–3.

The Paranoid Style. The *paranoid* manager is characterized by suspiciousness and mistrust of others. This type of manager is hypersensitive and hyperalert. He or she is ready to counter perceived threats and exhibits concern over hidden motives and special meanings. The paranoid

TABLE 6–1 Characteristics of Neurotic Personal Styles

NEUROTIC STYLES	PERSONAL STYLES
Paranoid	Suspiciousness and mistrust of others; hypersensitivity and hyperalertness; readiness to counter perceived threats; overly concerned with hidden motives and special meanings; intense attention span; cold, rational, unemotional.
Compulsive	Perfectionism; preoccupation with trivial details; insistent that others submit to own way of doing things; relationships seen in terms of dominance and submission; lack of sponteneity; inability to relax; meticulousness, dogmatism, obstinancy.
Dramatic	Self-dramatization; excessive expression of emotions, incessant drawing of attention to self; narcissistic preoccupation; craving of attention and excitement; alternation between idealization and devaluation of others; exploitative incapacity for concentration or sharply focused attention.
Depressive	Feelings of guilt, worthlessness, self-reproach, inadequacy; sense of helplessness and hopelessness; of being at the mercy of events; diminished ability to think clearly; loss of interest and motivation; inability to experience pleasure.
Schizoid	Detachment, noninvolvement, withdrawal; sense of estrangement; lack of excitement or enthusiasm; indifference to praise or criticism;lack of interest in present or future; cold, unemotional

manager has an intense attention span and is cold, rational, and unemotional. Fantasies include perceptions that there is a menacing superior force that is out to get the person and that one had better be on one's guard. Managers with this style may become preoccupied with confirming their suspicions. There is also the danger that the manager's defensiveness will lead to a loss in the capacity for spontaneous action.

The paranoid organization emphasizes organizational intelligence and controls. Chief executives tend to react rather than anticipate. Managers, concerned about being perpetually vigilant and prepared for emergencies, develop sophisticated information systems to identify threats. Accompanying paranoia is conservatism, fear of innovation, and avoidance of risk-taking. Suspicion is institutionalized.

The Compulsive Style. The *compulsive* manager tends toward perfectionism and preoccupation with trivial details. These people insist that others submit to their way of doing things, and they perceive relationships in terms of dominance and submission. Compulsive managers lack spontaneity, exhibit an inability to relax, and are meticulous, dogmatic, and

TABLE 6–2 Dangers of Neurotic Styles

NEUROTIC STYLE	DANGERS
Paranoid	Distortion of reality due to a preoccupation with confirmation of suspicions; loss of capacity for spontaneous action because of defensive attitudes.
Compulsive	Inward orientation, indecisiveness; and postponement; avoidance due to fear of mistakes; inability to deviate from planned activity; excessive reliance on rules and regulations; difficulties in seeing the big picture.
Dramatic	Superficiality, suggestability, heightened risk of operating in a nonfactual world; action based on hunches; overreaction to minor events; feelings of use and abuse by employees.
Depressive	Overly pessimistic outlook; difficulties in concentration and performance; inhibition of action, indecisiveness.
Schizoid	Frustration of dependency needs of workers caused by emotional isolation of manager; resulting bewilderment and aggressiveness.

obstinate. The fantasies of the compulsive manager emphasize fears of being at the mercy of events. Such people strive to master and control as many things as possible affecting their lives. The dangers of this style are that the manager turns inward in his or her orientation, is indecisive, and tends to postpone decisions. His fear of making mistakes, combined with his inability to deviate from planned activities, leads him to an excessive reliance on rules and regulations. The compulsive manager often has difficulty seeing the big picture.

In compulsive organizations, ritual, detail, and careful planning dominate decision making. With compulsive chief executives, controls are also emphasized, but to obtain the goals of efficiency and cost control rather than to monitor suspicious activites and potential threats. Operations are standardized. Elaborate sets of formal policies and procedures are evolved. Compulsive managers strive to reduce uncertainty and to avoid surprises at all costs.

The Dramatic Style. The *dramatic* manager is given to self-dramatization, excessive expression of emotion, narcissistic preoccupation, and incessant drawing of attention to oneself. Compulsive managers crave activity and excitement, alternating between idealization and devaluation of others. They can be exploitative and they show incapacity for sharply focused attention and concentration. Dramatic managers fantasize on how to get attention from and how to impress people who are im-

TABLE 6–3 Characteristics of Neurotic Organizational Styles

NEUROTIC STYLE	ORGANIZATIONAL CHARACTERISTICS
Paranoid	Primary emphasis on organizational intelligence and controls; environment is studied to identify threats and challenges; top managers are suspicious and wary of people both inside and outside the organization; there is a tendency to centralize power in the hands of top executives; key decisions come from the top; the locus of power is high in the organization; subordinates are employed to find out what is going on.
Compulsive	Wed to ritual; every last detail is planned in advance; thoroughness, completeness, and conformity are emphasized; operations are standardized with formal policies, rules, and procedures; organization is very hierarchical; strategy is carefully planned; reliance on an established theme.
Dramatic	Tend to be hypersensitive, impulsive, dramatically venturesome, and dangerously uninhibited; decision making reflects hunches and impressions rather than facts; address a wide array of diverse projects in desultory of fashion; dramatic flair causes top echelons to centralize power to be able to initiate ventures independently; themes are boldness, risk-taking, and diversification; decision making style is unreflective and impulsive.
Depressive	Inactivity, lack of confidence, extreme conservatism are characteristic; there is an atmosphere of extreme passivity and purposelessness with bureaucratically motivated insularilty; a sense of aimlessness and apathy among top managers preclude attempts to give clear direction, orientation, and goals.
Schizoid	Exhibits leadership vacuum; top executive discourages interaction for fear of involvement; leaders view world as unhappy, populated by frustrating people; second tier managers engage in gamesmanship from lack of leadership; schizoid organizations often become political battlefields; second tier managers engage in infighting because leader is insecure, withdrawn, and noncommittal; shifting coalitions try to influence indecisive leader; main characteristic is dispersal of some power and delegation of decision making power to managers just below top executive; independent fiefdoms arise with alienated departments and divisions; second tier managers rarely collaborate effectively.

portant in their lives. Among the dangers of this style are superficiality, suggestibility, and the risk of operating in a nonfactual world. Dramatic managers may take actions based on hunches and overreact to minor events. The people with whom they interact may feel abused and used.

In dramatic organizations, the chief executive is often hyperactive, impulsive, dramatically venturesome, and dangerously uninhibited.

Audacity, risk-taking, and diversification are management themes. Organizational goals reflect the top manager's narcissistic need and his or her desire for attention and visibility. Organizational structure is often too primitive for the broad number of policy areas in which the bureaucracy is involved.

The Depressive Style. In this neurotic style, the manager expresses feelings of guilt, worthlessness, self-reproach, and inadequacy. The person has a sense of helplessness and hopelessness, and of being at the mercy of events. There is a diminished ability to think clearly, a loss of interest and motivation, and an inability to experience pleasure. Fantasies of depressive managers are typified by a hopelessness about life and feelings of not being good enough and of not being able to control events. Dangers of this style include an overly pessimistic outlook, difficulties in concentration and performance, and indecisiveness.

In depressive organizations, formal authority is centralized and based on position rather than expertise. Depressive organizations are insulated and are characterized by inactivity, lack of confidence, and extreme conservatism. Depressive managers are content with the status quo, doing little to discover key threats and weaknesses. A sense of aimlessness, lethargy, and inactivity permeates organizational activities.

The Schizoid Style. This style manifests itself in feelings of detachment, noninvolvement, withdrawal, a sense of estrangement, and lack of excitement or enthusiasm. This type is indifferent to praise or criticism, appears to be cold and unemotional, and lacks interest in the present or the future. The schizoid manager's fantasy world affords few satisfactions, for this person is unhappy with the world of reality and feels that interactions with others will inevitably fail and cause harm. Schizoid managers conclude that the safest course is to remain distant from those around them. The dangers in this style are emotional isolation and frustration from dependency. Bewilderment and aggressiveness may result.

The schizoid organization suffers from a leadership vacuum. The chief executive has often suffered past disappointments, believes that most contacts will end painfully, and daydreams to compensate for lack of fulfillment. Infighting develops among lower-level managers as a result of the leadership vacuum, but the initiatives of one group of managers are often blunted and neutralized by competing groups. Divisions within the organization thwart effective coordination and communication.

MODERN PRESIDENTS

Historical events will be used to place modern presidents in the categories constructed by Kets de Vries and Miller. Including a president in this scheme does not mean that the president is a bad manager or lacks managerial skills. Rather, it means the president has exhibited some characteristics of the classified type. In reality, presidents are complex human beings who exhibit a variety of styles. The following discussion focuses upon their primary styles. A later discussion will supplement this with an identification and discussion of their secondary styles.

TABLE 6–4 Tendencies of Presidents toward Neurotic Management Styles

MISMANAGEMENT STYLE IN THE WHITE HOUSE	PRESIDENTS
Paranoid	Richard Nixon Lyndon Johnson
Compulsive	Herbert Hoover Harry Truman Jimmy Carter
Dramatic	Franklin D. Roosevelt John F. Kennedy Ronald Reagan
Depressive	Gerald Ford
Schizoid	Dwight Eisenhower

PARANOID PRESIDENTS

Managers who exhibit paranoid tendencies are suspicious and mistrustful of others. They are hypersensitive, hyperalert, and ready to counter perceived threats. At least two modern presidents—Richard Nixon and Lyndon Johnson—have demonstrated paranoid tendencies at some time during their presidencies.

Richard Nixon

Of all modern presidents, Nixon exhibited the strongest tendencies toward paranoia. Noted presidential scholar James David Barber argues that much of Nixon's emotional energy was spent resisting the temptation to lash out at his enemies (Barber, 1985, p. 313). Nixon was widely perceived as cold and unemotional. He presented an image, if not the reality, of rationality. His first term aide, William Safire (1975, p. 275), ventured the thought that Nixon was the first political paranoid with a majority.

Events that illustrate Nixon's paranoid tendency while president include Watergate and his decision to invade Cambodia.

Events before Nixon's election to the presidency, however, demonstrated manifestations of a worldview in which he saw himself pitted against evil forces out to undermine his own righteous position. Early in his career, Nixon became known for his almost fanatical anticommunism, perceiving himself as a lone underdog in the fight to combat its worldwide dissemination. For example, when involved with the Alger Hiss case, Nixon said no one could fight communism without "expecting to pay the penalty for the rest of his life" (Barber, 1985, p. 301). When running for the Senate in 1950, Nixon described himself as a sad underdog whom the world was out to get. When defeated for governor of California in 1962, he proclaimed that his departure from politics would mean that his opponents would not be able to kick him around anymore.

Vietnam brought forth early tendencies toward paranoia in the Nixon White House. Nixon made the decision to intervene unilaterally in Cambodia without extensive consultation with either his cabinet or foreign affairs advisors. Without the countervailing perspective of counselors with a more detached view, Nixon's paranoid impulses caused him to infringe on Cambodian neutrality in violation of international law. When word leaked out in the *New York Times* about secret B-52 raids over Cambodia, Nixon claimed that the leaks were endangering national security and ordered telephone taps on at least thirteen members of his own national security staff and on at least four journalists.

By 1971, Nixon kept an "enemies list" of opponents of the White House position on the war, which included members of the "Eastern establishment," politicians, lawyers, journalists, television commentators, preachers, and professors. The intent was "to screw" the political enemies on the list. The Nixon White House was ready to and did resort to illegal measures to combat perceived threats. One illegal effort on the part of the White House was to counter the leaking of secret documents on the extent of U.S. involvement in Vietnam to the media. The infamous "plumbers unit" committed many of these illegal acts, including the break-in of the office of Daniel Ellsberg's psychiatrist in search of damaging evidence.

But the one event that evoked Nixon's paranoid tendencies more than any other was Watergate. Employing an ex-CIA agent and Cuban malcontents, Gordon Liddy, general counsel of Nixon's reelection committee, authorized that the headquarters of the Democratic National Committee be burglarized. The capture of these burglars set into motion an elaborate cover-up within the White House. The cover-up expanded like a spider's web, eventually encompassing the CIA, the FBI, the Committee to Reelect the President, and the White House staff. The president and his closest advisors were both entangled in this web of deceit. Except for the discovery of the White House tapes which revealed, in the president's own words, the extent of paranoid perceptions and behavior in the White House, the entire Watergate cover-up might have been successful.

Nixon's paranoid style had a major impact on the management of the White House. Power was centralized for the purpose of controlling both the government and policy. Foreign policy was controlled by Henry Kissinger at the National Security Council. Domestic policy was centralized in the hands of John Ehrlichman. Access to the White House was controlled by Bob Haldeman. Nixon loyalists were placed in departments and agencies throughout the government. Decisions were made in the White House, often bypassing cabinet officers. Nixon used the Internal Revenue Service (IRS), the CIA, and the FBI to political advantage by collecting information on his political enemies and aiding in the attempted Watergate cover-up. Nixon became increasingly isolated from the public and from Congress. Toward the end of his ill-fated administration, an atmosphere of fear and paranoia gripped the White House. With ever-increasing preoccupation of major White House players with outside attacks, Haig, Schlesinger and Kissinger began to fear irrational acts by Nixon himself. In a fascinating, even extraordinary, footnote on Nixon in the second and third editions of *The Presidential Character*, Barber (1977, 1985) describes the scene as follows:

> At the end of the Nixon regime there was a coup: the Presidency was run by a general [Alexander Haig] who, by the luck of the draw, had a passion for reason, if also a certain lack of moral imagination. The general, who more than a year previously had ripped out Nixon's taping systems without permission, in the summer of 1974 entered into negotiation with the Vice-President [Gerald Ford] regarding conditions under which he could come to power—the general again acting on his own. Another military leader, the Secretary of Defense [James Schlesinger] established a system by which he could veto the Commander-in-Chief's order to the armed forces. A Presidential order conveyed to the Secretary of State [Henry Kissinger] elicited the reply, "Tell the President to fuck himself." (Bob Woodward and Carl Bernstein, *The Final Days* [New York, Simon & Schuster, 1976], p. 199.) No tanks in the street, no bearded madman gesticulating from a balcony. Just some quiet little arrangements to keep things going—without the interference of the People's Choice. Fortunately it was one of the Nixon's administration's few Horatios, rather than one of its many Iagos, who grabbed power. A system that has to depend on that kind of future is dangerous. (Barber, 1977, p. 551; 1985, p. 552.)

Watergate and Nixon's rampant paranoia, which brought forth Watergate, undercut the president's attempts to restructure power between the executive and legislative branches. According to Arthur

Schlesinger, Jr. (1973), the impressive range of Nixon's actions—from his aggrandizement of presidential war-making powers to his battles with Congress over impoundments—revealed an underlying larger design to rebalance constitutional powers in favor of the executive. Schlesinger (1973, p. 266) argues that had Nixon limited his executive aggrandizement to war-making, treaty-making, impoundments, executive privilege, and the pocket veto, he might have succeeded in his revolt against the separation of powers. However, Nixon's paranoia was his downfall, and ultimately it was the nation's salvation. His willingness to perceive enemies in every newsroom, classroom, and government office created a fearful and distrustful atmosphere. In a terrifying innovation, Nixon transferred the techiques of espionage and covert warfare from foreign policy to domestic politics. This distrustful atmosphere fueled greater paranoid behavior and perceptions on his part, leading to extreme and illegal actions that ultimately brought about his downfall by the Congress. His resignation, under the threat of impeachment, ended the rule of fear.

Lyndon Johnson

Lyndon Johnson also exhibited many paranoid attitudes and behaviors. He was frequently unpredictable and idiosyncratic. Johnson placed great stress on personal loyalty, and he demanded that subordinates be faithful. At times, his treatment of advisors and subordinates bordered on the humiliating and demeaning. Johnson's style of government was personal, he was given to overpersonalizing both the Great Society and the Vietnam War. He viewed critics of these programs as levying personal attacks against him. This personalization of the presidency led him to break with previously close advisors, including Bill Moyers, Robert McNamara, and George Reedy.

While Johnson's overcommitment to detail served him well in domestic policy, this tendency led to his isolation and undoing in the arena of foreign policy. Vietnam built up Johnson's "we versus they" mentality. It isolated him from critics and, in the end, according to Hess (1976, p. 110), it turned his presidency into a bunker. Johnson was deeply suspicious of the media, the "Eastern establishment," the Kennedy clan, antiwar demonstrators, and various "nervous Nellies" who might undermine his presidency. At times his paranoia led him to distort reality, as in his description of the Gulf of Tonkin incident in 1964 when he alleged American destroyers were attacked off the coast of North Vietnam. Using this event as evidence of North Vietnamese enmity, he pushed through Congress the Gulf of Tonkin Resolution, which asserted that Congress "approves and supports the determination of the President, as Commander-in-Chief, to take all necessary measures to repel any armed attack against the forces of the United States and to prevent further aggression." Subsequent events proved Johnson's account of the incident was dubious at best and deceitful at worst and led to Congress' repudiation of "this functional declaration of war." It also led Senator J. William Fulbright to break with his long-time friend, Lyndon Johnson. Ultimately, Johnson's perception of an undefeatable opposing force committed to undermining his reelection led him to announce that he would not run for reelection in 1968.

As a result of Johnson's unpredictable and sometimes demeaning penchant for creating strain and tension among subordinates, the White House staff experienced high turnover during his tenure. At times the Johnson White House was hyperactive, seeking to develop major new programs on both the foreign and domestic fronts. This placed an inordinate amount of strain on Johnson's relations with his staff and his cabinet. As in the Nixon White House, power was centralized. New agencies were added to the Executive Office of the President, with responsibilities given to those most loyal to Johnson and those closest at hand. The inability to extricate his administration from Vietnam isolated Johnson from the rest of the country, and toward the end of his term this even restricted his freedom of travel. To avoid antiwar protestors, he refused to appear in public except on military bases. His sense of siege was so great that he even declined to appear at the 1968 Democratic National Convention in Chicago.

In the end, even his refusal to run again was couched in terms that implied he could end the war by the time he left office. Instead, the war dragged on for another four years. Johnson left office a sick and embittered man who blamed the collapse of his dreams of a Great Society on "that bitch of a war."

COMPULSIVE PRESIDENTS

Compulsive presidents are perfectionists. They wallow in details and rarely relax. Their extreme meticulousness kills spontaneity. Often they are dogmatic and obstinate. Sometimes their attention to detail is so overwhelming that they become indecisive and postpone decisions. They frequently turn inward. Three modern presidents have exhibited compulsive managerial styles while in the White House—Herbert Hoover, Harry Truman, and Jimmy Carter.

Herbert Hoover

Throughout his career, Herbert Hoover's style reflected order, accountability, and hard work. Hoover demonstrated an appetite for detail and a penchant for facts. This, combined with industry and a gift for organization, marked Hoover as one of the most conscientious and dutiful of modern presidents. As Barber (1985) suggests, Hoover was compulsive in his management style. He combined extreme individualism with a sense of responsibility for others. Hoover thought that the presidency could be managed through hard work and attention to detail.

In addition to some of the more desirable features of a compulsive managerial style, Hoover exhibited many of its weaknesses. Like many compulsive managers, his absorption with detail frequently prevented him from seeing the big picture. While Hoover did take some action to combat the Great Depression, such as the establishment of the Reconstruction Finance Corporation, he never grasped the fact that the magnitude of the Depression required a new form of government involvement. In the face of 25 percent unemployment, widespread hunger and misery, extensive business bankruptcies, foreclosures, and economic collapse, Hoover continued to adhere to the tenets of rugged individualism and unfettered free enterprise. The only vision Hoover could provide to restore the country to economic health was an orthodox one of balanced budgets and expenditure cuts.

Unable to combat worsening economic conditions, Hoover turned inward and became increasingly depressed, rigid, and indecisive. In spite of the visible proof that his orthodox plan was not working, Hoover remained unable to deviate from it. His indecisiveness spilled over into his management of international affairs. He was reluctant to commit to any action stronger than protesting Japanese aggression in Manchuria. Nor was he decisive in formulating efforts to stem growing trade protectionism. During his presidency, some of the strongest protectionist barriers ever adopted were put into place, including the Hawley-Smoot Tariff Act of 1930.

The Hoover White House was oriented toward detail, conformity, and adherence to rules and regulations. Despite the great pressure on Hoover, he never succumbed to illness and never missed a day's work. Hoover, the manager, frequently surrounded himself with bank reports and statistics. Barricaded in his study, he viewed himself as defending the Republic against disaster. He repeatedly reiterated the traditional themes of free enterprise and the sanctity of private property. Schlesinger (1957, p. 247) viewed Hoover as a man of high ideals whose intelligence froze into inflexibility, with a dedication tarnished by self-righteousness. These characteristics resulted in a hierarchical and rigid White House that was unable to rise to the problems of the day.

Harry Truman

Of the three compulsive presidents in the modern presidency, Harry Truman is the least clear cut example of this management style. Nonetheless, Truman did exhibit many compulsive attitudes and behaviors. Truman was very hard working, diligent, and persistent. Some have called him a twentieth-century James K. Polk, who was famous for devoting extraordinary hours and effort to his presidential duties. Like Polk, Truman had dramatic moments in which he rose above his compulsive attention to detail.

Truman is known for keeping a sign at his desk that stated, "The Buck Stops Here." This symbolized his willingness to take responsibility and make final decisions, but also showed a reluctance to delegate authority. Compulsive managers often fail to distinguish between large and small decisions, sometimes devoting the same time and attention to trivial details as they do to decisions of considerable magnitude and impact. An example of this behavior was Truman's decision to drop the atomic bomb on Hiroshima and Nagasaki. When asked if he agonized over those decisions, Truman responded that he did not, that he made the best decision he could under all circumstances, and that he slept soundly in the knowledge that he had done his best.

Prior to becoming president, Truman's hard work and attention to detail led to a series of early jobs that demanded such an orientation. While in the army he managed a canteen and eventually worked his way up to captain. Upon his discharge he opened a haberdashery, a business requiring detailed record keeping. Later he entered politics and was elected to a county judgeship in Missouri, another job that focused more on detail than on higher-level policies.

Truman was feisty, dogmatic, and persistent. His 1948 presidential campaign, perhaps more than any other single event of his presidency, showed his grit and determination to overcome obstacles. Running as an underdog he stormed the country on a campaign train before the election, giving rousing speeches to initially skeptical crowds. This campaign earned him the nickname of "Give 'em hell, Harry," reflecting his promise in the heat of the campaign to stand strong and be unyielding.

Compulsive managers, more than other types, are deeply committed to principle. Truman was willing to withstand pressure for unpopular but principled decisions. Another one of his favorite quotes was, "If you can't stand the heat, get out of the kitchen." Truman himself was willing to stand the political heat for upholding the principle of civilian control of the military when he fired the very popular General Douglas MacArthur, then commander-in-chief of the United Nations forces in Korea, who appeared willing to circumvent presidential authority on questions of military strategy in Korea.

Truman's compulsive behavior was also manifested in his personal life. His perfectionism caused him to postpone marriage to the only woman he ever loved until he was thirty-five. He was dogmatically and obstinately loyal to his family, an attitude that sometimes caused him to overlook their inadequacies. His attack on a *Washington Post* music critic for giving Margaret Truman, his daughter, a harsh review of her singing debut was grounded more in his emotional loyalty to her than in a realistic assessment of her abilities as a singer.

The organizational impact of Truman's compulsive style was considerable and long lasting. His attention to detail and his penchant for neatness and order helped crystallize the institutionalization of the modern presidency begun under Roosevelt. As a "clean desk" type of manager, Truman took giant steps toward creating an orderly government after the effective but haphazard Roosevelt administration. Many important agencies were established during Truman's administration. Among these were the Council of Economic Advisors, the National Security Council, the Central Intelligence Agency, and a unified defense establishment. Compulsive organizations are absorbed with standardizing operations and developing formal policies, rules, and procedures. Truman strongly supported rationalization of executive organization and commended the Hoover Commission on Executive Organization for its efforts to achieve this goal. Compulsive organizations also exhibit an established theme. The Truman White House consistently pushed the theme of anticommunism in foreign affairs. In pursuit of this goal, Truman made many excellent appointments, including those of Dean Acheson, George Marshall, Clark Clifford, and Paul Nitze. Although much of Truman's compulsive behavior caused him to be widely criticized at the time, from the vantage point of history, he has come to be viewed as a conscientious, decisive, honest, and competent chief executive.

Jimmy Carter

Jimmy Carter's one term in the White House is a classic case of compulsive management. Carter demonstrated an extraordinary proclivity for detail and meticulousness. Carter felt compelled to control the details of White House operations, even to the point of scheduling the use of White House tennis courts. He was an avid reader of government reports. As Governor of Georgia, he pledged to read all bills passed by the legislature—an overwhelming volume of material—and did his best to uphold that promise. He continued the practice of mastering the substantive details of a huge array of policy areas when campaigning for the presidency and while occupying the Oval Office. This mastery helped him in the presidential debates with Gerald Ford in the 1976 campaign.

Carter's obsession with substantive detail, however, sometimes caused him to lose sight of larger policy goals. Overloading the legislative agenda with an excess of detailed proposals, he overwhelmed the Congress and the public without establishing a clear sense of priorities. Trying to achieve many goals at once, it often appeared that his administration was directionless. Carter's first hundred days were characterized by attempts to act on a laundry list of campaign promises. The thrust of his presidency became increasingly blurred as he set deadlines, ran into obstacles, retreated, then changed directions.

With increasing lack of direction came a reduction in Carter's ability to inspire and persuade. According to James Fallows, Carter's speech writer, "You can't inspire people with a jigsaw puzzle" (Johnson, 1980, p. 295). Carter himself was sensitive to the problems created by his tendency to pursue many things at once. He wrote in his diary after his first month in office that "everybody has warned me not to take on too many projects so early in the administration, but it is almost impossible for me to delay something that I see needs to be done" (Carter, 1982, p. 87).

Carter also exhibited other compulsive behavior traits besides his attention to and mastery of detail. Whatever he did, he did intensely. He worked hard, logging long hours in the Oval Office. He was conscientious almost to a fault. As problems multiplied, he became increasingly indecisive and changed his positions on policies. Initially, Carter planned to withdraw U.S. troops from Korea. Later he changed his mind. He originally intended to support enhanced radiation weapons, but later retreated from that position, much to the chagrin of Helmut Schmidt, the West German chancellor.

Beginning his administration with liberal ideals, he shifted to a policy of increasing political realism as a result of domestic and international events. He reinstated cuts in the Department of Defense; CIA activity was revived; arms sales were increased. The Soviet Union was restored to its place as the great disturber of international peace.

As is typical of compulsive managers, Carter was very principled but lacked a unifying political philosophy. As Barber (1985, p. 440) has noted, Carter "came to office with large principles and an eye for detail, but in between, where a coherent program might have been, was lots of air." Carter's principles were founded in an underlying religious belief which he often discussed. He was a born-again Christian who managed to find time while in the Oval Office to teach Sunday school. The sincerity of his religious beliefs led him to have great empathy for blacks and for those abroad whose human rights were violated. Despite his tenacity, however, Carter's pragmatism prevented him from becoming a religious zealot. While compulsively principled on some issues, he remained more flexible than Woodrow Wilson (Stoessinger, 1979, p 284).

At times, Carter lacked spontaneity. He was dogmatic, obstinate, self-reliant, and inflexible. With the exception of the Camp David agreements between Israel and Egypt, he was not skilled in the art of negotiation. During the Iranian hostage crisis, he developed a "Rose Garden" campaign strategy of isolating himself in the White House. Critics contend that he adhered to this strategy to the point of counterproductivity. A challenge for the presidency from within his own party by Edward Kennedy finally forced Carter to abandon this strategy. As the Kennedy challenge against an incumbent president in the same party illustrates, Carter did not serve as an effective broker for the myriad interests within the Democratic party.

Perhaps Carter's greatest failing at negotiation occurred when he first came to Washington. He was unable to develop a rapport with the Washington power elite, especially with his fellow Democrats in Congress. Carter's campaign as a Washington outsider, coupled with his lack of negotiating skill, left him hamstrung in playing the Washington power game. Influential Democrats such as House Speaker Tip O'Neill, Senator Robert Byrd, Representative Al Ulman, Senator Russell Long, and Senator Gary Hart all felt abused and betrayed by Carter's early actions in the White House.

The organizational ramifications of Carter's compulsive management style were major and often detrimental. He carried loyalty to a fault, surrounding himself with fellow Georgians which precluded his seeking advice from experienced Democrat loyalists in Washington. He failed to rid his administration of political liabilities such as Bert Lance, the director of the Office of Management and Budget, and Frank Moore, the White House liaison with Congress. Lance finally resigned under a cloud of suspicion, and Moore painfully learned his job through trial and error.

Carter found it hard to delegate authority. He wished to retain control over the political agenda, but his inability to manage effectively resulted in a undisciplined and loosely coordinated White House staff. Carter tried to be president, secretary of state, and chief of White House staff simultaneously. His desire to control White House operations prevented him from centralizing power in a strong administrator. Only belatedly did Carter make Hamilton Jordan his chief of staff, but Jordan was not particularly suited to this role. Only in the twilight months of the Carter administration, when Jack Watson became chief of staff, and Al McDonald staff director, did the Carter White House finally develop an operative hierarchical structure run by competent administrators. His noble experiment in cabinet government soon proved ineffective because members of his cabinet developed their own political agenda. The result was the ousting of two cabinet members—Joseph Califano and Michael Blumenthal.

As a one-term president, Carter did not have a second chance to improve these compulsive managerial deficiencies. In the final analysis, the successes and failures of the Carter administration depended most of all upon Jimmy Carter himself.

DRAMATIC PRESIDENTS

Dramatic managers crave activity and excitement. Sometimes they tend toward narcissistic preoccupation with their own performances. They excel at self-dramatization and emotional expression. They rarely concentrate on detail and at times may exhibit an abbreviated attention span. They operate on intuition and hunches and may be accused of being exploitative. Three modern presidents have demonstrated a dramatic managerial style—Franklin Roosevelt, John Kennedy, and Ronald Reagan.

Franklin Roosevelt

Roosevelt's administration represented a dramatic departure from that of his predecessor, Herbert Hoover. From his inaugural address when he told the nation that "The only thing we have to fear is fear itself," to the completion of the revolutionary "Hundred Days"; from his fireside chats to his twice weekly press conferences; and from his tilted cigarette holder to his stories about his dog, Fala, Roosevelt was the personification of the dramatic managerial style in the White House. Quick witted and full of energy, he was given to shifting quickly from one subject to another. He relied upon personal conversations to collect his information. According to British Prime Minister, Winston Churchill, meeting Roosevelt was like opening a bottle of champagne (Barber, 1985, p. 201). Even a crippling bout with polio failed to extinguish Roosevelt's ability to project drama and excitement. His carefully staged public presentations were so skillfully managed that few ordinary citizens realized that their hearty president could not walk.

Roosevelt was a great wartime leader who played a key role in an unsurpassed historical drama. During his administration he deftly moved from "Dr. New Deal" to "Dr. Win the War" in the presidential roles he played. His wartime meetings with Churchill and Stalin were the focal point of world attention. His proposals for exchanging U.S. destroyers for British military bases, his "Bundles for Britain" campaign, the Atlantic Charter, which laid the groundwork for the postwar United Nations, and his decision to pursue an unconditional surrender policy toward the Axis powers all had the essence of high drama.

Roosevelt's dramatic role was not limited to being the leader of the wartime coalition for the Free World. He also played the part of a manager who radically and fundamentally changed the role of government in American society. The idea of a balanced federal budget gave way to a new perception that government should counter depression with government spending to create consumer demand and employment. The notion that an unfettered marketplace was the ultimate economic arbiter fell to new Keynesian ideas that government fiscal policies should provide a counter-cyclical force to business cycle swings. The belief that human welfare was best served through the voluntary efforts of churches, families, charities, and communities was overthrown and replaced by a newer notion that government should provide a minimum floor for those hit by hard times.

Under Roosevelt, Social Security was adopted for the elderly, blind, and disabled. Public works programs, such as the Civilian Conservation Corps (CCC) and the Works Progress Administration (WPA), were adopted for the unemployed. Farmers received aid through the Agricultural Adjustment Act (AAA). The Tennessee Valley Authority (TVA), criticized by many as a socialist plot, was created to bring that region of the country out of the depths of poverty by providing cheap electricity and flood control. Government regulation became accepted as a way to correct market abuses. The Securities and Exchange Commission (SEC) was established to regulate the nation's stock markets. The Wagner Act revolutionized labor relations, making it possible for labor unions to bargain collectively under protection of the law.

Perhaps the most dramatic breaks with precedent undertaken by Roosevelt was his decision to run for a third and fourth term and his willingness to alter the structure of the Supreme Court. With his reelection in 1940 and 1944, he broke a two-term precedent that had stood for a century and a half since the presidency of George Washington. Not only was Roosevelt the first president to break this tradition, but because of the Twenty-second Amendment, which has been called "the Republicans' revenge," he will be the only president to have done so unless the amendment is repealed.

When the "nine old men" of the U.S. Supreme Court struck down much of his New Deal legislation on the grounds of substantive due process, Roosevelt undertook an ill-fated attempt to "pack the Court." He proposed to augment the number of Supreme Court judges by the number of sitting justices over the age of seventy who refused to retire. Although his efforts met with considerable resistance and ultimate failure, as a result of "the switch in time that saved nine," the Supreme Court began to rule more favorably on subsequent New Deal legislation.

Roosevelt's impact on the organization of the White House was profound. He was a very unconventional manager who frequently violated hierarchical chains of command and the tenets of good administration. He practiced a competitive theory of administration that stressed philosophical pluralism and pitted advocate against adversary in both his staff and cabinet. He felt that the result was an eclectic collection of ideas that represented the best thinking of the time. This management style also allowed Roosevelt to personally dominate his administration, even to the extent of being his own secretary of state. Many of his appointments were old friends and colleagues from younger days when he was governor of New York and assistant secretary of the navy. One of the lasting impacts of Roosevelt on government organization was the implementation of the recommendations of the famous Brownlow Commission, which advocated strengthening the office of the presidency. The commission concluded that "the president needs help," thus beginning the process of the institutionalization of the modern presidency.

John Kennedy

Youthful, handsome, rich, witty, and personable, John Kennedy was the epitome of the dramatic management style. Kennedy represented a return of excitement, drama, and style to the White House. Kennedy represented many "firsts" in the presidency. He was the first Roman Catholic ever to reside in the White House. He was also the youngest man ever to be elected to the Oval Office. He was the first president born in the twentieth century, and he represented the ascension of a new generation into power. Kennedy and his strikingly beautiful wife created the mythology of a new Camelot. His appeal brought the best and the brightest to Washington to tackle the nation's problems. Kennedy was able to attract some of the best speech writers ever to serve the presidency, including Ted Sorenson and Arthur Schlesinger. The social and artistic life of Washington revived under the Kennedy spell, flowering into a renaissance.

Kennedy's eloquent inaugural address called for a "New Frontier." He challenged the American public to think not of what the country could do for them but to think of what they could do for their country. One of his most dramatic achievements was to convert public service from a duty to a high calling. Perhaps never before and certainly not since Kennedy had government service been held in such high esteem. He challenged young people to serve their fellow humans and to represent the United States abroad by joining the Peace Corps. In his administration, the push to implement civil rights for blacks began in force, especially in the South. Unlike previous administrations, which had downplayed the problems of racial inequality, the Kennedy administration was supportive of efforts to attain equal rights for blacks.

From the depths of defeat in the ill-fated Bay of Pigs invasion to the heights of tension in the Cuban missile crisis, Kennedy's management of foreign affairs was riveting and dramatic. According to Dean Rusk, Kennedy was eyeball to eyeball with the Russians in the dispute over the housing of Soviet missiles in Cuba, and the Russians blinked first. The youthful president exuded personal style and a sense of presence in both defeat and victory, taking blame for the former and sharing credit for the latter. When the Soviets built the Berlin Wall, barricading in the citizens of East Berlin, Kennedy visited that troubled and divided city at the height of the cold war and declared in German that "I am a Berliner." The West Germans responded with gratitude by showering him with affection. Other dramatic initiatives under Kennedy's administration were the Alliance for Progress, manned space flights, the creation of the hot line to the Kremlin, the Limited Test Ban Treaty, sending additional troops as military advisors to Vietnam, and the famous speech at American University calling for interdependence, arms control, and an end to the cold war.

Kennedy's management of the White House represented a reinstatement of the Roosevelt style. He rejected the institutionalized presidency and the organizational arrangements of Eisenhower, much as Roosevelt had rejected the agency status quo of Hoover. Kennedy's chief transition advisor, Richard Neustadt, whose model of appropriate presidential style was that of Roosevelt, gave encouragement to the looser form of presidential management. Kennedy had little interest in formal organization and the detailed operations of the executive branch. His disdain for routines and set procedures undoubtedly hurt him in his conduct of the Bay of Pigs operation. Kennedy, according to Stephen Hess (1976, p. 91) showed "a generational chauvinism toward Eisenhower, Johnson, and the old boys network." Emphasis was placed on crisis management. The presidency once again became the focal point of government. In the Kennedy era issues were handled centrally within the White House itself, in part because "the best and the brightest" drew departmental policies into the Oval Office. Kennedy found cabinet meetings to be virtually useless, preferring to meet instead with smaller groups of close advisors on a functional basis. The personalized presidency under Kennedy exuded charisma, skillful public relations, and dramatic and entertaining press conferences. However, the government had changed since Roosevelt's times. The federal bureaucracy had grown larger, more complex, and more difficult to manage. Some argued that Roosevelt's style of personalized management had outlived its usefulness, and that Kennedy's loose but charismatic administration could not meet the growing responsibilities of an increasingly bureaucratized federal government.

Ronald Reagan

An actor in the White House? Who is better suited to display a dramatic management style than a bona fide (although, some would contend, grade B) actor. Ronald Reagan has lived up to this expectation of the American public. Some supporters argue that his White House curtain calls surpass any he received in Hollywood. Reagan is the third, and only Republican, president with a dramatic management style since Hoover.

Galbraith (1985) argues that as our first president with a theatrical background, Reagan has adapted well to the script of the presidency, a script that stresses art over reality, style over substance, and spirit over facts. Reagan has earned the accolade of "the great communicator" after long years of well-honed practice before a variety of audiences. Although his style frequently is stronger in image than content, he retains the remarkable ability to reassure the public of his decency and good intentions.

Dramatic managers at their worst are superficial, suggestible, and risk operating in a nonfactual world. At times, Reagan has demonstrated these characteristics. His views of the American economy and of foreign policy have been criticized as throwbacks to an earlier era. Reagan's presidential role model is Calvin Coolidge, who presided over a period of unfettered free markets and naivete in foreign policy. Reagan clings to the beliefs espoused by free enterprise theorists, despite one of the heaviest flurries of corporate mergers and takeover bids since the 1920s. His continuing belief in his supply side policies has led to a doubling of the national debt. Moreover, during his administration, the rhetoric of the cold war returned, and one of the largest arms buildups since the World War II was begun.

Reagan's lack of concern for facts has led him to make a number of egregious errors and has forced his staff to develop strategies for damage control. According to Reagan biographer Lou Cannon (1982, p. 19), when Reagan was young and went off to play by himself, he entered a "make-believe world" in which imagined heroic deeds had the capacity to transform reality. Reagan carried these traits with him throughout his political career and into the White House.

Reagan appears to enjoy his job as president, especially those which involve leading public ceremonies and meeting with adoring admirers. He is less comfortable when confronted with the details of daily administration and the nuts and bolts of complex policies. He relies heavily upon his staff, but is uncomfortable with disagreements and tensions among his advisors. When disputes arise, his wife, Nancy, frequently intervenes and confronts him with the necessity of making unpleasant decisions, especially in regard to personnel. In October 1985, Reagan, unhappy with the performance of his secretary of health and human services, Margaret Heckler, showed his reluctance to engage in unpleasant confrontations and his affinity for gaining dramatic attention by offering her an ambassadorship to Ireland rather than removing her totally from his administration.

Dramatic presidents excel at press conferences, and Reagan has been no exception. In the Heckler incident, Reagan called a press conference to reassure Heckler, the press, and the public that there was no dissatisfaction with her performance or demotion intended, in spite of the well-known fact that his White House advisors disapproved of her managerial capabilities and her lack of enthusiasm for Reagan's conservative social agenda.

Dramatic presidents have short attention spans and are unable to focus attention sharply. Reagan exhibits an oscillating energy level that undercuts his ability to concentrate his attention for an extended period of time. He alternates among disinterest, lassitude, and passivity on the one hand, and sudden bursts of energy, interest, and vigor on the other. His own advisors report that President Reagan frequently has lapses of attention during long and detailed staff meetings. He has been known to fall asleep during meetings with his cabinet staff and world leaders, including the Pope. Nor is Reagan good at detailed homework in preparation for meetings with staff, his own cabinet, or other leaders. Reagan remains more enamored of presidential pageantry than with the hard reality of governance.

During Reagan's bursts of energy, he is most effective as a dramatic manager. He responds positively to the approval, affection, and applause of the public. Barber argues that Reagan's most successful moment in the presidency occurred with the passage of the 1982 Tax Equity and Fiscal Responsibility Act, but that the Reagan revolution owed its success to a conjunction of atypical factors that were not likely to recur. As a result of the great Reagan electoral victory in 1980, Congress was willing to go along with the idea that Reagan had a mandate, pushing through many of his first term policies. In addition, Reagan used his considerable charm on the Washington establishment. The good will generated by his personal appeal and affability was reinforced by sympathy for him when he was wounded in a 1981 assassination attempt. During this time, the Democrats were in disarray and were unable to mount effective counterstrategies to the Republican initiative to grant Americans, especially well-to-do Americans, a sizable tax cut. Reagan's love of drama and ceremony served him well then as he effectively manipulated the media to his own advantage.

Reagan's dramatic managerial style resulted in a change of mood in Washington and a change of government policy. He brought new "old" ideas to a country tired of the Carter malaise. His administration reversed direction from the Carter administration on issues of civil rights for blacks and women, social spending, and government regulation. He reconfigured East-West relationships by using confrontational rhetoric against "the evil empire" of the Soviet Union and by proposing a five-year defense buildup in the amount of a one and a half trillion dollars to restore the balance of military forces.

However, the organizational dangers of a dramatic managerial style are a litany of the management problems in the Reagan administration. The organizational momentum of the first two years soon dissipated, and Reagan did not have the focused attention to restore it. Dramatically run organizations often display inconsistencies in policies and strategies that, in turn, result in dissipation of resources and high turnover. Among the early casualties of the Reagan administration were Secretary of State Alexander Haig and National Security Advisor Richard Allen. David Stockman, who headed the Office of Management and Budget, while not a casualty, was reprimanded for indiscreet public comments. Later, James Watt, Anne Burford, and Raymond Donovan all found themselves out of a jobs as their policies and personal idiosyncrasies fell from favor.

One personnel shift that undercut effective operation of the White House was the replacing of James Baker, the president's chief of staff, with Donald Regan, the former secretary of the treasury and previous chief executive officer of Merrill Lynch. These two men arranged on their own an exchange of offices at the beginning of Reagan's second term. This was later ratified by the president. The move undoubtedly proved a tonic for Baker, who quickly assumed charge of all monetary policy. In Donald Regan's case, the adjustment was difficult, stormy, and contentious. The organizational style of the new chief of staff for the White House was often abrupt, arbitrary, and lacking in political sophistication. As a consequence of the Iran-Contra scandal, Donald Regan resigned and former Senator Howard Baker replaced him. Baker's previous experience as Senate Majority Leader helped smooth Reagan's relationships with the Congress and the public.

Perhaps the best example of inconsistent strategies advocated by President Reagan was his supply-side attempts to cut taxes, raise defense spending to an all time high, and to balance the budget and cut deficits, all simultaneously. As time progressed and the size of the national debt doubled, additional revenues were not forthcoming from economic recovery, as predicted by supply-siders. The consequence of these inconsistences absorbed White House attention at the beginning of Reagan's second term. Perhaps the greatest danger of the Reagan managerial style, however, is its inability to marshal resources to deal with continuing and exacerbating problems, including the mounting federal and trade deficits, the overpriced dollar, the expense of his strategic defense initiatives, and the growing West European fears of U.S. exaggeration of the power and evil intentions of the Soviet Union. In large part because of his dramatic skill, Reagan's approval ratings remain high, independent of the success of his policies.

DEPRESSIVE PRESIDENTS

Depressive managers exhibit feelings of a lack of self-worth, of inadequacy and helplessness. They often view themselves as being at the mercy of events. Frequently they are inhibited and indecisive. Although not completely exemplifying this presidential mismanagement style, Gerald Ford at times showed depressive characteristics.

Gerald Ford

Gerald Ford was an accidental president who succeeded to the presidency under the unfortunate circumstances of Watergate and the clouded resignation of Richard Nixon. Spiro Agnew, Nixon's vice-president during his first term, was forced to resign under threat of criminal prosecution stemming from his earlier tenure as governor of Maryland. Agnew was charged with accepting payoffs in the awarding of state contracts. He pleaded *nolo contendre* to one charge of income tax evasion, and he resigned the vice-presidency in exchange for a promise that he would not be sent to prison. Ford, the Republican minority leader in the House, was chosen in October 1973 to replace Agnew as vice-president under the provisions of the Twenty-fifth Amendment. Ford was sworn into that office in December 1973. Perhaps in the largest accident in the history of the presidency, Ford was catapulted from the vice-presidency to the presidency in August 1974 when Richard Nixon resigned. Ford was bothered throughout his tenure by the fact that he was an unelected president, especially toward the end of his term during the bicentennial of the country.

The problems at the time of his appointment were immense and depressive. Ford was often at the mercy of events created by others. According to his press secretary, Ford's role in history was to clean up the mess made by others. In addition to Watergate, the problems he inherited included the lingering war in Indochina, a sick economy, and the excesses and abuses of the nation's intelligence agencies. After all the turmoil and scandal of the Nixon administration, Ford was viewed by the press as "Mr. Clean." He projected a likable image, one of candor and common sense. As the cloud of Watergate slowly lifted and the country became acclimated to the decency of the new president, a new cloud was formed by Ford's pardon of his former boss. Ford's decision to pardon Nixon took the early bloom off his administration, destroying his high hopes and expectations for accomplishment. His popularity plummeted. The public's confidence in him was undermined. Even his good friend and press secretary, Jerry ter Horst, resigned in protest. Ford, depressed at the departure, referred to his former friend in private discussions as "that son of a bitch" (Nessen, 1978, p. 10). Ford was never able to recover fully from the pardon decision, which contributed to his electoral defeat in 1976.

Characteristic of depressive managers and their organizations is an indecisiveness and an inhibition to use forceful action. Ford appeared unwilling or unable to grapple with rising and increasingly distressful inflation. Rather than use formal government controls and existing tools, Ford attempted to combat inflation through a voluntary program called "Whip Inflation Now" (WIN). A large number of WIN buttons were distributed. The day after Ford spoke to Congress on the issue, WIN enlistment forms were printed in newpapers all over the country to recruit volunteers for a citizen's campaign against inflation. This action proved to be no action. Unemployment continued to rise and auto sales continued to drop. As the country moved increasingly into an ever-deepening recession, Ford's policies were altered. A major tax cut replaced an earlier $5 billion tax increase as a means to fight inflation.

Ford's personal management style also exhibited inaction and indecisiveness at times. He did not like to fire people and was reluctant to show his anger when his cohorts and subordinates made egregious mistakes. Once asked what he considered to be his greatest flaw, he responded that his easygoing nature kept him from getting angry and swearing at people (Nessen, 1978, p. 162). Ford's indecisiveness caused him first to renounce his candidacy for election in 1976 and later to change his plans as he grew accustomed to the prerogatives of the presidency and had begun appreciate the advantages of incumbency.

Ford was unskilled at dealing with the press. His public image was that of an awkard and uncoordinated bumbler. He was alternately called Bozo the Clown or our "top fall-down comic." This image suggested mental ineptitude. When speaking about Ford, Lyndon Johnson said that "he played football too often without his helmet" and that "he was so dumb he couldn't walk and chew gum at the same time." However unfair these accusations, they generated an image of inadequacy and undermined public respect. The reality was that Ford had graduated in the top third of a brilliant Yale Law School class, had ascended to the top leadership of the Republican party, and was a well coordinated athlete. Yet he seemed helpless to change the image of a good-natured klutz, which seriously damaged his political fortunes.

Many organizational problems occurred in the Ford White House. Ford had inherited some of these problems from Nixon and generated others of his own. After Nixon's last chief of staff, Alexander Haig, departed, chaos reigned at the White House. Feuding among Ford staffers was a constant problem throughout his administration. Notorious rivalry erupted between Ford's staff and the staff of Nelson Rockefeller, whom Ford had named as his vice-president. Leaks were frequent and created pessimistic public images of White House operations. Chief of Staff Donald Rumsfeld was half jokingly referred to as a "smiling Haldeman." While Ford complained bitterly about staff leaks and dissension, he failed to clean house or to reshuffle his advisors and cabinet until October 1975. Then in the so-called Sunday night massacre, he fired Secretary of Defense James Schlesinger and CIA Director William Colby, announced that Henry Kissinger would no longer be national security advisor, and revealed that Rockefeller would not run for vice-president in 1976. He removed Elliot Richardson from his post as ambassador to Britain and named him secretary of commerce. He recalled George Bush from Peking to head the CIA. Ford's indecision, however, had lingered too long and his corrective action came too late. He should have won public approval for replacing Nixon appointees with his own, but premature leaks and speculation extended the image of mismanagement in the White House. By a narrow margin, Ford, with all the advantages of incumbency, was defeated in the 1976 election by a Georgia peanut farmer who campaigned effectively against mismanagement of the Oval Office and the nation's affairs.

SCHIZOID PRESIDENTS

Schizoid managers exhibit these characteristics: They are detached, non-involved, withdrawn, and have a sense of estrangement from events. They may show a lack of excitement or enthusiasm and are often indifferent to praise or criticism. At times they appear cold and unemotional. Eisenhower has been classifed as a schizoid president.

Dwight Eisenhower

The fit of Eisenhower into the schizoid managerial category is a loose one. Although he demonstrated some schizoid tendencies, they are only marginally descriptive of his White House performance. Nonetheless, the traditional depiction of Eisenhower is that of a detached and even indifferent president. He had an aversion to partisan politics and approached the presidency as a patriotic duty to be borne but not enjoyed. He was frequently bored or fatigued by the demands of the Oval Office. These demands, in Eisenhower's calculus, outweighed the pleasures and joys. Eisenhower was basically an apolitical president who appeared to rise above partisan politics. He presented an avuncular image to the American public. Like a benevolent but distant uncle, he appeared removed from the daily operations of government.

Eisenhower's social policies were generally conservative and, at times, even negative. They sought to halt the further spread of "New Deal socialism," which Eisenhower felt was undermining American individualism and threatened to bankrupt the economy. While his foreign policy stance was strongly anticommunist, he delegated much of its direction to his secretary of state, John Foster Dulles. Progressive critics of

Eisenhower have argued that his administration of domestic affairs smacked of "luxurious torpor." Foreign-policy experts have criticized him for his loose handling of foreign affairs and for his failure to exercise operational control over the conduct of American foreign policy.

Eisenhower's press conferences were viewed as rambling exercises without syntax or intellectual coherence. Even his addiction to golf symbolized, for many, presidential indifference and lack of dedication to the job. Other criticisms of Ike's indifference as president have been cited. He has been critiqued for his failure to use his personal popularity to build up the Republican party and to wean it away from isolationism and Hooverism. Although annoyed and frustrated by the role and policies of California Senator William F. Knowland, the "Senator from Taiwan," Eisenhower was ineffective at neutralizing Knowland's disrupting influence.

Eisenhower exhibited similar indifference and inaction toward Wisconsin Senator Joe McCarthy, even when McCarthy attacked Eisenhower's good friend and mentor, General George C. Marshall. Eisenhower failed to rally to Marshall's defense. Yet another example of Eisenhower's detachment and disinterest was his disbelief that his chief of staff, Sherman Adams, could be guilty of any improprieties. When confronted with accusations of Adams' malfeasance, Eisenhower asserted that he needed his chief of staff and was distressed when Adams chose to resign and to return to New Hampshire.

Rather than emulate the role model of the hand-shaking, baby-kissing politician, Eisenhower idolized detached and aloof corporate executives of large firms as the epitome of American success. In his initial cabinet, he surrounded himself with eight millionaires and a plumber. Eisenhower continued to feel comfortable with these executives and their management style despite their mixed reviews in the press and accusations that they and he were out of touch with the nation's problems.

New revisionist historical research on Eisenhower presents a more involved and complicated picture of his personality and his administration. Instead of an indifferent chief executive who governed by committee and let domestic and foreign problems accumulate, revisionist historians now paint a picture of Eisenhower as a strong-willed, well-organized manager capable of cogent analysis and balanced judgment. This new view holds that Eisenhower was humane, optimistic, full of common sense, and quite capable of making hard decisions. What seems to be emerging is evidence that shows Eisenhower as much more involved behind the scenes in political decisions and policy choices than previously thought. He showed a sense of balance about the size of the military budget and the Soviet threat, resisted the isolationsts in his own party, and set the tone, if not the organizational strategy, for the emergence of a more modern Republicanism. The new research stresses his natural leadership capabilities and his understanding of and willingness to use political and military power with finesse and a sense of its limited efficacy (Ferrell, 1981; Cook, 1981; Greenstein, 1982).

Current historiography depicts a president who warned the country of the growth of the military industrial complex, who gave the nation eight years of peace and prosperity, and who was firm on defense and the threat of communism without being an extremist on either. The contrasting pictures between the old and new Eisenhower suggest the two faces of the man. On the one hand is the image of the smiling benign war hero reluctantly performing his duty in behalf of an adoring electorate. The old Eisenhower was an "earth smoother" rather than a "earth mover." On the other hand is the emergence of a more recent image of a dedicated, hardworking, and engaged Eisenhower given to fits of anger and chagrin behind the scenes when confronted with attacks from the far right, including the McCarthyites. The true Eisenhower may lie somewhere between the old and the new images.

Organizationally, Eisenhower imposed the military model of a chief-of-staff hierarchy upon the White House. He delegated responsibilities and considerable power to both staff and cabinet members. For example, Eisenhower organized the National Security Council into an efficient and structured organization. He established an executive secretariat to provide institutional memory and to rationalize policy planning. A great believer in cabinet collegiality, Eisenhower used his cabinet for general policy guidance. Eisenhower did not, however, provide strong direction except in military matters. His delegation without direction sometimes led to inertia and committee recommendations at the lowest common denominator. Eisenhower's Whiggish philosophy of the presidency led him to be aloof from many of the pressing social problems of the country. A civil rights revolution was building up under his feet, yet he did not sympathize with or enforce the *Brown* v. *Board of Education* desegregation decision. Eisenhower's general detachment and frequent indifference also led him to react to congressional initiative rather than to provide leadership to that divided and sometimes obstreperous national body. Overall, behind the image of the grinning avuncular Eisenhower lies a man frequently depressed by the onus of the presidential office who took only fleeting pleasures from its responsibilities and activities. This contributed to Eisenhower's detachment and schizoid management style.

SECONDARY NEUROTIC TENDENCIES

On occassion presidents exhibit countervailing tendencies in their primary management styles. The complexity of the human personality does not readily lend itself to simplified classification schemes despite the insight

TABLE 6–5   Primary and Secondary Neurotic Tendencies

PRESIDENT	PRIMARY TENDENCY	SECONDARY TENDENCY
Hoover	Compulsive	Depressive
Roosevelt	Dramatic	Compulsive
Truman	Compulsive	Dramatic
Eisenhower	Schizoid	Depressive
Kennedy	Dramatic	Depressive
Johnson	Paranoid	Dramatic
Nixon	Paranoid	Schizoid
Ford	Depressive	Compulsive
Carter	Compulsive	Dramatic
Reagan	Dramatic	Schizoid

and order that these schemes may provide. Presidents may alter their management styles based on experiences in office, especially those involving crises. In addition to their primary neurotic styles, modern twentieth century presidents have exhibited secondary neurotic styles.

Whereas Hoover was primarily a clear-cut case of compulsive management, he sometimes showed depressive characteristics. As the economic crisis of the 1930s deepened and his strategies proved ineffective, he often felt that he was at the mercy of events. He withdrew from public life and isolated himself at his desk. He developed a sense of helplessness and hopelessness and became psychologically depressed. This depression further inhibited his ability to undertake decisive action.

Roosevelt, at times, was compulsive in addition to being dramatic. Like compulsive managers, he eschewed any intimation of being at the mercy of events and attempted to control things affecting him and his administration. This need to continue his control of events contributed to his violation of the tradition of the two-term president. He could be assertive and domineering, especially on questions of policy. His struggle with the Supreme Court approached obstinacy. His unsuccessful efforts to purge Democrats in Congress who opposed him showed his dogmatism and need to control.

Truman was sometimes dramatic as well as compulsive. In a dramatic clash with the management of the Youngstown Sheet and Tube Company Truman ordered federal troops to take over and run the company in order to maintain war production during the Korean War. The Supreme Court ultimately struck down Truman's assertion of presidential prerogative. Truman's conflict with General MacArthur also demonstrated his dramatic flair. In his Wake Island meeting with MacArthur and his subsequent firing of that popular and distinguished military leader, Truman drew national and international headlines. His early-morning walks each day with newspaper reporters were another way to gain attention.

Though his primary neurotic management tendency was schizoid, Dwight Eisenhower also showed depressive characteristics. His sporadic but accelerating physical problems, his concern about the health of his wife, the loss of his close confidant and chief of staff, Sherman Adams, and his conflict with the right wing of the Republican party all took a toll on Eisenhower's optimism. The U-2 incident, which propelled Nikita Khrushchev to cancel a scheduled summit meeting, also contributed to a pessimistic outlook and a loss of motivation, especially in his second term.

Although the public image of Kennedy is of a dramatic and exciting president, Kennedy, like Eisenhower, occasionally demonstrated secondary depressive characteristics. Like Eisenhower, Kennedy also had physical problems that contributed to a depressive outlook at times. Although disguised at the time, the seriousness of his physical ailments have surfaced. But unbeknownst to the public at the time, the youthful president, who projected vigor and vitality, had Addison's disease—a marked adrenal-cortical deficiency. He also had major back pain from an injury sustained in World War II. Kennedy expected to die early.

A second source of personal stress for Kennedy was family tragedy. His infant son, Patrick, died after a premature birth in August 1963. His father, Joseph P. Kennedy, suffered a stroke and subsequently was unable to communicate with his son. His marriage was sometimes stormy and rocky. Nor was Kennedy immune to or insensitive to failure, as the Bay of Pigs fiasco showed. Theodore Sorensen (1965, p. 410) has testified that while Kennedy was mostly a happy president, he sometimes became frustrated and wearied at the continual pressures of office. When Kennedy was about to reveal the Cuban missile crisis to the public via the national media, congressional leaders presented him with numerous objections and no solutions. Kennedy expressed deep bitterness about the demands of the presidency, stating that if congressional leaders wanted his job, they could have it.

Johnson's secondary management tendency was dramatic. His height of six feet four inches and his large frame and Texan expansiveness were eye-catching and imposing. Johnson was given to dramatic gestures and almost hyperbolic statements. Johnson's programs and goals provided further evidence of his dramatic characteristics. He planned to build a Great Society in both the United States and Southeast Asia. He launched a war on poverty, expecting to eliminate it by 1975. He demonstrated an almost flamboyant flair in his dealings with Congress. His masterful "stroking" and "treatment" were among the most dramatic manifestations of legislative leadership by a president in the twentieth century, comparable only to that of Franklin D. Roosevelt and Woodrow Wilson. When journalists visited Johnson at his Texas ranch, he would sometimes drive them around the back roads at a hundred miles an hour. Often these drives were accompanied by the consumption of alcoholic beverages. Many other incidents, such as showing his operation scar to photographers and lifting his pet beagle by the ears, illustrated Johnson's dramatic flair.

In addition to his primary paranoid management style, Nixon sometimes was schizoid. Always fairly withdrawn, Nixon's tendencies toward isolation were exacerbated by Vietnam and especially by Watergate. Nixon felt under siege by war protesters and Watergate investigators both in Congress and in the courts. He came to rely more and more upon his gatekeeper, Bob Haldeman, to screen out unwanted distractions and intruding visitors. Nixon was consistently cold and unemotional in the performance of his official duties. He did not relish conflict or combat with his staff. While comfortable with realpolitik in the international arena, Nixon became increasingly detached from domestic events and strife. As he became more isolated, his domestic world shrank to the size of his famous legal pads which he used to write his own speeches, political directives, and interpretation of events.

Ford's secondary characterisitic was compulsive. His daily energy output was remarkably high for a man in his early sixties. According to Barber, Ford was hyperactive all of his political life (Barber, 1985, p. 390). While clearly not an intellectual or a creative legislator, Ford was a hard and diligent worker who conscientiously met the demands of the office of the presidency. He did not shirk confrontation with the Congress, as his many vetoes attest. From his congressional experience, Ford learned the hard details of the federal budget. He took both interest and pleasure in studying and mastering the fine points of fiscal politics.

Like Truman, Carter was primarily a compulsive manager who had a flair for the dramatic. From his break with tradition by going on an "inaugural walk" following his swearing-in ceremony to his fireside chats in which he wore a cashmere sweater, Carter emphasized the plebian side of the presidency. He eschewed aristocratic trappings, including "Hail to the Chief" and first-class travel for his top aides. The number of chauffeured limousines for top government officials fell dramatically. However, the most dramatic event of his presidency was his staging and negotiation of the Camp David agreements. He not only brought Menachem Begin and Anwar Sadat together but he used forceful persuasion to get them to agree. The first Middle East settlement in twenty years was announced from the White House with great fanfare.

Reagan sometimes demonstrates contradictory tendencies, which border on the schizoid. Perhaps the most salient manifestation of this tendency is his public image of strong leadership, dramatic activity, and excitement, in contrast with the image of the private man who detests unpleasant confrontation, is reluctant to dismiss incompetents, and appears more interested in the trappings of the presidency than in the hard details of legislation. Senior Republicans in both the Senate and the House have complained bitterly about Reagan's lack of involvement in the development of workable solutions to many national problems, including the federal deficit. Reagan's private dealings with the Democratic leadership have often left his fellow Republicans exposed and vulnerable. As the second term of the Reagan administration winds down, Reagan's dramatic style appears to be losing ground to his secondary tendencies. As deficits, trade, and interest rate problems continue to mount, his dramatic style appears to be less successful. Increasingly, it is at odds with the hard realities of staff dissension, political opposition, summit diplomacy, and rising protectionism.

With the expansion of the institution of the presidency, presidents are increasingly expected to be skillful managers as well as masterful politicians. Yet an examination of presidents as corporate managers is relatively new. Inquiries to date have focused mostly on positive managerial styles. It is common knowledge though that neurotic behavior does occur within the White House, and the presidency is as susceptible to mismanagement as any large organization. One need only recall the mistakes in economic and fiscal policies of the 1920s and 1930s, the political scandal of Watergate, and the military tragedy of Vietnam to recognize the dangerous and deadly consequences of mismanagmeent in the Oval Office.

Our analysis in this chapter has dwelt at some length and detail on an explanation of the neurotic model of managerial behavior. This application of the neurotic model to presidents has been suggestive and not definitive. There is ample room here for further study and research. The neurotic categories used are not meant to be rigid, but rather to imply tendencies, not degree, in management style. These tendencies can and do change during the course of a presidential administration.

REFERENCES

ABRAHAMSEN, DAVID, *Nixon vs. Nixon: An Emotional Tragedy*. Bergenfield, N.J.: New American Library, Signet Books, 1978.

BARBER, JAMES DAVID, *The Presidential Character: Predicting Performance in the White House*, 3rd edition. Englewood Cliffs, N.J.: Prentice-Hall, 1985.

BRODIE, FAWN M., *Richard M. Nixon: The Shaping of His Character*. New York: W.W. Norton & Co, Inc., 1981.

BURNS, JAMES MACGREGOR, *Presidential Government: The Crucible of Leadership*. Boston: Houghton Mifflin, 1966.

CANNON, LOU, *Reagan*. New York: Putnam's, 1982.

CARTER, JIMMY, *Keeping Faith.* New York: Bantam, 1982.

COOK, BLANCHE WIESEN, *The Declassified Eisenhower.* New York: Doubleday, 1981.

CYERT, RICHARD M., and JAMES G. MARCH, *A Behavioral Theory of the Firm.* Englewood Cliffs, N.J.: Prentice-Hall, 1963.

FERRELL, ROBERT H., ed., *The Eisenhower Diaries.* New York: W.W. Norton & Co., Inc., 1981.

FREUD, SIGMUND, and WILLIAM C. BULLITT, *Thomas Woodrow Wilson: A Psychological Study.* Boston: Houghton Mifflin, 1962.

GALBRAITH, JOHN KENNETH, *"Reagan's 'Facts'—Artistic License."* *The New York Times,* September 27, 1985, p. 21.

GEORGE, ALEXANDER L., and JULLIETTE L. GEORGE, *Woodrow Wilson and Colonel House.* New York: John Day, 1956.

GLAD, BETTY, *Jimmy Carter: In Search of the Great White House.* New York: W.W. Norton & Co., Inc., 1980.

GREENSTEIN, FRED I., *The Hidden-Hand Presidency: Eisenhower as Leader.* New York: Basic Books, 1982.

HARGROVE, ERWIN C., *Presidential Leadership.* New York: Macmillian, 1966.

HARGROVE, ERWIN C., and MICHAEL NELSON, *Presidents, Politics, and Policy.* New York: Knopf, 1984.

HESS, STEPHEN, *Organizing the Presidency.* Washington, D.C.: The Brookings Institution, 1976.

HYMAN, SIDNEY, "What Is the President's True Role?," *The New York Times,* September 7, 1958, p. 25.

JOHNSON, HAYNES, *In the Absence of Power: Governing America.* New York: Viking, 1980.

KEARNS, DORIS, *Lyndon Johnson and the American Dream.* New York: Harper & Row, 1976.

KETS DE VRIES, MANFRED F.R., and DANNY MILLER, *The Neurotic Organization: Diagnosing and Changing Counterproductive Styles of Management.* San Francisco: Jossey-Bass, 1984.

KOENIG, LOUIS W., *The Chief Executive,* 4th edition. New York: Harcourt Brace Jovanovich, 1981.

LOWI, THEODORE, *The Personal President: Power Invested, Promise Unfilled.* Ithaca, N.Y.: Cornell University Press, 1985.

MARCH, JAMES G., and HERBERT SIMON, *Organizations.* New York: Wiley, 1958.

MAZLISH, BRUCE, *In Search of Nixon: A Psychological Inquiry.* New York: Basic Books, 1962.

NESSEN, RON, *It Sure Looks Different from the Inside.* Chicago: Playboy Press, 1978.

NEUSTADT, RICHARD, *Presidential Power.* New York: John Wiley, 1960.

ROSSITER, CLINTON, *The American Presidency.* New York: Harcourt Brace & World, 1956.

SAFIRE, WILLIAM, *Before the Fall: An Inside View of the Pre-Watergate White House.* Garden City, N.Y.: Doubleday, 1975.

SCHLESINGER, ARTHUR M., JR., *The Crisis of the Old Order, 1919–1933.* Boston: Houghton Mifflin, 1957.

SCHLESINGER, ARTHUR M., JR., *The Imperial Presidency.* Boston: Houghton Mifflin, 1973.

SIMON, HERBERT, *Administrative Behavior.* New York: Macmillan, 1947.

SORENSEN, THEODORE, *Kennedy.* New York: Harper & Row, 1965.

STOESSINGER, JOHN, *Crusaders and Pragmatists: Movers of Modern American Foreign Policy.* New York: W.W. Norton & Co., Inc., 1979)

CHAPTER SEVEN
IN SEARCH OF HEROES:
When Presidents Are Great

The nation has lived through trauma and trying times during and since the assassination of President John F. Kennedy. The twin tragedies of Vietnam and Watergate were the cause of some of the severest troubles in the history of the country and in the institution of the presidency in modern times. These tribulations were accompanied by economic stagflation, OPEC shocks to gas and oil prices, deteriorating international competitiveness, and the rise of the Soviet Union to military parity with the United States. These blows to the American body politic have created a crisis of confidence among Americans in the ability of their institutions and leadership to cope with problems.

A youthful and charismatic president who promised the country a "New Frontier" was assassinated. Five years later his brother and presidential candidate Robert Kennedy met the same fate as did Martin Luther King, Jr., a famous black leader, who articulated the hopes of a suppressed minority. John Kennedy's successor, Lyndon Johnson, was virtually driven from office by the agony of war in Southeast Asia, only to be succeeded by a president who was forced to resign in order to prevent an almost certain impeachment. Following this, Gerald Ford became an unelected president who ascended to the office by accident and was in power during the bicentennial of the Republic. In spite of high hopes that Jimmy Carter would restore vigor, honesty, and competence to the White House, his term of office proved to be a major disappointment, paving the way for the election of a former movie star who promised to restore America to greatness by revitalizing its faith in itself, in its people, its institutions, and its way of life. Whether or not Ronald Reagan fulfilled the role of a valiant and fearless national leader, the American public's hunger for heroes and greatness remains.

As the twentieth century draws to a close, the desire and the need for great presidential leadership has never been more apparent. But when are presidents great? Since John Kennedy raised American hopes and spirits only to have them dashed in one split second by an assassin's bullet on a November day in Dallas, have modern presidents fulfilled the expectations of greatness? Critics would argue that the gap between performance and promise is large. Lyndon Johnson's egomania and questionable business dealings have raised doubts about his character and the reasons for his rise to power. Richard Nixon has been characterized as obscuring the truth to the point of pathological lying and abusing the power of the presidency. Gerald Ford, in spite of his nostalgia and high regard for Harry Truman, displayed few of the characteristics of his role model and represented institutionalized mediocrity. Perhaps never has the gap between promise and performance been greater than in the Carter White House, where high hopes were dashed upon the jagged rocks of big league politics in Washington and Moscow. Emphasizing rhetoric over reality, Ronald Reagan's affability and "Mr. Nice Guy" image enabled him to maintain the affection and respect of the American people while mortgaging the future of its children and passing the buck of hard decisions about the domestic and international economies to his successors.

The hero worship of Kennedy, Eisenhower, Truman, and Roosevelt suggest a nostalgia for the days of strong presidential leadership combined with respect for their character and their achievements. The growing complexity and tensions in the world make the exercise of presidential greatness more demanding, onerous, and difficult, but the need for effective and strong leadership (and the craving for great presidents to meet that need) is stronger than before. In addition to traditional leadership qualities, greatness requires a high degree of selling and management skills. This chapter will use the selling and management scores developed in previous chapters to classify modern presidents. Particular attention will be devoted to those presidents who exhibited great leadership.

TYPES OF PRESIDENTIAL LEADERSHIP

The dimensions of selling and management skills so crucial to the success of the modern presidency may be combined to form a typology of presidential leadership. (See Table 7–1.)

TABLE 7–1   Types of Presidential Leadership

		SELLING SKILLS	
		Operational Leadership	Great Leadership
Management Skills	*High*		
	Low	Innefective Leadership	Political Leadership

Ineffective Presidents

Ineffective presidents are those who are low on both selling and management skills. Often unusual political circumstances surround the election of an ineffectual leader. He or she may be perceived as the more attractive candidate when pitted against a candidate who has made major mistakes during the campaign or one who is held responsible for the sins of one's party or one's predecessors. Some ineffective presidents are accidental, that is, thrust unexpectedly into the presidency upon the death or resignation of the incumbent president. Until recently, the vice-presidential selection process has been casual, haphazard, and political, with vice-presidents selected mostly for their ticket balancing qualities rather than their competence and their ability to perform as president. Recent presidential nominees have employed a more rigorous examination process to select their running mates, thus placing the days of unqualified vice-presidential candidates in the past. Yet the possibility, even the probability, of ineffective presidential leadership unfortunately remains. When that happens, the country almost invariably suffers.

Operational Presidents

Operational presidents are good managers but poor communicators and salespeople. Under fortuitous circumstances, modern media-marketing efforts in political campaigns may allow operational presidents to be packaged like commercial products and sold to the public so that, despite low personal selling skills, they are elected. Once in office, however, their lack of these personal skills becomes more apparent and detrimental to the achievement of their policy goals. As their communications with key audiences falter, the administrations of operational presidents likewise falter. Although operational presidents in their purest form may become an endangered species in the Oval Office, the need for competent management skills in the White House increases across time. Early in their administrations, before their lack of selling and communication skills becomes apparent, their skill at management may allow them to be effective in achieving policy goals. It also may help them establish a solid reputation within the Washington community, which, in turn, may radiate outward through columnists and television news anchors to the general public. Because of their managerial focus and emphasis, operational presidents communicate better with elites and other managers than they do with the public or the public's representatives.

Political Presidents

Presidents who exhibit political leadership are high on selling skills but low on management skills. *Political presidents*, like great presidents, are effective communicators who are good at the manipulation of verbal symbols. They inspire and lead important constituencies and have at least a competence in, if not a mastery over, television. Political presidents are good campaigners and relish the excitement and crowds of the campaign trail. Ranking low on management skills, it is their misfortune to be unable to translate effectively their personal charisma and the political momentum they generate into coherent and well-managed public programs. Chaotic, inconsistent, and even contradictory programs with little effective presidential oversight often result.

Great Presidents

Great presidents have a high degree of both selling skills and management skills. Great presidents, as good salespeople, can both persuade salient audiences to follow their policy initiatives and conceptualize and devise strategies to implement and manage those policies. They communicate effectively with the public and have good working relationships with the media. Increasingly, they must be able to project both their own image and their policies effectively through television. Without these abilities to convince and persuade, it is nearly impossible to become a great president and even a marginally effective one.

As good managers, great presidents recruit and select good people to work in their administrations. Because the scale of government dwarfs even the largest of private corporate structures, a great president must rise above the daily operations to delegate authority effectively, to set overall policy objectives, and to motivate subordinates to carry out those objectives. In essence, the great president must walk a fine line between being too informed about the details of government operations and being too ignorant about them. Great presidents need to be experienced and competent professionals who understand micromanagement but excel at macromanagement.

METHODOLOGY

Previously, modern presidents have been ranked high, medium, or low on four aspects of selling ability—selling to the media, to the public, to Congress, and to world leaders—to derive overall selling scores. These scores are summarized in Table 7-2.

Six of the modern presidents evaluated rank high on selling ability. Roosevelt, with a score of 3.00, ranks the highest, followed by Kennedy, Eisenhower and Reagan (2.50), Johnson (2.25), and Truman (2.00). Four modern presidents rank low on selling ability. Nixon and Ford (1.75) are the highest in the low category, while Carter (1.25) and Hoover (1.00) have considerably lower scores.

TABLE 7-2   Presidential Selling Scores

		SELLING SCORES	
		LOW	HIGH
	High	OPERATIONAL LEADERSHIP	GREAT LEADERSHIP
Management Skills		Nixon (1.75)	Roosevelt (3.00) Kennedy (2.50) Eisenhower (2.50) Truman (2.00)
	Low	INNEFECTIVE LEADERSHIP	POLITICAL LEADERSHIP
		Ford (1.75) Carter (1.25) Hoover (1.00)	Reagan (2.50) Johnson (2.25)

Range for scores: 1 to 3

Presidents were also ranked high, medium, and low on four types of policy management—defense, foreign, social, and economic policies. Again, overall scores were computed, this time for management skills. Five presidents were accorded high management scores, and five were rated low. (See Table 7-3.)

Among those presidents with high management scores are Roosevelt (2.50), Truman (2.50), Nixon (2.25), and Eisenhower and Kennedy (2.00). Those presidents with low management skills include Carter and Johnson (1.75), Reagan (1.50), and Hoover and Ford (1.25).

TABLE 7–3   **Presidential Management Scores**

		SELLING SCORES	
		LOW	HIGH
	High	OPERATIONAL LEADERSHIP	GREAT LEADERSHIP
Management Skills		Nixon (2.25)	Roosevelt (2.50) Truman (2.50) Eisenhower (2.50) Kennedy (2.00)
	Low	INEFFECTIVE LEADERSHIP	POLITICAL LEADERSHIP
		Carter (1.75) Hoover (1.25) Ford (1.25)	Johnson (1.75) Reagan (1.50)

Range for scores: 1 to 3

These rankings are necessarily qualitative in nature, but, according to John Van Maanen (1983, p. 10), qualitative and quantitative methodologies are not necessarily mutually exclusive. The two approaches differ primarily in overall form, focus, and emphasis of study. Van Maanen argues that "qualitative methods represent a mixture of the rational, serendipitous, and intuitive. . . qualitative investigators tend also to describe the unfolding of social processes rather than the social structures that are often the focus of quantitative researchers." Presidential selling and management skills are more akin to processes than to fixed institutions, and like most qualitative research, both the meaning and the significance of specific actions are largely determined by the context.

The rankings on the four dimensions of selling—to the media, to the public, to the Congress, and to world leaders—and on the four dimensions of management skills—defense, foreign, social, and economic policies—may be averaged to derive overall selling and management scores. When a high score is assigned a rating of 3, a medium score a rating of 2, and a low score a rating of 1, the range for overall selling and management scores is 1 to 3. Selling and management scores may be added, as in Table 7–4, to produce total presidential leadership scores. These selling and management scores may also be averaged, to produce average leadership scores as displayed in Table 7–5. The range for the total presidential leadership scores is 2 to 6, whereas the range for the average presidential leadership scores is 1 to 3.

TABLE 7-4　Total Presidential Leadership Scores

		SELLING SCORES	
		LOW	HIGH
	High	OPERATIONAL LEADERSHIP	GREAT LEADERSHIP
Management Skills		Nixon (4.00)	Roosevelt (5.50) Kennedy (4.50) Truman (4.50) Eisenhower (4.50)
	Low	INEFFECTIVE LEADERSHIP	POLITICAL LEADERSHIP
		Ford (3.00) Carter (3.00) Hoover(2.25)	Johnson (4.00) Reagan (4.00)

Range for scores: 2 to 6

Presidents range from 2.88 to 1.13 on their average leadership scores. (Table 7–5.) Rankings, in descending order, are: Roosevelt (2.75); Kennedy, Truman and Eisenhower (2.25); Nixon, Johnson, and Reagan (2.00);

TABLE 7-5　Average Presidential Leadership Scores

		SELLING SCORES	
		LOW	HIGH
	High	OPERATIONAL LEADERSHIP	GREAT LEADERSHIP
Management Skills		Nixon (2.00)	Roosevelt (2.75) Kennedy (2.25) Truman (2.25) Eisenhower (2.25)
	Low	INEFFECTIVE LEADERSHIP	POLITICAL LEADERSHIP
		Ford (1.50) Carter (1.50) Hoover(1.13)	Johnson (2.00) Reagan (2.00)

Range for scores: 1 to 3

Ford and Carter (1.50); and Hoover (1.13). When actual selling and management scores are used to divide presidents into one of the four leadership types, each category has at least one representative from each political party, with the exception of the operational leadership category, which has only one individual in it, Richard Nixon.

INEFFECTIVE PRESIDENTIAL LEADERSHIP

Three presidents exhibit ineffective leadership styles—Herbert Hoover, Gerald Ford, and Jimmy Carter. All three presidents are low on both selling and managerial skills. Hoover ranks the lowest on average leadership (1.13), while Ford and Carter both rank moderately low (1.50). (See Table 7–5.)

Herbert Hoover

Unfortunately and somewhat surprisingly, Herbert Hoover ranks at the very bottom of overall selling scores, scoring low on all four categories of selling ability. Sadly, he did not do much better on management skills, ranking low on his management of foreign, social, and economic policies, and ranking moderate on management of defense policy. Many of the standard presidential performance evaluations have ranked Hoover as being average, and he does not appear on any of the lists among the ten worst presidents. Perhaps the more recent poor performances of Nixon and Carter have tended to eclipse the memory of Hoover's failures in both selling ability and policy management.

Upon closer examination, however, Hoover was unable to convince any important audiences after 1930 that more of his same policies would solve the nation's mounting and massive problems. Nor was he able to fashion bold policies to deal with the troubled times. In foreign policy, in spite of his good intentions, his unwillingness to back up his words with firm action and force did little to arrest aggressor nations in the late 1920s and early 1930s.

Gerald Ford

Gerald Ford, the accidental president, was also an ineffectual one. Ford was somewhat better at selling (1.75) than he was at managing (1.25). (see Tables 7–2, 7–3). He ranked low in selling to world leaders but medium in other selling categories. On management skills, he ranked consistently low with the exception of foreign policy, where he ranked medium. In the 1982 Murray-Blessing survey, Ford was rated average, and he places among neither the ten best nor the ten worst presidents in a 1982 *Chicago*

Tribune poll. His term was so short, so consumed by Watergate and the aftermath of the Nixon pardon, and so unplanned, that his performance often appeared ad hoc and lacking in direction.

Unlike nonaccidental presidents, Ford had no agenda. Unlike most presidents who had to formulate a national agenda years in advance of running and to develop communications skills to articulate that agenda to a wide range of audiences, Ford assumed the White House without a platform. His "good guy" personal characteristics did not make up for this lack of conceptualization nor for the absence of finely honed skills. His blandness did not allow him to transcend or to solve the manifold problems he inherited.

Jimmy Carter

Like both Hoover and Ford, Jimmy Carter also was an ineffectual leader, exhibiting low selling and low managerial skills. Except for dealing with world leaders, where he ranked medium, Carter ranked low in selling to the crucial audiences of the media, the public, and Congress. Scoring medium in managing defense, foreign, and social policies, and low in managing economic policy, Carter's management skills were somewhat higher (1.75) (Table 7–3) than his selling skills (1.25) (Table 7–2) but still ranked low (below 2.00). Because Carter was slightly better at managing than at selling, his talents were the reverse of his predecessor, Gerald Ford, who was slightly better at selling than managing. However, neither was very good at either.

In the Murray-Blessing poll, Carter is rated just behind Ford, but in the *Chicago Tribune* poll, he is rated the tenth worst president in U.S. history. His overall leadership score here is not the lowest possible (1.50) (Table 7–5) but still places him in the ineffectual leadership category, tied with Ford. Carter assumed the White House as a Washington outsider anxious to strip the office of imperial trappings, to restore it to the common people, and to revive a sense of national morality after Watergate. He also sought to achieve world peace and to place human rights once again on the foreign-policy agenda. As with other ineffectual presidents, good intentions were not enough and did not offset a lack of selling and management skills. Carter, the one term president, found that playing minor league softball in Georgia did not qualify him for Washington hardball politics.

OPERATIONAL PRESIDENTIAL LEADERSHIP

Only one president, Richard Nixon, falls in the category of operational leadership. This leadership style is more common in the corporate than in the political world, particularly among managers who rise from corporate financial divisions, watching profits and losses. Yet occasionally, operational leadership is observed in politics, and in at least one instance in modern times, operational leadership even ascended to the White House.

Richard Nixon

As an operational president, Nixon ranks low on selling ability (1.75) (Table 7–5) and high on management skills (2.25) (Table 7–5). The range of Nixon's selling skills is very great, running low to high. He received low rankings for selling to the media and the public, medium to Congress, and high to world leaders. His performance was very uneven, but was not uniformly bad. In management, Nixon ranked medium in managing defense, social, and economic policies, and ranked high in his management of foreign policy.

Nixon's average leadership score is 2.00 (Table 7–5), placing him considerably above his rating in the Murray-Blessing and *Chicago Tribune* polls, where he is rated at the bottom of all presidents, along with Grant and Harding. One of the reasons for this ratings gap is the greater emphasis placed by those two polls on integrity and morality. At least one historian has called Nixon the most corrupt president in U.S. history (Murphy, 1985, p. 443). His corruption is hard to deny, but actual performance in office, rather than personal characteristics, remains the focus of this study. When the focus in on performance, Nixon looks better than when personal characteristics are more heavily weighed. Nixon continues to be one of the most controversial of presidents, alternately blamed for undermining the Constitution and praised for foreign policy successes, including the opening up of Communist China. Refusing to fade away like an old soldier, Nixon still wrote informative and provocative books long after his disgraceful exit from the presidency. He advised both President Reagan and the Republican party on politics and foreign policy throughout the Reagan presidency.

POLITICAL PRESIDENTIAL LEADERSHIP

Only two modern presidents—Lyndon Johnson and Ronald Reagan—have shown a political leadership style, exhibiting high selling but low managerial skills. As a type, political leadership might be assumed to be a common category, for politicians without selling skills may have a difficult time getting elected. Politicians do not have extensive managerial experience, especially in supervising and managing large bureaucracies, but most politicians have at least to sell themselves before they achieve any success.

Lyndon Johnson

Lyndon Johnson ranks moderately high on overall selling ability (2.25) (Table 7–2), scoring a high only on selling to Congress, and medium on selling to the media, the public, and world leaders. On managerial skills, Johnson ranks low on managing both foreign policy and defense policy, but ranks medium on economic policy and high on social policy, giving him an overall management score of 1.75 (Table 7–3). If Vietnam had not consumed so much of Johnson's time and energy, his management performance almost certainly would have improved. Johnson was clearly a president of immense talents, but a possessor of fatal flaws, including a massive ego and a rigid perspective on foreign policy. These flaws undercut his management of both foreign policy and defense policy, making him a political president rather than a great leader. Johnson's overall leadership score, based on his selling and managerial skills, is 2.00 (Table 7–5). In contrast, the 1970 Maranell Presidential Accomplishment Poll ranked Lyndon Johnson ninth, just after Andrew Jackson and just before James K. Polk and three places above John Kennedy. In the Murray-Blessing poll of 1982, Johnson was ranked tenth, one place above Eisenhower and two places above Kennedy.

Ronald Reagan

Ronald Reagan's obvious selling skills rank him high with the public and with Congress and moderate with the media and world leaders, for an overall score of 2.50 (Table 7–2). His title "great communicator" is based upon these considerable skills. In the management of his policies, Reagan rates considerably lower, especially on foreign policy and social policy where he ranks low. On economic policy and defense policy, he performs moderately, providing an overall management score of 1.50 (Table 7–3).

Reagan's simplistic and often old-fashioned worldview sold well to a public that wanted to return to older and more traditional values and was anxious to restore America to its former reputation of being number one. This simplistic worldview, however, has not facilitated policy management to the same degree as his selling ability. Reagan's ebullient optimism contributed to his "Teflon" quality, and he often described the way he would like the world to be rather than the way it was. His speeches, which were soothing to the public, were not often taken seriously by politicians of either party because of the large gulf between rhetoric and reality.

Despite this, Reagan's overall leadership score, based on both selling ability and managerial skills, is 2.00 (Table 7–5). Reagan's overall leadership rating is identical to Johnson's, although the gap between Reagan's selling and managerial skills (1.00) is greater than the equivalent gap for Johnson (0.50). (See Tables 7–2, 7–3.) Historians and political scientists have not yet evaluated Reagan's long-term contribution to American history and the presidency.

GREAT PRESIDENTIAL LEADERSHIP

The fourth, final, most significant, and most desired category of presidential leadership is *great leadership*. This style consists of high selling ability with high managerial skills and represents the best of both. When presidents combine high ratings in both categories, they have the necessary set of skills to succeed in one of the most complex, important, and difficult political offices in the world today. Four modern presidents may be classified as great: Roosevelt, Truman, Eisenhower, and Kennedy. Of these four, Roosevelt ranks the highest on overall leadership (2.75), followed by Kennedy, Truman and Eisenhower (2.25). (See Table 7–5.) Clearly the gap between Roosevelt and the other three presidents is appreciable. Two of these presidents—Roosevelt and Truman—are among the ten best presidents in the U.S. Historical Society poll. Three of the presidents—Roosevelt, Truman, and Eisenhower—are among the ten best presidents in the *Chicago Tribune* poll.

Harry Truman

Harry Truman was a slightly better manager than salesperson. On both of these dimensions, he was good but not outstanding, ranking 2.00 on overall selling ability and 2.50 on overall management. (See Tables 7–2, 7–3.) In selling to crucial audiences, Truman actually ranked low at selling to the public, but high on selling to world leaders. His ability to sell to the media and to Congress was average or moderate. On management, Truman scores high on defense and foreign policy, and medium on both social policy and economic policy. His overall score on management ranks him with Franklin Roosevelt on this dimension.

Truman's rating in presidential performance evaluations is remarkably consistent. He was ranked eighth in the Schlesinger poll of 1962, sixth in the Maranell poll of 1970, and eighth in the U.S. Historical Society poll of 1974. The *Chicago Tribune* poll of 1982 and the Murray-Blessing poll of 1982 both also ranked him eighth. Truman's reputation has grown since he left office. In professional polls he is usually ranked as a near great president. When selling ability and management skills are the primary criteria for ranking presidents, Truman falls into the category of great presidents, but he runs considerably below Roosevelt, tying with Eisenhower and Kennedy. His high rankings here illustrate the importance of achievements in both foreign policy and defense policy, areas where Truman excelled. Successes here partially offset more lackluster performances elsewhere. Time has helped Truman's reputation, as it may eventually help Nixon, and has helped Eisenhower.

Dwight Eisenhower

Dwight Eisenhower has been the beneficiary of revisionist scholarship, which has raised his professional standing from average in the Schlesinger and Maranell polls to a ranking of ninth best in the *Chicago Tribune* poll and eleventh best in the Murray-Blessing poll. This is a remarkable shift in presidential performance evaluations over the past twenty years. When selling and management are the primary dimensions considered, Eisenhower ranks in the great leadership category, with a score of 2.25, behind Roosevelt and tied with Truman and Kennedy. (See Table 7–5.)

On selling ability, Eisenhower performed moderately well with the media and Congress. His performance with the public and world leaders was high. On the scale of management, Eisenhower ranked medium in both foreign and economic policy, low in social policy, but very high in defense policy. Surprisingly, Eisenhower's overall selling score is 2.50 (Table 7–2) and his management score is 2.00 (Table 7–3). This research confirms that Eisenhower's earlier rankings were artificially low, perhaps because of the greater activism of later periods and perhaps because newer historical sources of information were not then available.

John F. Kennedy

John Kennedy, the youngest American president, was also one of the best. On the axis of selling ability, Kennedy rated high on his ability to sell to the media, the public, and world leaders. Only on selling to Congress did he rate low, producing an overall selling score of 2.50 (Table 7–2). His youth, charisma, style, ironic sense of humor, good looks, and wit were all qualities that enabled him to sell the policy products of his administration. On the axis of management, Kennedy ranked medium in all four categories, for an overall management score of 2.00. (Table 7–3) Kennedy was a better salesman than manager.

According to the Maranell Accomplishment Poll, Kennedy rated twelfth just behind John Adams and ahead of James Monroe and Grover Cleveland. The Murray-Blessing poll ranks him as number thirteen, just after Eisenhower and James K. Polk. He is not listed among the ten best presidents by either the U.S. Historical Society poll or the *Chicago Tribune* poll. Many of the top-ranking presidents in these polls, however, were not among the modern presidents evaluated here.

Considering the short length of time that Kennedy was in office, it is remarkable that his performance evaluation continues to rank high, in spite of new works that have viewed his administration, record, family, and personal life from a more jaundiced perspective. With the passage of time, the Kennedy myth and the Kennedy reality have begun to merge, and the more lasting accomplishments of the promising, but truncated, Kennedy presidency remain. Perhaps more lasting, and in the long run more important, than any particular solitary policy achievement was his contribution to the American spirit. His idealism, youthful energy, and sense of public service inspired a generation of America's youth to consider sacrificing self-interest for causes greater than themselves.

Clinton Rossiter (1960, pp. 102–103) observed of Lincoln that he was "the martyred Christ of democracy's passion play," and that "the final greatness of the presidency lies in the truth that it is not just an office of incredible power, but a breeding ground of indestructible myth." While Kennedy was not a Lincoln, his martyrdom created a myth not yet indestructible, but nevertheless still powerful twenty-five years after his presidency. The myth of Camelot was that America could draw forth its brightest and best to serve the nation and the world and to grapple with the unending challenge of making the American dream of equality and justice for all a reality.

Franklin Roosevelt

Franklin Roosevelt, America's only four term president, is in a class by himself. Of the ten modern presidents examined here, his leadership score is significantly higher than any other. On selling ability, he ranks high in all four categories—excelling at selling to the media, the public, Congress, and world leaders, for an overall score of 3.00. (Table 7–2.) He ranks almost as high on overall management with a score of 2.50. (Table 7–3.) Roosevelt ranks high except in foreign policy and economic policy, performing well in his management of social and defense policies. Yet Roosevelt was not without flaws, especially in management. His highly idiosyncratic management style, which was casual, individualistic, and opportunistic, allowed conflict between subordinates to smoulder and sometimes flare into the open. In spite of his sloppy administrative style, however, "in the end, his deficiencies as an administrator were nearly swallowed up in his genius for bringing politics in the support of policy" (Rossiter, 1960, p. 144).

Another area in which Roosevelt has been criticized was his conduct of foreign policy. The criticisms of historical revisionists, while hardly sustainable in many instances, nonetheless raise legitimate doubts about policies toward the Japanese in the 1930s, the Germans in the 1940s, and the Soviets during World War II. Overall, these are minor compared with the magnitude of his accomplishments, which have earned him the highest of ratings of any modern president in all of the major polls taken since

World War II. He consistently rates among the top three, behind Lincoln and Washington. Some of Roosevelt's social policies are beginning to show their age and are in need of major surgery, but they set the tone of the political agenda for half a century and laid the foundations for a more humane society. He influenced all subsequent presidents, even those of opposite ideological orientations such as Ronald Reagan (Leuchtenberg 1983). His were the toughest of times—he faced economic devastation and despair in peacetime and hostile aggression from both East and West in wartime—and yet, in spite of his own severe physical handicaps, he was able to inspire the nation to believe in itself. Personally unthreatened by others' abilities, criticism, or controversy, F.D.R. was able to attract and harness some of the best talent to address some of the most vexing problems of the time. His unsurpassed ability to sell his programs and manage a peaceful social revolution clearly ranks him among the greatest of presidents.

THE SEARCH FOR HEROES

America continues its search for heroes, but the pickings have been sparse in the White House in recent times. After Kennedy, no modern president has been ranked great, with both high selling and managerial skills. Two presidents—Ford and Carter—have been undistinguished at both, while two others—Johnson and Reagan—have excelled primarily at selling, and one—Nixon—ranked high only on management.

The four presidents ranked great all shared World War II experiences in different ways, and they came to power in the White House in chronological succession. Three—Roosevelt, Truman, and Kennedy—were so-called strong presidents, or "earth movers." One—Eisenhower—was a conservative "earth smoother." The three strong presidents were Democrats, whereas Eisenhower, the less active, was a Republican.

When are presidents great? Is it coincidental that the four great modern presidents followed one another in office, or did something about their troubled times bring forth their greatness, which otherwise would have been obscured? Perhaps the answer is a qualified yes to both questions. The ratings developed here were based on actual performance of persuasive and administrative skills while in office, but of course the exercise of skill levels is always evaluated against the backdrop of the times. If the times are troubled and turbulent and the issues momentous, more virtuoso performances are called for than if the times are peaceful and placid. However, evaluating the skill level of presidents diminishes the significance of the times as much as possible. Indeed, among the presidents rated great for their manifestation of high selling ability and managerial skills, both Eisenhower and Kennedy held office in relatively prosperous and peaceful periods, although in a modern world of tension, strife, and regional warfare, it is questionable whether there are any peaceful times anymore. The modern era is not a period of either peace or war, but a twilight zone between the two.

If America is searching for heroes, how do ineffectual leaders ascend to the White House? Hoover rode in on the crest of economic prosperity and prejudice, benefiting from a strong anti-Catholic bias against his Democratic opponent, Al Smith. In prosperous times, the rigidity and fixed mind-set that handicapped his selling ability and management in times of dire crises were not apparent. Ford was an accidental president, ascending to the presidency not out of a craving for the office or tested in the fires of heated presidential campaigns and primaries, but from being in the right place at the right time, picked by a wounded and soon to be disgraced president. Carter appeared as a folk hero prepared to lead a populist revolt against an insensitive and heavy-handed Washington establishment. Drawing on the regional pride of his native South, he was able to arrest briefly the slippage of middle-class white voters in that region from the Democratic fold. His victory was short-lived when his lack of selling ability and managerial skills undercut both his and the people's hopes for a heroic president.

Nixon, the sole operational president, who was a good manager but a poor salesman, succeeded in spite of himself. If Nixon could have confined himself to the conduct of foreign affairs, his talents would have been better utilized and perhaps maximized. In a lower office, his character flaws may have passed unnoticed, but in the fishbowl of the White House, they were exposed under the magnifying glass of Watergate, which produced a heat so intense it inflamed the nation's resentment, consuming and destroying his presidency.

Both Johnson and Reagan exhibited strong selling abilities. They were skilled at persuading crucial audiences, but their views of the world and the goals of their policies were dramatically different. Johnson's great abilities were in domestic affairs, and his fatal policy flaws were in the field of foreign relations. Magnanimous in his conceptualization and creation of a new and great society, he often was small-minded and mean in his treatment of subordinates and colleagues.

By contrast, Reagan, always sensitive to the personal dilemmas and tribulations of individuals, has been criticized for slashing spending for social programs to the bone and for raising the incidence of poverty. According to Joseph Lowery, head of the Southern Christian Leadership Conference, "while the president's words are soft like a lamb, his programs bite like a wolf" (Barber, 1985, p. 497). Reagan represents the return of the two term presidency, a phenomenon absent from American politics since the days of Eisenhower. In his first term, Reagan was more pragmatic than ideological in domestic policy, and more ideological than pragmatic in foreign policy. In his second term, due in part to the replacement of staff pragmatists by conservative ideologues, domestic policy grew more ideological. At the same time, the pressure of allies and domestic public opinion softened Reagan's hard-line ideological stance in foreign policy. Reagan's rhetoric fitted the heroic mold, but his management of important policy areas and lack of innovative solutions to the long-term problems of distribution and growth did not measure up to greatness. In the final analysis, he was a political president, not a great one.

If this analysis has any validity, it should not only help in a better understanding of when and why presidents are great, but also in finding and choosing the right candidates to compete for this high office. As Barber argues in his book *The Presidential Character*, a better understanding of a candidate's character, worldview, and style can help us choose future presidents more wisely. While there is no substitute for presidential performance, it is nevertheless reasonably clear that if presidential candidates do not show considerable skills in both selling and management, they are unlikely to be successful, let alone great presidents.

REFERENCES

BARBER, JAMES DAVID, *The Presidential Character Predicting Performance In the White House*, 3rd edition. Englewood Cliffs, N.J.: Prentice-Hall, 1985).

LEUCHTENBERG, WILLIAM E., *In the Shadow of FDR: From Harry Truman to Ronald Reagan*. Ithaca, N.Y.: Cornell University Press, 1983.

MURPHY, ARTHUR B., "Evaluating the Presidents of the United States," in *The American Presidency: A Policy Perspective From Readings and Documents*. David C. Kozak and Kenneth N. Ciboski, eds. Chicago: Nelson-Hall Publishers, 1985.

ROSSITER, CLINTON, *The American Presidency*. New York: Harcourt Brace & World, 1960.

VAN MAANEN, JOHN, ed., *Qualitative Methodology*. Beverly Hills, Calif.: Sage, 1983.

CHAPTER EIGHT
THE PRESIDENCY TOMORROW:
The Challenges and Promises of the Twenty-first Century

FUTURE TRENDS AND THE PRESIDENCY

Many challenges await the presidency of the twenty-first century—challenges created in part by major economic and demographic trends that have their roots in the present. Among these are ongoing changes in the economic status of the United States, population composition, the shifting tides of international power, and quality of life for the average citizen. Many of the domestic problems confronting current presidents will become increasingly intertwined with foreign problems, creating what Lincoln Bloomfield has called an "interdependency agenda." Among these are foreign trade, resource management, civil rights, and immigration policy. Several current problems will persist and magnify. Political parties will become less relevant for decoding political messages, thus augmenting the need for the president to be a media salesperson and a communicator.

Economic Trends

Structural rigidities currently in the economy will not abate in the future, making tensions between labor and management an important issue and compulsory arbitration an increasingly viable option. Tensions between the contradictory trends of continued nationalization and a decentralized government structure will raise and heighten age-old questions about the viability of the federal system. America's headlong rush into debt will continue as both the consumer debt and the national debt reach all-time highs. Presidents must sooner or later grapple with the problem of mortgaging the future economic welfare of the country for the present convenient deficits. This problem may worsen a negative balance of payments as America borrows abroad to finance its credit habit—a habit that may threaten its superpower status. The world financial system confronts the ominous trends of high indebtedness of third-world nations, thus increasing protectionism within major industrial nations and increasing disparities between rich and poor nations.

After three decades of unprecedented peacetime improvement in economic productivity following World War II, the U.S. economy began to decline in the early 1970s. Productivity fell to its lowest point in decades. Despite the weakening of OPEC, economic conditions improved only superficially and spun downward dramatically in the early 1980s in a recession rivaling the Great Depression of the 1930s in its severity and intensity. From slow escalation in national debt, the flow of red ink reached a torrent during the Reagan era, doubling the national debt with deficits exceeding $200 billion annually. The annual trade deficit was not far behind, approaching $170 billion in 1986.

Contributing to and compounding the general economic decline was the deterioration of specific industries, particularly agriculture, textiles, steel, automobiles, and other traditional manufacturing segments, thus creating policy decisions about whether to prop up failing industries with subsidies for purposes of national defense. One consequence of industrial failure is heightened pressures for protectionist legislation by both labor unions and industry lobbyists, accelerating protectionist repercussions overseas. The shift to services is often accompanied by a decline in required skills and wages, raising questions among "baby-boomers" about their ability to afford the same living standard as their parents.

In many modern industrialized countries around the world, a partnership has developed between government and industry that has helped industry compete abroad. American presidents, however, must deal with a greater antagonism between these two giants at home. To compete, the United States may need to develop a national industrial and investment policy. The successful implementation of such a policy will require greater public investment in research and development. Managing scientific inventions and their dissemination may become a new presidential function, requiring an expansion in the Office of Science and Technology. A major overhauling of outdated patent and antitrust legal systems looms on future presidential agenda. Critical to national economic development is continued American access to the remaining frontiers of oceans and space. The skill of future presidents in negotiating international agreements, as well as protecting the interests of the United States in those negotiations, will be critical. New technologies, such as genetic engineering, life-prolongation, and communications inventions will present new dilemmas for government oversight and regulation.

Demographic Trends

In the latter part of the twentieth century, immigration, both legal and illegal, as well as differential birth rates among racial groups, began to change the complexion of America. This trend is projected to continue into the twenty-first century when whites are predicted to no longer be a majority of the population. Higher reproductive rates for blacks, Hispanics, and Asians promise to change radically the contours of both the American political and demographic scene, making the rainbow coalition of minorities a majority. As the ethnic background of both legal and illegal immigrants shifts from European ancestry to Hispanic and Asian, the melting pot may no longer be conducive to melting. The issue of bilingualism will continue to rear its head, threatening to sever America into two separate and distinct cultures, if not nations.

Along with racial changes, the American population has continued its trend of getting older, causing some demographers to predict a life expectancy of ninety-one by the year 2000. An older population raises the specter of intergenerational conflict and has already caused financial stresses on the Social Security system, Medicaid, and Medicare. An older population is linked to increasing health costs as well as labor shortages in certain areas.

A third population trend is the significant but sometimes subtle and overlooked shift of interregional migration. Well chronicled is the shift from the industrial Frostbelt to the service-oriented Sunbelt. Less obvious is a shift in resources to the periphery along the country's coastlines where high-tech industries are bringing a newfound wealth. One repercussion of this has been an economic and intellectual drain on the agricultural and industrial heartland of America.

International Trends

Rising to superpower status in the years following World War II, the United States shared the world stage only with the Soviet Union. Throughout the decades of the fifties and sixties, other nations played secondary roles or bit parts. In the seventies and eighties, however, challenges to superpower status began to come from Japan and China, leading international economists to predict the Pacific basin as the next major growth area, perhaps surpassing the industrial capacities of Western Europe and the United States. Economic challenges came from a revitalized Common Market with West Germany as its cornerstone. Accompanying America's changing economic status in the international arena was its shift from a creditor to a debtor nation. Only in military affairs did bipolarization continue to cast the United States and the Soviet Union as the two major players. In economics and politics, the superpowers were washed by the waves of regionalization and decentralization, which symbolized the growth of power centers in Western Europe, East Asia, and the Middle East. The U.S. role as peace keeper of the world and protector of the free world diminished, despite an upsurge of militancy under the Reagan administration to support anticommunist insurgency movements against Marxist regimes.

The absence of an effective international government to help control nuclear weapons and to prevent global holocaust will continue to plague U.S. relations with other countries. Presidents will be crucial in the leadership role that the United States plays in dealing with such international problems. In addition to these overriding concerns are the continued growth of terrorism (accelerated by the ever-greater miniaturization of explosives and lethal weapons), management of finite resources and energy supplies, and uncertainty about long-term climatic changes and their impact on future food supplies and living environments. Localized conflicts and increasing radicalization of third-world politics will carry the potential for instability and violence. Population growth will cause the world to bulge at its seams by the end of the millennium, forcing this issue upward on future presidential agenda.

Quality of Life Trends

Besides economic, social, and international trends, changes in the quality of life will confront and challenge future presidents. The baby-boom generation born between 1946 and 1964 created special problems for the nation. Their large numbers placed pressure on all social institutions through which they passed, beginning with schools and portending future difficulties for institutions that care for the elderly when the baby-boomers pass into old age. Additionally, this generation was the first in a long time to confront the possibility of stagnant or even declining living standards. Baby-boomers suffered a sharp decline in their ability to purchase new homes, to assure their financial security, and to educate their children. Some baby-boomers temporarily maintained living standards by developing families with two wage earners and incurring greater amounts of personal debt. This generation heightened the urgency for public policies to enhance productivity and encourage long-term growth.

Other trends affecting the quality of life that confront and challenge modern presidents include the widespread abuse of drugs and alcohol throughout all sectors of American society, an accompanying growth in crime, and increased concerns about health and health costs as the population experiences longer life expectancies. Alcoholism remains the number-one problem, but presidential efforts, especially of the Reagan administration, have been directed toward stemming the flow and use of cocaine and crack. Close on the heels of the explosion of cocaine use was an expansion of the use of synthetic or so-called designer drugs.

Crime is directly fueled by drug abuse, especially in decaying urban centers. Estimates have placed the annual narcotics traffic in the United States as high as $110 billion a year in the mid-1980s. In Washington and New York, studies revealed that over half of all persons arrested were using drugs at the time of their arrest. Government efforts to suppress the use of illegal drugs increased dramatically but with little notable success. The spreading use of illegal drugs into the middle and professional classes threaten the legal framework of American society. Newer forms of crime, including industrial espionage, computer theft, and white collar crime, will present new challenges to the president as chief law enforcer, raising the distinct possibility of a national police force.

An additional concern over the quality of life focused on health and environment-related issues. With the development of vaccines for most infectious diseases, the incidence of long-term systemic diseases such as cancer, heart disease, and Alzheimer's disease as cause of death rose. These diseases (in contrast to infectious diseases that were cured on a more rapid basis) often require long-term and expensive treatments. The AIDS epidemic finally caught a President's eye in 1987 when figures showed over 22,500 dead, a million and a half infected with the virus and an estimated 179,000 dead by 1991 (cited in *Newsweek* August 10, 1987, p. 22). Along with the shift in the nature of diseases affecting most Americans came a rise in health care costs. Concern over health contributed to renewed focus on environmental pollution from nuclear waste, toxic wastes, and manufacturing by-products that create acid rain and air and water pollution. Despite significant strides in addressing certain facets of pollution, many areas of concern remain for future presidents, including global issues such as pollution of common oceans, underground reservoirs, and outer space.

These and other so-called future forces will create a full agenda for coming presidents. The difficult and often intractable nature of these problems will tax presidential leadership skills to the limit. Like good managers of large, diverse, and technologically oriented corporations, future presidents will need to be cognizant of trends in science and technology and their implications for the solution of global problems on Planet Earth. Like good salespeople in the modern era, future presidents must communicate complex, sophisticated, and often technical and difficult information through symbols and the effective use of multiple media to a variety of audiences both at home and abroad. In the late twentieth century and early twenty-first century, presidents will not be able to afford the luxury of thinking that smaller is better. Global problems call for global thinking in the Oval Office.

FUTURE TRENDS AND PRESIDENTIAL SELLING SKILLS

Future problems confronting modern presidents will only grow more complex, complicated, and interrelated. Similarly, the solutions to future problems will also become more complex and complicated. Both problems and solutions will be more difficult for the average citizen to comprehend, thus placing an additional onus on the communication and selling skills of the president. If presidents are to cope successfully with problems created by current trends and future forces, they will need the support and cooperation of all the audiences to whom presidents must sell their ideas, policies, and programs. The effectiveness of future presidents will be deeply affected by their capacity to simplify and clarify not only the problems but also their solutions. The consequences of the failure to communicate effectively with important audiences will be increasingly devastating, not only to the president personally but also to the nation as a whole.

Future Trends and Selling to the Media

Especially important to the ability of future presidents to cope with problems of mounting complexity and interdependence will be their ability to sell their policies and programs to the national media. With a larger population having diminished inclinations to read and to write, large segments of the citizenry have developed an increased reliance upon the electronic media to keep abreast of political, economic, and international events. Along with a decline in the influence of newspapers, magazines, and other print media, political parties will likely experience a similar decline. Unless future decades see an unlikely and near miraculous recovery of political parties into their former mediating role between citizens and politicans, the media will play an increasing role in the selection, election, and evaluation of future presidents. The media will become the major conduit through which the president approaches the public.

Complicating presidential selling skills has been a growth in media skepticism and investigative reporting. An additional complication has been the growing conviction by wide segments of the populace that the media wields undue influence in the determination of presidential elections and policies. This has led to concern over "media conspiracies." This public skepticism creates the temptation for presidents to blame the media for their problems. A recent example of this would be President Reagan's constant complaint that he might have gotten more hostages of terrorists released if the press had just "Backed off." Such confrontational politics between presidents and the media is a political dead end street, for presidents come and go whereas major institutional players among the media, who are less vulnerable to the four years shifts of power, persist.

Examples of the growing power of the media, the increasing importance of selling to it, and the consequences of presidential candidates failing in this endeavor existed in the recent past. In 1984, Walter Mondale, the Democratic nominee for president, blamed his massive defeat on his own inability to project effectively through the media, especially on television. Ronald Reagan's electoral victories in 1980 and 1984 have been attributed to his skill at such projection. The entrance of electronically effective presidential candidates such as the Rev. Jesse Jackson and the Rev. Pat Robinson into the limelight of presidential politics both altered the strategies and prospects of other candidates and further highlighted the significance of skillful selling and media communication. The failure of future presidential candidates to sell their policies to the media effectively will most likely abort their candidacies and eliminate their chances for election.

Traditionally, successful presidential candidates have had to shift the focus of their selling efforts once they assumed office. During the campaign, their selling skills must be directed toward convincing the media. Through the media they must convince the public that they have the requisite personality and leadership abilities to be successful in the Oval Office. Once in office, they must refocus on selling solutions to the many and varied problems the nation confronts. This distinction between selling presidential performance from the campaign office and presidential policies from the White House may become more obvious. Even greater degrees of communication and selling skills will be required to accomplish this without undermining perceptions of sincerity and stability.

In all likelihood in the future, the media will pay increased and closer attention to the selection, election, and evaluation of presidents because of the president's growing role as national problem-solver. In spite of recent emphasis on decentralization, deregulation, privatization, and decreased public programs in the Reagan era, there is every expectation that future presidential cycles will result in renewed pressures on the federal government to deal with mounting national and international problems. Little prospect exists for long-term solutions that do not involve a major federal role.

Future Trends and Selling to the Public

Independent of current trends toward ever more complex and interdependent challenges to presidential problem solving, many barriers exist to presidential communication with the public within the American system. George Edwards has observed in his book, *The Public Presidency* that the president's "problems in meeting the public's expectations are aggravated by a number of features of American politics and policymaking that provide formidable obstacles to his achieving his goals, including Congress, the courts, our decentralized party system, the executive branch, and limits on rational decision making" (Edwards, 1983, p. 6). Few observers anticipate that these fundamental obstacles will change in the near future. An effective future president must continue to sell programs to the public in spite of these impediments.

Superimposed on these structural barriers to presidential public interchanges are the current and future trends discussed above. The depth and scope of the resulting problems will inevitably affect the general public in profound ways, heightening demands upon the body politic in general and the presidency in particular. Presidents must sell viable solutions to the public in order to meet these demands or their reputations for effective leadership will be undermined. Failure to address these problems in a timely fashion will contribute to serious fissures in American society. Yet selling solutions is complicated by a growth in the number of symbols that presidents must use, as well as the need to modify the collective meaning of old symbols. In simpler eras, symbols representing good and evil often captured the guts of political conflicts, both domestically and internationally. Presidents manipulated such symbols as communists versus anticommunists, the free world versus the Iron Curtain countries, and democracy versus totalitarianism. Domestically, conflict was simplified by such symbols as "robber barons" versus "The Man in the Street," Wall Street versus Main Street, the farmer versus the big city, and the immigrant versus city hall. In a more technical, sophisticated, and interdependent world, blatant distinctions between good and evil and gross simplifications of conflict often obscure the subtle distinctions required by risk assessment, environmental impact statements, measured growth, and international negotiations. Symbols reflecting extreme positions, such as a total abolition of nuclear weapons on the one hand or an unconstrained arms race on the other, or free trade versus protectionism, often ignore the dire consequences such positions reflect. Great presidential skill is required to use these symbols without obscuring the needed subtlety and moderation.

At the same time that symbols have become more numerous and complex, the average citizen has become more sophisticated in separating the real message from the electronic massage by a manipulative messenger. Increasingly, selling involves not just technical communications and acting skills but also sincerity and honesty and astuteness in selecting sound policies to sell. Illustrative of increasing skepticism by both the senders and receivers of mass media communications concerning presidential affairs is the reluctance of the American people to believe President Reagan's story on "Iranscam," a major presidential crisis that developed during the latter part of 1986 and the early months of 1987. The widespread knowledge that Reagan was contradicting his publicly stated policy against arms sales to Iran by selling weapons to Khomeini's government in exchange for American hostages and future political leverage resulted in a dramatic drop in Reagan's approval rating. In spite of Reagan's technical skills in communication, the duplicity surrounding the arms to Iran and the siphoning of the profits to Contra rebels in Nicaragua—against the explicit prohibitions by Congress—undermined Reeagan's ability to sell his foreign policies in general. Iranscam created a major credibility gap among a majority of the American people who doubted Reagan's veracity concerning his lack of knowledge about this affair.

Future Trends and Selling to the Congress

National legislators have always been relatively independent of the president compared to other systems. Current developments in American politics accentuate this independence. Political action committees have supplanted political parties in financing congressional campaigns. The decline in political parties, which has heightened the role of the media in presidential communications with the public, has also undercut the dependence of members of Congress upon the presidency. With the media playing an increased role, members of Congress, like the president, can communicate more directly with the public.

The trends in economics, demography, internationalism, and the quality of life support the expectation of greater demands on Congress for legislation and money to deal with their implications. Little possibility exists that the influence of Congress on these areas will diminish in the future. Realizing the importance to their constituencies of the resolution of some of these problems, it is most likely that Congress will jealously guard its prerogatives in the future.

In addition to the natural distrust between the executive and the legislative branch bred by "separated institutions sharing powers," which is coeval to the American system, the residue of Vietnam, Watergate, and Iranscam further fuel this distrust. Moreover, as problems multiply in their number and complexity, the executive temptation to "go it alone" and bypass the Congress will increase. Under these somewhat stressful circumstances and the desperate need for increased comity between the two dominant branches, demands for effective presidential selling to Congress will be greater than ever before. By the late 1980s, the public's distaste for infighting between the president and the Congress, as well as the sacrifice of the national interest for personal interest, created an increasing demand for executive-legislative teamwork for the common good. Such teamwork, in turn, rests heavily upon a high level of political expertise combined with effective communication and persuasion from the White House.

Future Trends and Selling to World Leaders

The trends toward increasing complexity and interdependency elevate the importance of effective presidential selling ability to world leaders perhaps more than to any other audience. The implications of not dealing successfully with these trends have profound consequences both domestically and internationally. According to one observer, the debt crisis alone "is affecting the health of the U.S. economy, the conduct of U.S. foreign policy, the stability of the U.S. financial system, and the rate of U.S. unemployment—not to mention . . . national security" (Watkins, 1986, p. viii). The redress of many of the problems confronting the world today, including the arms race and economic growth and distribution, require coordinated efforts among the major world powers, particularly the United States, the Soviet Union, the Common Market countries, China, and Japan. Congress is not likely to go along with common solutions perceived to be antithetical to American interests. Thus, presidential selling to other world leaders becomes important concerning policies favored by Congress and the American public.

Current and future trends are precipitating new challenges to U.S. leadership in world affairs, thus intensifying the need for persuasive presidents who can communicate effectively with their international peers in the international arena. The emergence of new, younger, more progressive leadership in the Soviet Union promises to offer increased competition to the American president for the spotlight in world leadership. The Iceland summit in 1986 and the Iran-Contra escapade offered Mikhail Gorbachev opportunities to exploit U.S. weaknesses and indecision. The halting moves toward political and economic freedom in China opened new and expansive vistas for Chinese growth and dynamism in world affairs. An active, modernizing China promises to challenge the ingenuity and leadership of any future American president. Last but not least, the continued challenge of Japan for industrial and economic leadership of the world must inevitably be reckoned with by the White House. Even more true in the future than in the past is John F. Kennedy's observation that domestic errors will only wound us, but errors in foreign affairs can kill us. International configurations of the future will demand forceful and enlightened U.S. leadership personified by a president who can persuasively and effectively sell.

The Consequences of a Nonpersuasive Presidency in the Future

As the magnitude of problems confronting future presidents increases, the consequences of a nonpersuasive presidency also increase. Future presidents will be called upon to do more rather than less. As a result, presidents who behave like ineffectual Milquetoasts, other-directed Vacillators, rigid True Believers, and power-hungry Godfathers will be poorly typecast in the role of the nation's chief salesperson. Presidents who adhere too rigidly to preconceived beliefs and values will not maintain the flexibility to explore the numerous options that future complexity may demand. Presidents who are too flexible will be perceived by the public as lacking the vision to lead the nation through trying times. In relatively safe, secure, and prosperous times, the nation can occasionally afford a nonpersuasive president, but if the future is uncertain and challenging as current trends indicate, then election of a nonpersuasive president might spell disaster and stagnation when the times require action and vision. The margin for error in presidential selling ability is shrinking at an accelerating rate. As the stakes of national and international politics increase, today's tolerable mistakes may be magnified into tomorrow's intolerable misfortune.

FUTURE TRENDS AND PRESIDENTIAL MANAGEMENT

As with selling ability, presidential management increases in importance as the number, complexity, interdependence, and scale of problems grow. The need for more efficient, wise, and equitable solutions mounts. To survive effectively, government must recognize and possibly embrace some trends affecting management in the private sectors. These include the growth of "entrepreneurs" who develop new ventures within existing institutional frameworks; increased emphasis on employee well-being; democratization of the decision-making process by incorporation of employee input; and the development of an information society. Government capacity to manage the "megatrends" that John Naisbitt has described is crucial to the achievement of foreign, defense, social, and economic policy goals and to compete effectively with the emerging Japanese superstate.

Future Trends and Defense-Policy Management

The importance of management of defense policy is highlighted by the Reagan administration's trillion and a half dollar defense buildup since 1980 and its proposal of a further trillion-dollar program in the development of the Strategic Defense Initiative (SDI), also called "Star Wars." With such stupendous funds involved, careful cost-effective management was never more crucial. If Star Wars and the MX missile system prove to be of dubious value, both the direct cost and opportunity cost of wrong policy management choices will be phenomenally high. In spite of widespread scientific misgivings about the viability of SDI, the Reagan administration worked long and hard for its research and development, even to the point of rupturing negotiations with the Soviets at the Iceland summit meeting of 1986. The result was a temporary breakdown of superpower negotiations over arms control. The sudden and unexpected escalation during this summit of the negotiating stakes apparently caught President Reagan ill-informed and unprepared to deal with the consequences of proposals for universal nuclear disarmament. This raised serious questions among U.S. allies over the viability of their own defense systems without a future nuclear deterrent.

These examples illustrate the great dimensions of the problems involved in judicious defense management in the coming decades. Such problems only promise to increase in scope and intensity as we push toward the twenty-first century. The implications for mismanagement in defense policy are so profound as to stagger the imagination, not only because of the tremendous financial costs and economic sacrifices, but also because of the security risks that would result from miscalculation and misadventure. As armaments become more costly, more complex, and more numerous, the stakes involved grow higher and higher. The president's capability to successfully manage the arms race, arms control, arms reduction, or disarmament becomes crucial to the peace of the world. Ill-conceived and ill-managed defense systems, arms negotiations, and great-power summits can not only disrupt diplomatic relations and threaten to bankrupt economies, but they also threaten both the United States and the world with the dire prospects of nuclear conflicts, nuclear winters, and nuclear extermination.

Future Trends and Foreign Policy Management

If defense policy is the cutting edge of national power, foreign policy is the shield of the Republic and diplomacy is its advance buffer. The failure of competent foreign policy management leads to the use of military power as a solution to international problems. Successful foreign policy management is indispensable to the nation's security. Change, the everlasting law of international relations, guarantees new presidential challenges, not only in selling policies to world leaders but also in managing their implementation. New power configurations will rise, new economic relationships will emerge, and new and dangerous troublespots will flare up. Perhaps as never before the president must be the diplomat-in-chief (Plischke, 1986).

The president's future success or failure in this role will determine whether the country goes forward, downward, or upward. President Carter's mismanagement of foreign policy in the neutron bomb controversy and the Iranian hostage crisis proved injurious to the prestige of his presidency. The infighting between Secretary of State Cyrus Vance and National Security Advisor Zbigniew Brzezinski during Carter's term of office exemplifies the negative fallout when management of foreign policy is ineffective.

President Reagan's difficulties with foreign policy management in the first nine months of his first term, when Secretary of State Alexander Haig and National Security Advisor Richard Allen both resigned under fire, were only a prelude to even more serious problems of mismangement in this area in his second term, when he was forced to transfer his national security advisor, Admiral John Poindexter, and fire Poindexter's deputy, Lt. Col. Oliver North. In that unhappy situation the president's chief of staff, Donald Regan, and his director of the Central Intelligence Agency, William Casey, came under intense criticism for misleading the president as to the implications of conducting secret diplomacy from the basement of the White House in opposition to the advice of Secretary of State George Shultz and Secretary of Defense Caspar Weinberger. That fiasco is a classic case of what can go wrong when a president is uninformed and fails to provide wise policy leadership. The repercussions of that bad management still reverberate in the diplomatic corridors of Western Europe and the Middle East. The tragic lesson again appears to be that there is no substitute for presidential knowledge and experience in foreign-policy management coupled with the wisdom to choose and rely upon wise and experienced advisors. Reagan's failure to maintain a top-flight national security staff, his failure to have a politically sophisticated chief of staff, and his failure to rely upon his highly qualified secretary of state proved a disaster in this instance.

There is little if any reason to think that the problems experienced by Carter and Reagan will not be replicated in the future if presidential foreign policy management is similarly lacking. Any president can make errors in judgment of policy, but the errors can be minimized in their incidence and impact with good management skills attentive to both the organizational structure that implements foreign policy and the caliber of people that staff those organizations. American presidents since Nixon have failed at crucial times in crucial ways to manage the nation's foreign policy effectively. If future presidents cannot emulate or exceed the performances of Eisenhower and Nixon, America's future is precarious and uncertain.

Future Trends and Social Policy Management

Many future trends, especially demographic trends and changes in the quality of life, are closely linked to national social policy. After years of the Reagan administration's emphasis on slowdowns and cutbacks in funding social welfare programs, on deregulation of wide areas of the economy, and on increased reliance on unrestrained competition, many areas of America's social policy have suffered neglect, left to the untender mercies of unfettered markets. The consequences of the Reagan legacy for successive presidents is that wide areas of America's social fabric will be in need of considerable repair. The problems of the poor and the homeless in large urban centers promise to loom larger in the future. The problems of urban decay and minority rights similarly have not lessened appreciably. It is patently clear that future presidents will face increasing pressure from minority and interest groups to redress some of the inequities and lost opportunities experienced by earlier generations. Future presidents will be challenged to prevent drug smuggling and illegal immigration from undermining the basic structure of American society. Skyrocketing medical costs and years of underfunding for education have long-term consequences that are not easily reversed.

Under Reagan's leadership, America experienced an unleashing of rampant individualism and privatization of many areas of social policy. Benign neglect was practiced in the areas of civil liberties, civil rights, poverty programs, and federal support for higher education. In an attempt to lower the national deficit, the administration sold off natural resources on federal lands and offshore. Safety requirements for automobiles were relaxed and postponed in an attempt to stimulate auto production and sales. Air traffic controllers, overworked and under stress, numbered less than full force years after Reagan clashed with the industry union and fired striking controllers. Nonaggressive positions on enforcement of environmental standards were taken in the areas of toxic waste and air quality.

If Richard Reeves in *The Reagan Detour* (1985) and Arthur Schlesinger, Jr., in *The Cycles of American History* (1986) are even partly correct, the country can anticipate a national mood change by the 1990s that will be sympathetic to increased governmental action on the social policy front. Moreover, the action-reaction syndrome that occurs across presidencies further supports speculation that Reagan's successors will undertake steps to correct the excesses of Reagan's attempted social revolution. Almost certainly, future presidents will be called upon to exercise leadership in confronting many of these problems that have been exacerbated rather than solved by Reagan's "hands off" stance. The changing demographic patterns will reflect themselves in changing political patterns, which will almost certainly create greater support for active presidential social policy management. Even by the late 1980s, Republican party professionals were reaching out to blacks and ethnic minorities in order to broaden their political base and challenge the Democrats for political allegiance of minorities. To the extent the Republicans will be successful in these efforts, concessions will be made to accommodate minority demands in exchange for their loyalty, regardless of the party in power in the White House. In the face of trends toward greater ethnic diversity and the decline in importance of the white Anglo-

Saxon American, future presidents will confront the need to manage social policy amidst numerous and sometimes conflicting demands, maintaining a moving social equilibrium. Presidents must be sensitive to the significance of social policy to social change. They must demonstrate their competence to recognize, organize, and manage social change in a fashion that elevates the quality of life. They must prevent any social disruption resulting from the failure to satisfy demands for change. The social agenda of future presidents will be composed of a raft of continuing problems left over from previous presidencies but will also include new and serious issues resulting from the changing social fabric and political culture.

Future Trends and Economic Policy Management

If economic trends in the late 1980s continue, future presidents may wonder why they sought the office. Facing future presidents are debts in both the federal budget and the balance of trade. Despite such efforts as the Gramm-Rudman-Hollings deficit-reduction bill, despite accounting chicanery of shifting expenditures forward to the next fiscal year, and despite a short-run strategy of selling off invaluable and irreplaceable national resources, federal deficits and the national debt continue to loom as larger-than-life problems. The cost of servicing the national debt grew to 15 percent of the annual federal budget, a figure exceeding $150 billion annually in 1987. During the 1980s, corporate, household, and consumer debts rose almost as fast as the national debt.

Correspondingly, savings have declined and American sources of lending have failed to keep pace with the need for investment dollars. Foreign investment in America, which was expected to be $1 trillion by the end of the decade, may still be insufficient as budget and trade deficits and low dollar value scare off foreign investors. If that happens—and the Japanese are already deeply concerned about the ability of the United States to cope with its debt problems—the consequences would be profound. In the late 1980s, President Reagan's Teflon armor on economic issues showed definite signs of wear, with the full impact of the disintegration of his economic policies coming home to roost for his successors.

Traditionally, economic and budgetary decisions have been secondary concerns of presidents, behind their major concern for foreign policy. The future promises to make economic policy management co-equal if not more important than foreign policy management for modern presidents. Indeed, as the United States is pulled, sometimes reluctantly, into a global economy, the lines between economic and foreign policy will become increasingly blurred. A major problem for future presidents will be how to make America competitive in the world economy. America's mounting trade deficit and negative balance of payments in part reflect the decline in the competitive edge. By 1986, the United States had surpassed Brazil as the largest debtor nation in the world, owing other countries almost $200 billion. In the 1980s the days of fixed exchange rates, which provide security in planning international economic endeavors, ended. Future presidents will be forced to deal with fluctuating currency values, making decisions about the tradeoffs between dollar devaluation to stimulate exports and maintenance of inflated values to attract foreign investment. Further indications of the linkage between economic and foreign policy management in the future are U.S. efforts to stimulate growth in other industrial countries to enable them to buy more U.S. exports to help American industry and to prevent the dollar from sinking further. However, the Japanese and the West Germans have blamed the disorders in the world monetary system and the large trade deficit on U.S. budget deficits maintained by the Reagan administration and the Congress. The failure to solve the issues of industrial growth abroad and budget deficits at home poses a grave threat to both the world economy and the national economy. Such issues promise to test presidential managerial skills to the utmost.

In addition to mounting trade deficits and increasing difficulty in competing in international markets, the U.S. economy has featured recent and recurrent recessions, high unemployment, double-digit inflation, and merger mania. The Reagan administration was successful in eliminating hyperinflation, cutting individual income taxes, modernizing the military, and restoring morale after the debilitating influences of Vietnam, Watergate, the Iran hostage crisis, and the energy shortage of the 1970s. However, significant economic issues remain for Reagan's successors, and one in particular is how to regulate insider trading on Wall Street. Indicative of the depth of the problem was the scandal created by financial magnate Ivan F. Boesky who admitted using insider information to make millions of dollars of profit. As Herbert Rowan (1986, p. 3) has written, "Encouraged by a national policy of deregulation... financial markets have transformed into what Henry Kaufman of Salomon Brothers calls a casino dominated by free wheeling speculators." Rowan also quotes Felix Roahtyn, a well-known investment banker, as saying, "I have been in business for almost forty years and I cannot recall a period in which greed and corruption appeared as prevalent as they are today."

Corporate mergers and the insider trading they sometimes surreptitiously foster reflect more concern with short run income statements than long-term productivity, making the maintenance of productivity a major issue on the agenda of future presidents. In 1986, American industry operated at 78 percent of capacity and the GNP increased at 2 percent, behind the levels exceeding 3 percent in earlier postwar years. The operating capacity rate was 3.4 percent below that of the previous two decades. On the issue of finding methods to improve productivity and to make America more competitive, future presidents may find that nothing less than a significant restructuring of the American economy will be called for, including greater partnerships among the normal adversaries of labor, management, and government. Major national research and development programs may be necessary to keep America competitive in supercomputers, microchip technology, fiber optics, and other newly emerging industries. National trade adjustment policies may help displaced workers find new jobs. Transferrable pension benefits may facilitate mobility from "sunset" firms and industries to "sunrise" enterprises. Future presidents will have to resist the temptation to protect uncompetitive industries at taxpayer expense and concentrate more on recapturing the competitive edge. The issue of how to make the United States more competitive became a leading issue for 1988 presidential candidates, who promised everything from a return to the gold standard to a $100 billion plan to have government retool basic education, upgrade research and retraining, and prioritize the commercialization of new technologies. With three out of four American workers vulnerable to foreign competition and with productivity growing less than that of Japan, West Germany, and France, the need for the United States to rediscover its competitive edge promises to be the number one political and economic issue of the 1990s. Finding answers to respond to that need will engage the mind and energies of any future president.

The Consequences of Future Presidential Mismanagement

Paranoid, compulsive, dramatic, depressive, and schizoid presidential managerial tendencies in the past have sometimes resulted in undesirable outcomes for the nation. Watergate and Vietnam are among them. Untrammeled expression of these tendencies in the future may have even more dire consequences. In the past the presidential selection process, faulty though it may be, has for the most part winnowed out the more bizarre types of presidential candidates. With increased attention paid to candidates' personalities and media styles rather than to managerial abilities, the danger will increase. A severely neurotic candidate may win the election, producing the paradox that the crumbling of old barriers to presidential selection might allow a demagogue into the White House at the same time the negative consequences of neurotic presidential mismanagement increase. Given economic, demographic, international, and quality-of-life trends, problems confronting future presidential managerial skills may be less tractable and more prolonged. If the problems become overwhelming and unsolvable, the pressures of the office of president may bring out neurotic mismanagement styles even more readily when the consequences of neurosis-induced mismanagement are even more severe. Advocating psychiatric screening for presidential candidates may in itself be a bit bizarre, but the day may come when the dangers of aberrant behavior may be so costly that a renewed emphasis is placed upon finding an integrated, well-adjusted personality capable of managing the nation's business.

THE FUTURE AND PRESIDENTIAL LEADERSHIP STYLES

In relating basic presidential leadership types to future trends and possible contingencies, candidates who are low on both selling and management skills will be unlikely to be elected president. They probably will not ascend to the White House unless they succeed a disabled, deceased, or terminally ill president. Even this possibility grows more unlikely as both presidential and vice-presidential candidates must exhibit superior selling skills at least to the media.

Operational candidates who are poor communicators but good managers are also unlikely to be elected. Only under extraordinary electoral circumstances where the public reacts to excessive and abusive use of selling skills bordering on demagoguery, or where patently obvious crises elevate public concerns over competence in policy management, will an operational president be elected in the future.

The leadership style most likely to win in the future will be political presidents who exhibit a high degree of selling ability but low managerial skills. With the shift to media campaigns, candidates who are not good salespeople will be less likely to be elected, whereas candidates who appear attractive and communicate persuasively will be more likely to become presidents. Rarely, however, are the managerial skills of presidential candidates tested before entering the White House on a scale comparable to what is needed once in office. Unfortunately, no advanced management schools exist for future presidents who must finely hone their skills through on-the-job training under fire. It used to be that the springboard to being president was being a state governor. Carter and Reagan may have revived this, but with indifferent results. Big state governors may be tested more and more for managerial skills, but President Reagan's political leadership style is probably indicative of the modal style for future presidents.

Plainly, the need for great presidents who combine both high selling ability and managerial skills will grow as problems become more complex and more interdependent. There always has been, is now, and will continue to be a preference for great presidential leadership. In the future, this preference may become a necessity. In the future more than ever, good intentions in the White House will not be enough. For future presidents, high competence in selling themselves, their programs, and their policies, coupled with high competence in managing the White House, the bureaucracy, and the defense establishment, equates with presidential greatness. For the United States to remain a vital, growing, prospering democracy that can maintain a leadership role in a troubled and interdependent world, great presidential leadership will be required. Without it, the country is in danger of slow demise in its quality of life at home and slow decline in its power position abroad. The future will present both dangers and opportunities to determine the worth of the American system. It will test the ability of its people to demand presidential greatness and the capacity of future presidents to deliver it.

REFORMS AND THE FUTURE PRESIDENCY

According to an old Chinese proverb, to prophesize is very difficult, especially with respect to the future. One of the uncertainties concerning future presidential performance is the degree to which the system will undergo significant structural and institutional reforms. Proposed reforms affecting future presidencies can be evaluated in light of existing knowledge about current problems and future trends. Ideas for political reform are currently popular as the country reevaluates itself and the Constitution during the 1987–1991 Bicentennial period while celebrating the drafting of the Constitution, its ratification, and the adoption of the Bill of Rights. The issue of how we choose presidents has two facets: the number and power of presidential primaries, which now dominate the presidential selection process, and the continued possibility that a close presidential election might be thrown into Congress, where unit voting by states might thwart an electoral majority. Many and varied proposals for changes in the Constitution and the political system have been promulgated and discussed. The focus here is on only those party, electoral, and institutional reforms that affect the presidency.

Proposed Party Reforms Affecting the Presidency

Running for president has become a full-time job what with the proliferation of state primaries and the institutionalization of what one observer has called *The Permanent Campaign* (Blumenthal, 1980). One of the most common party reforms proposed affecting the selection of the president is an alteration in the state-by-state primary system. Several advantages of presidential primaries fueled their adoption: They open the nominating process to a greater number of voters, they invite candidates from all regions as well as small and large states, and they are more representative than party caucuses or conventions.

The trend toward state-by-state primaries to select presidential nominees reached its acme around 1980 when a growing consensus emerged, especially in the Democratic party, that the point of diminishing returns had been reached. Critics contended that the quality of voter participation in primaries is low, with voters being more influenced by candidates' personalities and media appearance than by their policy positions. Critics also argued that the primaries are poorly scheduled and cover too broad a time frame. The first primary that is often decisive in determining which candidates continue the race typically takes place in New Hampshire, a small and unrepresentative state, while large states such as Pennsylvania, Michigan, California, and New Jersey hold their primaries much later. Yet another criticism is that primaries overstress media skills compared to the diversity of skills presidents need.

A growing awareness of the above criticisms has resulted in fewer state primaries and more demands for regional or at least clustered state primaries to reduce the time and expense involved in running for president. It is too early to evaluate the impact of regional primaries first introduced in the Democratic party in 1988. Against those who believe that a regional primary will be an efficient reform are many who find it cumbersome and too broad in its coverage of southern and southwestern states. Another criticism of the regional primary is that small states will get disproportionately less attention and the relatively unknown candidates will not be able to recover from a poor performance in an early regional primary, making the outcome of one day's polling too decisive. Opponents also contend that the scope of regional primaries will elevate, not decrease, the physical and financial stress on candidates.

While final judgments must await observation of actual regional primaries, and there is good reason to view their adoption with skepticism, the goal of consolidating state primaries and shortening the length and expense of nominating campaigns is eminently desirable. More than the current state-by-state primary system, regional primaries will certainly test the abilities of presidential candidates to sell themselves and their ideas to a diverse and heterogeneous public in a compressed amount of time and to manage their own time, campaign budgets, and enlarged campaign staffs.

An extension of the idea of regional primaries to select presidential nominees is the proposal for a national presidential primary, a nationwide election to be held by political parties in all states on a single day in late spring or early fall of the election year. Advocates of this reform argue that a national presidential primary would be most democratic, direct and easily understood. It would presumably attract widespread media coverage and diminish the length of campaigns. Opponents contend that this so-called reform would only enlarge the role of the media, would stress candidate showmanship rather than competency, and would hurt candidates lacking strong financial backing. However, the same arguments about testing the selling and managerial skills of presidential candidates that apply to regional primaries apply even more strongly to the national presidential primary.

Accompanying the rise of state primaries has been a diminution in the role of party elites and national conventions in the presidential selection process. Increasingly, nominee selection by national party conventions is a foregone conclusion even before the convention is held, leaving the party faithful with the role of cheerleader. Another proposed reform of the presidential nomination process is the reversal of the timetable for the national party convention and the state primaries (Cronin and Loevy, 1983). This idea, used in Colorado state nominations since 1910, would provide for a national preprimary selection that would choose two or three candidates who would then run in the state primaries. Party leaders could presumably place greater emphasis on selecting presidential candidates with high levels of both managerial and selling skills, thus enhancing the probability of great presidential leadership.

A combination of these reforms is also possible and, in fact, quite desirable. Especially appealing is the combination of reversing the input of the party elite through the national convention and the input of citizens through primaries, with the adoption of a national primary system. Critics of the preprimary convention argue that having party elites narrow the field of candidates for the nomination to two or three would result in the elimination of fringe or dark horse candidates. Only well known, well established, and more institutionally based candidates would be selected by party conventions. Supporters contend that the selection of more mainstream candidates is desirable, because successful party nominees must ultimately appeal to a majority of the entire population, and because party nominees with more extreme views in the past have gone down to disastrous defeat in the general election. The preprimary convention restores decision making power to the party elite and makes national party conventions more than morale boosters and media events, but it does not deprive citizens of having effective and decisive input into the final nomination. A national primary would cause candidates to focus on national issues and would eliminate the long and arduous campaigns that increasingly stress personality and physical stamina rather than the strength and quality of policy arguments and management skills. The persuasive skills required in a national primary are greater and more like those required by successful candidates in the general election and in the White House.

Proposed Electoral Reforms Affecting the Presidency

In the United States, the supposed cradle of democracy for the world, the president still is not popularly elected. The electoral college is interposed between the populace and the final determination of who is to be president. Established by constitutional framers fearful of too much direct input and possible mob rule, the electoral college still stands after 200 years. Defenders of the electoral college contend that, by and large, the system has worked well and promotes national unity and political legitimacy by generating majorities that magnify the often narrow margins of victory produced by the popular vote. They also say that the system favors the large urban state, which offsets the undue influence of rural small state constituencies that are favored in both the Senate and the House.

Critics argue that the electoral college overrepresents small states and large swing states and theoretically permits the election of a candidate who receives fewer votes than his or her opponent. Moreover, the failure of any presidential candidate to win a majority automatically throws the election into the House of Representatives where voting is by state delegation, not population. Electors are not legally bound to vote in accordance with the outcome of the popular vote in their states.

Many reforms and modifications have been proposed for the electoral college. Among the more important reforms that would retain some portion of the electoral college is the substitution of proportional allocation of electors within states for the current winner-take-all system. Another reform suggested is the abolition of the individual positions of electors, coupled with a retention of electoral votes allocated on either a proportional or winner-take-all basis. A third proposal would create 102 bonus electoral votes to be awarded to the winner of the popular vote. The bonus votes would be added to the winner's electoral college vote, virtually abolishing the possibility that a president would not have the largest number of popular votes. Supporters of this bonus plan contend it would decrease the probability of a deadlock in the electoral college and would encourage two-party competition in states where one party tends to dominate. None of these proposed reforms, however, have received much public support. Most likely only a crisis in the workings of the electoral college system will precipitate any major reforms.

Many people, including former President Carter, have recommended that a constitutional amendment be adopted that would provide for the direct popular elections of future presidents. Even this proposal, which in July 1979 received a majority vote in the Senate, seems unlikely to be adopted, although many political scientists argue that direct election is the most representative and democratic method of selecting presidents. Critics argue that direct election of the president would encourage third-party candidacies and increase the probability of no candidate receiving a majority of the popular vote. Supporters offer several solutions to this scenario. One is a runoff election between the top two vote getters. A second is to allow the plurality winner to assume the White House. A third solution, now possible with modern computer technology, is to record first, second- and third preferences of individual voters, reallocating the votes for the least popular candidate until a single candidate receives a majority vote.

Other criticisms of direct election of the president are that a national election would undermine the state-oriented system of federalism and that small states would be ignored and lose some of their current influence. Further, an undiluted majority rule would encourage political extremists who would stress television at the expense of direct contact with the voters. Some minority groups fear that they would lose their swing votes if the electoral college were abandoned. However, direct popular election is preferred to the current electoral college system on several grounds. Direct election would enhance the democratic principle of one-person one-vote, which has been a bulwark of American democracy. In comparison to the calculations involved in the electoral college, direct election would be simple and easily understood, and it would be more comparable to other electoral practices for national and state office. In an era where problems need nationwide solutions, a national campaign would result in highlighting and emphasizing comprehensive issues, rather than more parochial and state concerns, so that the good of the whole country is not sacrificed on the altar of regional, local, and specialized interests. Perhaps equally important, a national campaign becomes a test of candidate selling skills in a forum more closely approximating that which future presidents must face. The managerial skills required to run a successful nationwide campaign are greater than those required to run state-by-state efforts. Managing a national campaign represents a microcosm of the problems that a president must face in managing and implementing larger policies in large scale governmental bureaucracies.

Of the three systems for coping with a situtation where no candidate receives a majority vote, the reallocation of votes for less popular candidates is most preferred. Having plurality winners may be excluded as an option on the basis that officeholders should be the most preferred candidates of the remaining viable candidates of a majority of the voters. Runoff advocates contend that voters are deprived of issue debates that might arise in a reelection campaign if runoff elections are not held, and that a direct majority vote is the best basis for holding office. However, runoff campaigns are lengthy, expensive, and arduous on both candidates and voters. The turnout during reelection campaigns is often sparse. The candidate able to raise the largest amount of money in a short amount of time, often from special-interest groups, typically wins. Blacks contend that runoff elections are biased against them because the runoff election allows white majorities to coalesce behind the white candidate. Reallocating votes on the basis of second and third preferences of votes cast for less popular candidates has become more feasible with the development of supercomputers and computer networks that allow the temporary storage and rapid calculation of first, second, and third preferences for millions of voters.

Other proposed electoral reforms have involved the timing and sequencing of national elections. Most suggest some mechanism by which the terms of office for president and Congress can be more closely synchronized. Proposals for altering the timing and sequencing of Senate elections, especially those which call for shortening Senate terms to four years, have very poor prospects of being enacted politically because senators would be called upon to pass a constitutional amendment shortening their own terms and power positions. It is not without reason that the six year senatorial term has been called an unamendable part of the Constitution. As a way to circumvent this, the Committee on the Constitutional System, in their bicentennial report, called for extending the Senate terms to eight years.

Far more likely to be enacted are proposals that call for the abolition of midterm elections for the House of Representatives. Although these too would call for a constitutional amendment to lengthen the term of House members from two to four years, proponents of proposals that expand power bases find it easier to build coalitions for their ideas. It is not an impossible dream that, in the near future, harassed, overworked, and constantly campaigning members of Congress might be amenable to such a proposal. The abolition of midterm House elections would strengthen the president's party role by forcing House candidates of the president's party to run on the president's platform. The closer linkage of House and presidential elections would bolster the ability of presidents to sell their policies and programs to the Congress, thereby enabling presidents to be more effective. It would also increase accountability to citizens by tying congressional campaigns more closely to national platforms and issues.

A third set of proposals for electoral reform deal with the financing of campaigns. Most of these focus on the need for public financing of congressional campaigns to diminish the growing clout of special interest groups and their political action committees. In 1974, a sweeping campaign reform law established the Federal Election Commission and provided for public subsidies for presidential primaries and general elections. Public subsidies for presidential campaigns, long overdue, helped reduce the dependence of candidates on special interests and private funds. The experience of several elections has shown that some suggestions for reforming the 1974 law have merit. Under the current law, public subsidies for presidential campaigns are funded by a voluntary dollar per taxpayer checkoff on the federal income tax form whereby individuals may choose to allocate a dollar of their taxes to the subsidy fund. President Reagan has opposed this voluntary checkoff system, and contribution levels remain unstable. If the checkoffs were made mandatory, a steady predictable source of public funding of presidential elections would be available.

Some advocates of public subsidies contend that the public nature of television, especially the need to secure station licenses to assure programming in the public interest, justifies a mandatory donation of free television time to presidential candidates. If television networks were compelled to give free time to major party candidates, or time at reduced public service rates, a major cost of presidential campaigns would be reduced. At least network television could financially sponsor mandated debates between presidential and vice-presidential candidates of major parties.

Reformers who want to amend the 1974 law are concerned about its independent expenditure loophole. No provisions were made in the law to limit independent expenditures on behalf of presidential candidates as long as those expenditures are made without prior knowledge of the candidate and without coordinating directly with candidate campaign organizations. This loophole has led to a growth in outside expenditures in behalf of candidates, making the imposition of campaign expenditure limits on candidates accepting public subsidies considerably less meaningful. Suggested reforms to close the independent expenditure loophole include counting those expenditures within the candidate's allowable limits and greater disclosure of all election funding in behalf of candidates, including those funds spent without their knowledge.

Proposed Institutional Reforms Affecting the Presidency

Several proposals have been made to alter the institution of the presidency itself. Generally, these proposals are less appealing and less desirable than some party and electoral reforms also affecting the presidency. Calls for adoption of a parliamentary system, provisions for citizen recalls of the president, collegial executives where two or more persons share White House power, or even a dual executive with two presidencies all have major flaws and are politically unachievable except under conditions of upheaval and concomitant extreme and radical reform. Parliamentary variants that would allow legislators to serve in the executive or for the president to have a question and answer period with the legislature have more appeal, although in the case of executive-legislators, the resulting conflict of interest and the sheer demands on time and energy seem to preclude its adoption.

Some reformers who favor many features of the parliamentary system argue that presidential candidates should announce their cabinets before the election so the public would know the administrative team for which it is voting. This team ticket idea, however, undercuts the ability of the president to hire and fire cabinet members on the basis of performance, and it interjects political and ticket-balancing concerns just at it diminishes presidential flexibility. If other tests or indicators of the managerial skills of prospective presidents were available to the public, the cabinet team ticket would be unnecessary, for the president's ability to manage policy implementation in the bureaucracy would remain the primary concern.

The idea of a single six-year presidential term is as the old as the original Constitutional Convention. It has been periodically revived ever since that august assembly met in Philadelphia 200 years ago to shape the basic structure of American government. In the 1970s and 1980s, the idea resurfaced with considerable fanfare, receiving the endorsement of Presidents Carter and Reagan among others. This plan has proven particularly attractive to former cabinet members and White House staffers who have seen recent presidencies become mired in political reelection concerns when urgent questions of public and foreign policy cried out for courageous and nonpartisan resolution. Many others have felt that a president who did not have to worry about reelection could afford to be a president of all the people, rather than a broker between competing groups constantly maneuvering for political advantage in the next campaign. The underlying flaw of this proposal is that it tries to remove presidents from the political process, rather than assuring that they have sufficient selling skills to meet the challenges the process presents. Also implied is a distrust of the electorate to exercise judgment about presidential performance as policy managers. This plan would also lengthen the time period when the country is burdened by an ineffectual president weak on selling skills or managerial ability or both.

Although most political scientists are profoundly skeptical of the implications of such a constitutional amendment, its persistent recurrence suggests that the idea has some merit, especially in providing continuity and attention to foreign-policy issues and in allowing the president to rise above parochial and special interests to address national and global concerns. If such a constitutional amendment could be tested for one or two presidencies, subject to repeal, the advantages relative to its disadvantages would become more apparent.

Somewhat similar to a recall in impact but different in origination and more restricted are proposals for a congressional vote of no-confidence on presidential performance, an idea currently employed in parliamentary systems. Subsequent to a majority no-confidence vote, the Congress or the president or both would stand for reelection at an irregularly scheduled interval. Supporters contend that such a proposal would increase accountability to citizens, increase governmental efficiency, and force the president to maintain the confidence of Congress through consultation with members and leaders. The likelihood of a stalemate would be reduced. However, if only the president had to stand for reelection, Congress could become frivolous and seek to secure partisan political gains by voting out president after president. If only the Congress had to stand for reelection, the no-confidence vote would not be considered as an evaluation of presidential performance, and positive votes would be very unlikely. The most effective outcome would require both the president and Congress to stand for reelection, even though the use of this vote may be impaired by Congress not wanting to impose a reelection on itself. Richard A. Watson and Norman C. Thomas (1983, p. 413) have astutely and correctly observed that "grafting an essential feature of the parliamentary system onto the American separation of powers system would have highly destabilizing consequences."

The Twenty-second Amendment, the so-called Republicans' revenge against President Roosevelt's four term presidency, has been the subject of intense controversy ever since its inception. While, in fact, it has made little or no difference thus far in actually determining who occupies the White House, the case against it has been argued fully and eloquently by those who believe it is antidemocratic and handicaps the effectiveness of second term presidencies. The dean of American presidential scholars, Louis W. Koenig (1981, p. 92), has argued that "supporters of an effective presidency and the democratic ideal of free electoral choice ought to work for the repeal of the Twenty-second Amendment." The argument for its repeal is persuasive in theory but unconvincing in practice. Ever since its passage, only Dwight Eisenhower and Ronald Reagan have been in a position to be affected by its limitations. Most likely, Eisenhower's illnesses and Reagan's age would have precluded them from seeking third terms. Although Truman believed that the two term restriction would force him to govern with one hand tied behind his back, the evidence from Eisenhower's two terms suggests that the presidents with considerable selling skills and managerial ability are not hamstrung by this constitutional limit. Opponents of its repeal argue that without the limits imposed by the Twenty-second Amendment, political dynasties would become more likely and unscrupulous presidents might sustain themselves in office through the abuse of power. Sundquist (1986, p. 132) has argued convincingly that "while logic might suggest that the Twenty-second Amendment was unwise, both in denying the people a free choice of leaders, particularly in a time of crisis, and in depriving the presidency of one element of its power, its adoption does not appear to have had major consequences, nor is it likely to."

One suggested reform that impinges on the presidency is the abolishment of the office of vice president. This position has been eloquently argued by Arthur M. Schlesinger, Jr. (1986, pp. 337–372), who agrees with John Adams, the first vice president, who called the American vice presidency "the most insignificant office ever the invention of man contrived or his imagination conceived." Schlesinger advocates the outright abolition of the office. Should a vacancy occur in the presidency, the secretary of state would be acting president for ninety days when a new election would fill the vacancy. Schlesinger's position on this is somewhat idiosyncratic; most presidential scholars are inclined to believe that the vice presidency continues to serve a useful purpose by providing an immediate and available backup if the president dies, is disabled, declared incompetent, assassinated, impeached, or unexpectedly resigns. The vice presidency assures continuity and stability. The real problem of the vice presidency is how to improve its stature and to have it become integrated into an effective administration management team. Presidents with good management skills can integrate and effectively utilize their vice presidents within the current institutional arrangements. According to Joel Goldstein (1982) and Paul Light (1984), Ford, Carter, and Reagan have made significant strides toward better utilization of their vice presidents to expand and augment their own selling and managerial skills. Two requisites to continue the progress of upgrading the vice presidency are (1) the selection of able vice presidential candidates capable of assuming the presidency in the event of emergency, and (2) the recognition of the office and its holder by the incumbent president. On balance, the arguments for retaining and upgrading the office seem to outweigh the arguments for its abolition. What is important for future presidents is the development of the mangerial skills needed to recruit, integrate, and utilize high quality subordinates, especially the vice president. Nelson Rockefeller, Walter Mondale, and George Bush, all capable of assuming the presidency and at various times presidential candidates themselves, exemplified this caliber of vice presidential candidates. Some have contended that their selling abilities and managerial skills exceeded those of the presidents they served.

Another reform in the structure of the presidency that has gained substantial recognition under President Reagan, who repeatedly called upon the Congress for its enactment, is the presidential line item veto, the power to veto individual items in appropriations bills. Reagan argued that forty-three governors had the equivalent power to prevent wasteful overspending (Robinson, 1985, pp. 259–261). Reagan argued for a constitutional amendment to this effect, but he was opposed by many in his own party, including Senator Mark Hatfield, who was adamantly against its adoption on the grounds that it strengthened the president's budgetary powers at the expense of the Congress. Louis Fisher has also argued against this veto on the grounds that Congress does not appropriate the kinds of things presidents would veto line by line. Repeated attempts to find congressional remedies were introduced but were not successful. Reagan contended that he needed this power to balance the federal budget and reduce unnecessary spending, but many members of Congress were reluctant to surrender their power of the purse and felt that the president already had sufficient budget-cutting clout in the form of proposing budget cuts. A possible compromise is to try the presidential item veto for a two-year period and reassess it at that juncture. Because the item veto is a significant managerial tool that could possibly be used effectively by a president with well honed management skills to combat the continuing and serious problem of federal deficits, its adoption on a trial basis warrants consideration.

THE PRESIDENCY AND THE AMERICAN FUTURE

As the nation approaches the twenty-first century, plainly the structural problems of the American political system place severe constraints upon the capacity of the president to lead effectively. Our system of separation of powers, adequate two centuries ago when the demands upon national government were far less, is increasingly showing strain as the nation moves into its third century. Federalism, a dual form of government emphasizing local and regional government at the expense of national policy development and implementation, made more sense when local and regional cultural differences were sharp and distinct, than today when those differences have become blurred and all regions confront common problems. In the future, problems will transcend subnational boundaries even more. Bicameralism provided both territorial and population bases of representation but has increasingly become an obstacle to an efficient and responsive legislature. Pluralism originally made a virture of open, free, and available access in the American system but has increasingly become a source of obstructionist special interests who frustrate the achievement of the common good through lobbyists, political action groups, and iron triangles that threaten to dominate and control the legislative process.

The limits that these structural rigidities place on presidential ability to lead have become more obvious to presidential scholars. As we noted at the outset, Paul Light (1983) has spoken of the "no win" presidency, Harold Barger (1984) of "the impossible presidency," and Theodore Lowi (1985) of "the plebiscitary presidency." Bert Rockman (1984, p. xv) in his acclaimed book *The Leadership Question* thinks that much of the presidential literature has focused on the interplay of four elements. The first is the limited capacity for presidential direction in government. The second is the existence of exalted expectations for presidential direction. The third is the inevitable disappointment of those expectations, given the limited capabilities, and the fourth is the structural, situational, and personal conditions that influence presidential direction. Rockman contends that if we expect presidents to command the government and the government to do their bidding, these expectations will be frustrated, except in crises. Expectations that presidents will be influential participants in the policy process are more realistic, so that presidents not only can have a policy impact but can also engender trust in a system built on distrust. However, Rockman remains pessimistic, believing that strengthening the presidency in the absence of major structural reforms, probably unattainable, will not work. He concludes that "a resort to more presidentialism without a sufficient concern for making the whole of the government more effective hardly seems an appropriate prescription" (Rockman, 1984, p. 236–238).

While remaining fully cognizant of the severity of the structural limitations of the decentralized centrifugal American system in an increasingly interdependent world, we remain optimistic that the best way to make the system work is to combine effective presidential leadership with continuing efforts toward structural modifications that enhance the ability of national elected officials to develop, conduct, and implement both foreign policy and domestic policy. Short of total abandonment of the current system of separation of powers, however, the most urgently needed structural reforms are in the Congress, not the presidency. Lessening the impact of special-interest groups on the legislative process and freeing members of Congress from financial dependence on political action committees are more urgent concerns than modifications in formal presidential powers.

Party, electoral, and institutional reforms affecting the selection, election, and conduct of the presidency should be on the national agenda, but the most pressing problem of the presidency is identifying, encouraging, and electing presidential candidates with sufficiently high levels of both selling and management skills to meet the formidable tasks confronting the nation. Great future presidents must not only be active and positive, as James David Barber notes, but also must also have the requisite skills to be effective in an increasingly challenging environment. Character and good intentions alone will not allow future presidents to address the nation's needs adequately. Future presidents must have the ability to sell to the crucial audiences of the media, the press, the Congress, and world leaders. They must be effective managers of defense, foreign, social, and economic policies. The nation must demand no less than this. History will record the consequences if this goal is not attained.

Finally, future presidential greatness may not be only desirable and a popular preference but also a requisite for the survival of the United States as we now know it. Because leadership is interactive and democratic in America, the blame for leadership failure rests ultimately with the American people. Thus, the challenge of presidential greatness is a challenge for us all.

REFERENCES

ABRAHAMSEN, DAVID, *Nixon vs. Nixon: An Emotional Tragedy*. Bergenfield, N.J.: New American Library, Signet Books, 1978.

BAILEY, THOMAS A., *Presidential Greatness*. New York: Appleton-Century-Crofts, 1966.

BARBER, JAMES DAVID, *The Presidential Character: Predicting Performance in the White House*, 1st, 2nd, and 3rd editions. Englewood Cliffs, N.J.: Prentice-Hall, 1972, 1977, 1985.

BARGER, HAROLD M., *The Impossible Presidency: Illusions and Realities of Executive Power.* Glenview, Ill.: Scott, Foresman, 1984.

BERMAN, LARRY, *The New American Presidency.* Boston: Little, Brown, 1987.

BLUMENTHAL, SIDNEY, *The Permanent Campaign.* Boston: Beacon Press, 1980.

BRODIE, FAWN M., *Richard M. Nixon: The Shaping of His Character.* New York: W.W. Norton & Co., Inc., 1981.

BUCHANAN, BRUCE, *The Presidential Experience: What the Office Does to the Man.* Englewood Cliffs, N.J.: Prentice-Hall, 1978.

BURNS, JAMES MACGREGOR, *Presidential Government: The Crucible of Leadership.* Boston: Houghton Mifflin, 1966.

_____, *Leadership.* New York: Harper & Row, 1978.

BURNS, JAMES MACGREGOR, JACK PELTASON, and THOMAS E. CRONIN, *Government by the People*, 12th edition. Englewood Cliffs, N.J.: Prentice-Hall, 1984.

CANNON, LOU, *Reagan.* New York: Putnam's, 1982.

CARALEY, DEMETRIOS, "Major Trends in Research: 22 Scholars Report on Their Fields," *The Chronicle of Higher Education*, September 4, 1985, pp. xxxi.

CARPENTER, RONALD H., and WILLIAM J. JORDAN, "Style in Discourse as a Predictor of Political Personality for Mr. Carter and Other Twentieth-Century Presidents: Testing the Barber Paradigm," *Presidential Studies Quarterly*, 10 (Fall 1978), pp. 588–599.

CARTER, JIMMY, *Keeping Faith.* New York: Bantam Books, 1982.

COHEN, JEFFREY, "Presidential Personality and Political Behavior: Theoretical Issues and an Emprical Test," *Presidential Studies Quarterly*, 95 (Summer 1980), pp. 209–237.

Congressional Quarterly Almanac, 1981. Washington, D.C.: Congressional Quarterly Press.

COOK, BLANCHE WIESEN, *The Declassified Eisenhower.* New York: Doubleday, 1981.

CRONIN, THOMAS E., *The State of the Presidency*, 2nd edition. Boston: Little, Brown, 1980.

CRONIN, THOMAS E., and ROBERT LOEVY, "The Case for a National Preprimary Convention Plan," *Public Opinion* (December/January 1983), pp. 50–53.

CYERT, RICHARD M., and JAMES G. MARCH, *A Behavioral Theory of the Firm.* Englewood Cliffs, N.J.: Prentice-Hall, 1963.

DOWNS, ANTHONY, *Inside Bureaucracy.* Boston: Little, Brown, 1967.

EDWARDS, GEORGE C., *The Public Presidency: The Pursuit of Popular Support.* New York: St. Martin's Press, 1983.

FERRELL, ROBERT H., ed., *The Eisenhower Diaries.* New York: W.W. Norton & Co., Inc., 1981.

FISHEL, JEFF, *Presidents and Promises.* Washington, D.C.: Congressional Quarterly Press, 1985.

FREUD, SIGMUND, and WILLIAM C. BULLITT, *Thomas Woodrow Wilson: A Psychological Study.* Boston: Houghton Mifflin, 1962.

GALBRAITH, JOHN KENNETH, "Reagan's 'Facts'—Artistic License," *The New York Times*, September 27, 1985, p. 21.

GEORGE, ALEXANDER L., and JULLIETTE L. GEORGE, *Woodrow Wilson and Colonel House.* New York: John Day, 1956.

GEYELIN, PHILIP, *Lyndon B. Johnson and the World.* New York: Frederick Praeger Unger, 1966.

GLAD, BETTY, *Jimmy Carter: In Search of the Great White House.* New York: W.W. Norton & Co., Inc., 1980.

GOLDSTEIN, JOEL K., *The Modern Vice Presidency*. Princeton, N.J.: Princeton University Press, 1982.

GREENSTEIN, FRED I., *The Hidden-Hand Presidency: Eisenhoweer as Leader.* New York: Basic Books, 1982.

HARGROVE, ERWIN C., *Presidential Leadership*. New York: Macmillian, 1966.

HARGROVE, ERWIN C., and MICHAEL NELSON, *Presidents, Politics, and Policy*. New York: Knopf, 1984.

HESS, STEPHEN, *Organizing the Presidency*. Washington, D.C.: The Brookings Institution, 1976.

HOXIE, R. GORDON, "About This Issue," *Presidential Studies Quarterly*, 16 (Winter 1986), pp. 7–10.

HUGHES, EMMET JOHN, *The Living Presidency*. Baltimore Penguin, 1972.

HYMAN, SIDNEY, "What Is the President's True Role?," *The New York Times*, September 7, 1958, p. 10.

JOHNSON, HAYNES, *In the Absence of Power: Governing America*. New York: Viking, 1980.

KEARNS, DORIS, *Lyndon Johnson and the American Dream*. New York: Harper & Row, 1976.

KEGLEY, CHARLES W., Jr., *A General Empirical Typology of Foreign Policy Behavior.* Beverly Hills, Calif.: Sage, 1973.

KERBEL, MATTHEW R., "Against the Odds: Media Access in the Administration of President Gerald Ford." *Presidential Studies Quarterly*, 16 (Winter 1986) pp. 76–91.

KETS DE VRIES, MANFRED F.R., and DANNY MILLER, *The Neurotic Organization: Diagnosing and Changing Counterproductive Styles of Management*. San Francisco: Jossey-Bass, 1984.

KOENIG, LOUIS W., *The Chief Executive*, 4th edition. New York: Harcourt Brace Jovanovich, 1981.

LASCH, CHRISTOPHER, *The Culture of Narcissism: American Life in An Age of Diminishing Expectations*. New York: Warner Books, 1979.

LIGHT, PAUL C., *The President's Agenda: Domestic Policy Choice from Kennedy to Carter*. Baltimore: Johns Hopkins University Press, 1983.

_____, *Vice Presidential Power: Advice and Influence in the White House*. Baltimore: Johns Hopkins University Press, 1984.

LOWI, THEODORE, *The Personal President: Power Invested, Promise Unfilled*. Ithaca, N.Y.: Cornell University Preess, 1985.

MACCOBY, MICHAEL B., *The Gamesman: Winning and Losing the Career Game*. New York: Bantam, 1976.

MACGREGOR, DOUGLAS, "The Human Side of Enterprise,"*Management Review*, 46 (no. 11, 1957), pp. 22–28.

MANDELBAUM, MICHAEL, "The Luck of the President," *Foreign Affairs*, 64 (no. 3, 1986), pp. 393–412.

MARCH, JAMES G., and HERBERT A. SIMON, *Organizations*. New York: John Wiley, 1958.

MAYNES, CHARLES WILLIAM, "Lost Opportunities," *Foreign Affairs*, 64 (no. 3, 1986), pp. 413–434.

MAZLISH, BRUCE, *In Search of Nixon: A Psychological Inquiry*. New York: Basic Books, 1962.

MCCLELLAND, DAVID C., *The Achieving Society*. Princeton, N.J.: D. Van Nostrand, 1961.

MUELLER, JOHN E., *War, Presidents and Public Opinion*. New York: John Wiley, 1973.

NESSEN, RON, *It Sure Looks Different from the Inside*. Chicago: Playboy Press, 1978.

NEUSTADT, RICHARD, *Presidential Power.* New York: John Wiley, 1960.

Newsweek, August 10, 1987, p. 22.

OUCHI, WILLIAM G., *Theory Z: How American Business Can Meet the Japanese Challenge.* New York: Avon Books, 1981.

PETERS, THOMAS J., and ROBERT H. WATERMAN, Jr., *In Search of Excellence.* New York: Warner Books, 1982.

PLISCHKE, ELMER, *Diplomat in Chief: The President at the Summit.* New York: Praeger, 1986.

————, "Rating Presidents and Diplomats in Chief," *Presidential Studies Quarterly*, 15 (Fall 1985), pp. 725–742.

QUALLS, JAMES H., "Barber's Typological Analysis of Political Leaders," *American Political Science Review*, 71 (April 1977), pp. 182–211.

REEVES, RICHARD, *The Reagan Detour.* New York: Simon & Schuster, 1985.

RENKA, RUSSELL D., "Comparing Presidents Kennedy and Johnson as Legislative Leaders," *Presidential Studies Quarterly*, 15 (Fall 1985), pp.806–825.

RIESMAN, DAVID, *The Lonely Crowd: A Study of the Changing American Character.* New Haven, Conn.: Yale University Press, 1950.

ROBINSON, DONALD L., ed., *Reforming American Government: The Bicentennial Papers of the Committee on the Constitutional System.* Boulder, Colo.: Westview Press, 1985.

ROCKMAN, BERT A., *The Leadership Question: The Presidency and the American System.* New York: Praeger, 1985.

ROSSITER, CLINTON, *The American Presidency.* New York: Harcourt, Brace & World, 1956.

ROWAN, HOBART, "The Plummeting Morality Market," *The Washington Post National Weekly Edition*, December 29, 1986, p.5.

SAFIRE, WILLIAM, *Before the Fall. An Inside View of the Pre-Watergate White House.* Garden City, N.Y.: Doubleday, 1975.

SCHLESINGER, ARTHUR M., Jr., *The Crisis of the Old Order, 1919–1933.* Boston: Houghton Mifflin, 1957.

————, *The Cycles of American History,* Boston: Houghton Mifflin, 1986.

———— *The Imperial Presidency.* Boston: Houghton Mifflin, 1973.

SCHUBERT, DAVID, *Judicial Policy Making.* Glenview, Ill.: Scott, Foresman, 1974.

SHULL, STEPHEN A., *Presidential Policy Making: An Analysis.* Brunswick, Ohio: King's Court Communications, Inc., 1979.

SIMON, HERBERT, *Administrative Behavior.* New York: Macmillan, 1947.

SORENSEN, THEODORE, *Kennedy.* New York: Harper & Row, 1965.

SMOLLER, FRED, "The Six O'clock Presidency: Patterns of Network News Coverage of the President," *Presidential Studies Quarterly*, 16 (Winter 1986), pp.31–49.

STOESSINGER, JOHN, *Crusaders and Pragmatists: Movers of Modern American Foreign Policy.* New York: W.W. Norton & Co., Inc., 1979.

SUNDQUIST, JAMES L., *Constitutional Reform and Effective Government.* Washington, D.C.: The Brookings Institution, 1986.

TATALOVICH, RAYMOND, and BYRON W. DAYNES, *Presidential Power in the United States.* Monterey, Calif.: Brooks/Cole, 1984.

VOGLER, DAVID J., *The Politics of Congres,* 4th edition. Boston: Allyn & Bacon, 1983.

WALHKE, JOHN C., HEINZ EULAU, WILLIAM BUCHANAN, and LEROY C. FERGUSON, *The Legislative System: Explorations in Legislative Behavior.* New York: John Wiley, 1962.

WARREN, SIDNEY, *The President as World Leader.* Philadelphia: Lippincott, 1964.

WATKINS, ALFRED J., *Til Debt Do Us Part.* Washington, D.C.: Roosevelt Center for American Policy Studies andd University Press of America, 1986.

WATSON, RICHARD A., and NORMAN C. THOMAS, *The Politics of the Presidency.* New York: John Wiley, 1983.

WATT, DAVID, "As a European Saw It," *Foreign Affairs: America and the World, 1983,* 62 (no. 3, 1984), pp. 521–532.

WAYNE, STEPHEN J., *The Legislative Presidency.* New York: Harper & Row, 1978.

WEBER, MAX, *The Theory of Social and Economic Organization.* New York: The Free Press, 1964.

Index

defense policy, 105–6, 194–95
 economic policy, 127–29
 foreign policy, 113–14
 social policy, 121–22
mismanagement, 140, 162, 164–65
 dramatic, 153–57
salesmanship, 48–49, 53, 59, 67–71
Reedy, George E., 87
Reeves, Richard, 197
Reforms and the Future Presidency, 202–12
Reich, Robert B., 9, 92
Renka, Russell D., 57
Reisman, David, 22–23, 77
Robinson, Donald L., 211
Rockman, Bert A., 212–13
Roosevelt, Franklin Delano:
 leadership, type of:
  great, 171–73, 178, 180–81
 management, 96, 129–30
  defense policy, 100
  economic policy, 123
  foreign policy, 107–8
  social policy, 116
 mismanagement, 140, 162
  dramatic, 150–52
 salesmanship, 45–46, 50, 55, 61, 70–71
  non-persuasive, 75, 78, 85–87
Rose, Richard, 93
Rossiter, Clinton, 21, 25–27, 56, 180
Rourke, Herbert, 199
Rubin, Richard, 44–45

S

Safire, William, 140
Salomon, Lester, 121
Sawhill, Isabel V., 120
Schizoid presidents, 159–61
Schlesinger, Arthur M., Jr., 45, 143, 145, 197, 210
Schneider, William, 5
Schubert, David, 24, 26, 35
SDI, 18
Secondary Neurotic Tendencies, 161–65
Selling:
 to Congress, 54–57
 to the media, 43
 to the public, 49
 to world leaders, 60–69
Senior Executive Service, 95
Shull, Steven, A., 56–57

Siciliano, Rocco C., 95
Simon, Herbert A., 135
Skills:
 management, 37
 selling, 37
Smoller, Fred, 49
Sorenson, Theodore, 163
Stein, Herbert, 122–23, 126
Stoessinger, John, 64, 111, 148
Storybook presidency, 4
Sundquist, James L., 210

T

Tatalovich, Raymond, 32, 51
Textbook presidency, 93
Theory X, Y, Z, 25, 92
Thomas, Norman C., 57, 94, 210
Thurow, Lester, 11
Time, 12
Total Presidential Leadership Scores, 173
Trillion–Dollar Club, 40
Truman, Harry:
 leadership, type of:
  great, 171–73, 178
 management, 96–97, 129–30
  defense policy, 101
  economic policy, 123–24
  foreign policy, 108
  social policy, 116–17
 mismanagement, 140, 162
  compulsive, 145–47
 salesmanship, 46, 51, 55–56, 61–61, 70–71
  non-persuasive, 78, 85

V

Van Maanen, John, 172
Volger, David, 24

W

Wahlke, John C., 24, 26
Warren, Earl, 81
Warren, Sidney, 60–61
Waterman, Robert H., 41
Watkins, Alfred J., 193
Watson, Richard A., 57, 94, 210